Manga FOR DUMMIES®

by Kensuke Okabayashi

BICENTENNIAL 1807 WILEY 2007 BICENTENNIAL

Wiley Publishing, Inc.

Manga For Dummies®

Published by
Wiley Publishing, Inc.
111 River St.
Hoboken, NJ 07030-5774
www.wiley.com

Copyright © 2007 by Wiley Publishing, Inc., Indianapolis, Indiana

Published simultaneously in Canada

For general information on our other products and services, please contact our Customer Care Department within the U.S. at 800-762-2974, outside the U.S. at 317-572-3993, or fax 317-572-4002.

For technical support, please visit www.wiley.com/techsupport.

Wiley also publishes its books in a variety of electronic formats. Some content that appears in print may not be available in electronic books.

Library of Congress Control Number: 2006939589

ISBN: 978-0-470-08025-2

Manufactured in the United States of America

10 9 8 7 6 5 4 3 2 1

WILEY

About the Author

Kensuke Okabayashi is a professional freelance illustrator/sequential artist. Born and raised in Princeton, New Jersey, Kensuke has been inspired by manga artists such as Fujiko Fukio, Osamu Tezuka, and Rumiko Takahashi since childhood. While shopping his manga portfolio in Japan, he visited various animation and comic book studios to hone his skills. There Kensuke met with Matsumoto Leiji and Akazuka Fujio and interned with other manga artists.

After studying music and psychology at Wheaton College in Illinois, Kensuke shifted his focus from playing the piano to honing his art skills. He earned his BFA in Illustration at the School of Visual Arts in New York City after studying traditional painting and further developing his drawing skills. Upon graduating, he began picking up illustration and storyboard clients. His works eventually caught the eyes of several illustration agencies that currently represent him. His recent storyboard clients include Diesel Clothing, Diet Coke, Diet Pepsi, Dr. Pepper, Absolut Vodka, Wendy's, Allstate, State Farm, Canon Digital, All Nippon Airways, and Camel.

In addition to storyboards, Kensuke also actively illustrates for mainstream entertainment industry clients, including Wizards of the Coast, Takara Toys U.S.A., Kensington Books, Skyzone Entertainment, and Carl Fisher Music.

Inspired by his past experience of working long hours at a well-known coffee shop corporation, Kensuke developed and illustrated his creator-owned comic book series titled *JAVA!*, which portrays the quirky futuristic society of Neo Seattle, where mankind must consume coffee in order to live. The title attracted attention and was picked up by Committed Comics and published as a miniseries. His main character, Java (a high-power caffeine girl fighting crime), received positive reviews from major comic book review sites as well as from readers and distribution. Kensuke continues to work on creator-owned projects with other established colleagues and writers in the industry. His upcoming publication projects include Image Comics, Arcana Publications, and Archaia Press. His online portfolio is posted at his studio Web site at www.piggybackstudios.com.

On the side, Kensuke continues to draw from life and teaches art. He taught illustration courses at Mercer College of New Jersey for several years. He currently teaches studio art classes at the Education Alliance Art School in New York City. When not drawing or painting in his studio, Kensuke still enjoys playing the piano from time to time and honing his martial arts skills regularly at a local Tae Kwon Do club.

Dedication

This book is dedicated to my parents, Dr. Michio and Sahoko Okabayashi, for their unconditional love and support.

Author's Acknowledgments

I would like to thank my acquisitions editor, Michael Lewis, my project editor, Chrissy Guthrie, and my copy editor, Sarah Faulkner, at Wiley for all their hard work, advice, and support while I was writing this book. Big thanks to Wiley's composition department for scanning the illustrations and laying out the book. In addition, I want to thank my colleague, Takeshi Miyazawa, for his role as technical editor. My biggest thanks goes to my family, Michio, Sahoko, Yusuke, and Saichan, who have been my greatest supporters and fans. None of this would have been remotely possible without their help. Thank you and God bless you!

Publisher's Acknowledgments

We're proud of this book; please send us your comments through our Dummies online registration form located at www.dummies.com/register/.

Some of the people who helped bring this book to market include the following:

Acquisitions, Editorial, and Media Development

Senior Project Editor: Christina Guthrie

Acquisitions Editor: Michael Lewis

Copy Editor: Sarah Faulkner

Technical Editor: Takeshi Miyazawa

Editorial Manager: Christine Meloy Beck

Editorial Assistants: Erin Calligan, Joe Niesen, David Lutton, Leeann Harney

Cover Image: Kensuke Okabayashi

Cartoons: Rich Tennant (www.the5thwave.com)

Composition Services

Project Coordinator: Adrienne Martinez

Layout and Graphics: Carl Byers, Stephanie D. Jumper, Barbara Moore, Barry Offringa, Brent Savage

Anniversary Logo Design: Richard J. Pacifico

Proofreaders: John Greenough, Melanie Hoffman, Charles Spencer, Techbooks

Indexer: Techbooks

Publishing and Editorial for Consumer Dummies

Diane Graves Steele, Vice President and Publisher, Consumer Dummies

Joyce Pepple, Acquisitions Director, Consumer Dummies

Kristin A. Cocks, Product Development Director, Consumer Dummies

Michael Spring, Vice President and Publisher, Travel

Kelly Regan, Editorial Director, Travel

Publishing for Technology Dummies

Andy Cummings, Vice President and Publisher, Dummies Technology/General User

Composition Services

Gerry Fahey, Vice President of Production Services

Debbie Stailey, Director of Composition Services

Contents at a Glance

Table of Contents

Introduction

* *

Yōkoso (welcome) to *Manga For Dummies*. Manga is a cultural phenomenon that continues to grow in popularity not only in the United States, but also worldwide. Throughout this book, I focus on the basic skills you need to create your first manga characters for your own creator-owned manga series. Whether you're an aspiring artist or a professional illustrator wanting to explore a different style of drawing, this book is a great place to start.

About This Book

As you see throughout this book, more than 50 percent of the content is devoted to illustrations. I show you examples in the illustrations, and I tell you how to replicate them (or create your own examples) in the step-by-step instructions that accompany them.

All tips, advice, and drawings that I provide are based upon my own experience, both as a professional illustrator/sequential artist and as a former art student. I designed this book to take you through various drawing techniques and popular styles of drawing manga. Although you draw some manga characters realistically, others are more exaggerated. I encourage you to try out these different styles and find out which ones you like drawing most. As you become familiar with different faces and body types, you may want to combine different elements to come up with your own individual style.

Throughout this book, I cover a variety of popular manga topics. I introduce basic proportions and anatomy to demonstrate how to draw your first manga character from start to finish. I also cover different must-know character archetypes, including popular main protagonists, their supporting sidekicks, evil villains, wise ones, damsels in distress, and shōjo characters. In addition to characters, I show you how to create cool effects to apply motion and emotion to tell a story. For mecha fans, I also show you how to create your own mecha. Finally, I talk about some tips for self-publishing your first manga works and preparing to exhibit your works at your first manga convention.

Conventions Used in This Book

While writing this book, I used a few conventions that you should be aware of:

- ✔ Numbered steps and keywords appear in **boldface.**
- ✔ Whenever I introduce a new term, I *italicize* it and define it.
- ✔ Web sites and e-mail addresses appear in `monofont` to help them stand out on the page.

What You're Not to Read

Now, I didn't spend hours upon hours writing this book and drawing all the illustrations because I want you to skip over them. However, to be honest, you can skip over certain elements in this book and still get the gist of what's being covered. The sidebars (the gray boxes) throughout the book contain information that's interesting yet nonessential, so if you're pressed for time or just not into anything that isn't essential, feel free to skip them. Also, feel free to skip any information that has the Technical Stuff icon attached, because that info goes beyond what you absolutely need to know. You won't hurt my feelings (much).

Foolish Assumptions

When I sat down to write this book, I made a few assumptions about you, dear reader. This book is for you if

- ✔ You're really into manga, and you want to draw your own manga characters and come up with your own stories.
- ✔ You've never sketched anything other than a stick figure before, but you want to try your hand at this style of art because it seems pretty fun and easy to pick up.
- ✔ You're a fan of one kind of manga (maybe kodomo manga), and you want to know more about other kinds of manga (like shōnen or shōjo manga).
- ✔ You know very little about manga, but you want to know how it got started and what it's all about.
- ✔ You're an aspiring manga artist who hopes to be published someday.
- ✔ You don't care whether you're published or not. You just like to draw, and you like manga. So there!

While we're on the subject of foolish assumptions, allow me to take a moment to dispel a few foolish assumptions I've heard over the years:

✔ **After reading this book from cover to cover, I should become a successful manga artist.** One misconception of most reference books is that you should be able to master the art of manga by reading through the book from front to back. Drawing isn't an overnight phenomenon. Unlike those final exams in high school, you can't cram good art. My strong advice is not to be dissuaded if your drawings don't come out the way you want on your first try. Like many skills, practice is essential to getting good results.

✔ **I'm not as talented as my other friends — I may as well give it all up!** Nonsense! One of the glories of manga rests in its simplicity in line and form. Although having drawing skills or drawing lessons certainly helps, they aren't required. In my opinion, the key to achieving success isn't raw talent or even hard work, but passion. If you're not passionate about what you draw, no amount of talent or long hours you work will help you in the long run.

✔ **Like other comics, manga is for kids — people will make fun of me for taking this art form seriously (even more so if I pursue it as a career).** If this is your first time experiencing manga, this is an understandable false assumption. As I explain in the first chapter of this book, manga has a tremendous diversity of topics and genres (ranging from sports to politics to romance). It's no surprise manga is a multi-billion-dollar entertainment industry enjoyed by all ages and sexes.

How This Book Is Organized

This book is broken up into six different parts. Following is a summary of each of these parts, so that you can decide what appeals to you.

Part 1: Manga 101

Think of this part as your first day in a class for your favorite subject. This part provides an overview of manga's history and different genres, it tells you what tools you need to get started, and it wraps up with some basic drawing exercises to get your brain and your hand moving.

Part II: To the Drawing Board

Even though this book is set up to be modular (meaning that you can start anywhere you like), unless you've drawn manga before, you don't want to skip this part. Here I show you how to draw the essential components of any manga character: the head, eyes, body, and basic clothing. These chapters are the foundation for the rest of the book, especially Part III, where I show you how to draw specific types of characters.

Part III: Calling All Cast Members!

This is where things get juicy. Although you can find thousands of storylines and characters in today's popular manga world, most stories use certain archetypes as their protagonist or lead characters, sidekicks, antagonists, and so on. For whatever reason, this method has been a winning formula that's stood the test of time.

In this part, you take the basics and apply them to draw various types of characters, such as heroes, villains, and elders.

Part IV: Time to Go Hi-Tech

Like drawing those cool robots, machines, and weapons? How about those small sophisticated electronic devices? In this part, I cover the basics to get you started on drawing your own machines (referred to as *mecha*).

Part V: An Advanced Case of Manga

In this part, I go over the more advanced topics and manga subject matter. I start off with basic principles of perspective that allow you to add depth and interest to your drawings. I then show you how to create the illusion of motion and emotion by using different types of lines. Next, I cover backgrounds and storyboards. Finally, I tell you what goes into a good manga story and how to get your work noticed if you're looking to break into the biz someday.

Part VI: The Part of Tens

As a new manga creator, it's important to keep a look out for what other hot manga artists are drawing. As part of this section, I include ten of the most influential manga artists who continue to inspire the manga community worldwide. I also list ten places where you can present your work to the public.

Icons Used in This Book

Throughout this book, you see various icons in the left margins. These icons serve as flags to draw your attention toward important or helpful information. Each specific icon carries its own meaning, as listed here:

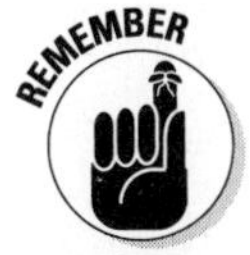
REMEMBER

As you may have guessed, this icon points out concepts or other information that you don't want to forget.

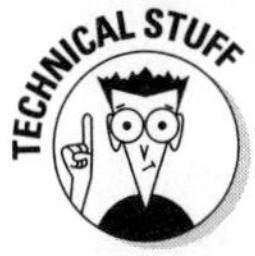
TECHNICAL STUFF

This icon points out information that goes a bit beyond what you absolutely need to know. If you're a thorough type of person, you'll likely enjoy these tidbits; however, feel free to skip them if you prefer.

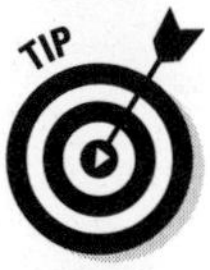
TIP

Look for this icon to provide you with helpful tricks and shortcuts to make your drawing life easier.

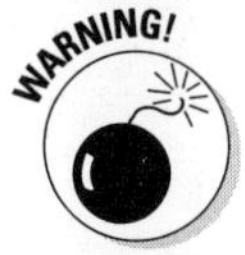
WARNING!

Don't skip this icon. It alerts you to various mistakes and pitfalls that you want to avoid.

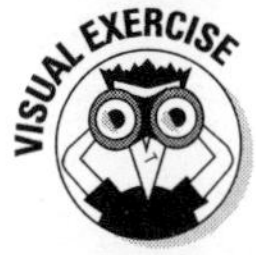
VISUAL EXERCISE

If you need some help getting the creative juices flowing, seek out this icon.

Where to Go from Here

Going from cover to cover in a strict sequential order isn't required. Based on your interests, you can visit chapters in any order, and you'll find that each section takes you step by step through accomplishing an objective. For those with drawing experience, the beauty of this format is that you can select whichever topic you want to know more about and dive into it.

However, for those of you who are new to manga or don't have prior drawing experience, I recommend starting with Part I and working your way through this book in order. Even if you're an experienced artist but new to manga, it's not a bad idea to brush up on your knowledge by starting with Part I and then choosing the section you're interested in.

Regardless of where you start, I recommend reading all the way through the chapter you choose before sitting down at the drawing table and working through its steps. Give yourself time to first digest different kinds of characters and techniques that are used in today's manga world. After that, go back and draw to your heart's content.

Finally, as if you don't have enough to keep you busy here in this book, be sure to check out some great bonus content online. Just go to www.dummies.com and search for *Manga For Dummies*.

Part I
Manga 101

The 5th Wave	By Rich Tennant

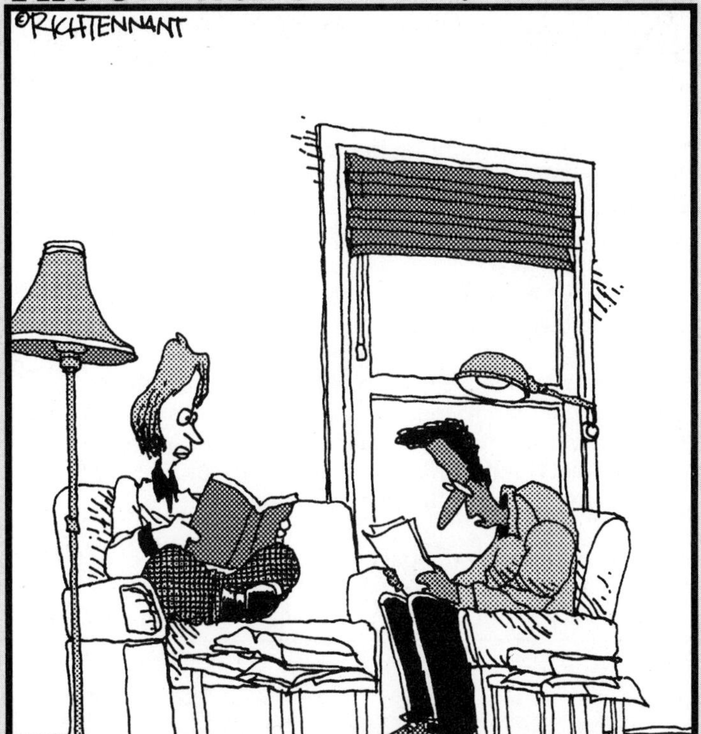
©RICHTENNANT

"I'd like to become a Manga artist. I'm just not sure I have that much whimsey in me."

In this part . . .

So, you want to draw manga? Whether you're drawing for the first time or you're a serious artist new to manga, this part is designed to get you started on the right foot. Maybe you're here as an experienced American comic book artist wanting to try something new. More likely, though, you're just really into manga and want to figure out how to draw your own characters. No matter what your background is, you're in for an awesome ride.

Here you get up to speed on the history of manga and how it's grown in popularity in recent years. You get the lowdown on the supplies you need to get started, and then you try some basic drawing exercises, which are designed not only to loosen your wrist, but also to help you become familiar with the tools. These exercises are widely prescribed by manga artists and their assistants; you can think of them as warm-up exercises.

If you're ready, turn the page and prepare to discover the world of manga!

Chapter 1

Welcome to Manga World

In This Chapter

- Discovering the origins and history of manga
- Exploring the different types of manga
- Evaluating the differences between American comics and Japanese manga

Welcome to the wonderful world of manga. From its humble beginnings after World War II, manga has grown to become an international phenomenon in the entertainment industry. Prestigious Japanese publishing houses (including the top three: Kodansha, Shueisha, and Shogakukan) release hundreds of titles translated into a multitude of foreign languages worldwide to promote the multi-billion-dollar industry.

Whether you're new to manga or a professional artist looking to try something different, this book is a great place to get your feet wet. Throughout this book, I take you step by step through exercises in drawing all sorts of characters, backgrounds, and useful special effects. I also give tips and pointers, most of which are based on my own experience. Although I recommend that beginners go through this book in sequential order, I designed the subject matter to be flexible so that you can navigate freely from chapter to chapter, depending on your interest.

In this chapter, I explore the history of manga, the various popular manga genres, and what makes manga so successful.

Tracing the Rise of Manga's Popularity

Humorous and satirical illustrations trace back to 12th century Japan. Although now understood to mean "comics originating from Japan," *manga* (pronounced MAHN-gah or MANG-ah) is literally translated as "whimsical pictorial." Katsushika Hokusai, a wood engraver and painter who lived from 1760 to 1849, coined the phrase in *Hokusai Manga,* one of his many publications. In a 15-volume series of sketches published in 1814, he covered various topics ranging from the informative to the comical aspects of the Edo period.

Despite the rapid growth and prosperity displayed in today's manga world, in truth, manga didn't see significant growth until World War II. Under the influence of the great manga artist Tezuka Osamu (1928–1989), manga began to gain not only national but also international recognition with works such as Astro Boy, Black Jack, Buddha, and many more. In the midst of a post-war economic struggle, Tezuka's manga adaptation of Robert Louis Stevenson's *Treasure Island* sold 400,000 copies to become the nation's top-seller.

During the 1960s, the generation that enjoyed reading manga as children grew up and brought their manga books and interests with them. People no longer viewed manga as something to be enjoyed only by children — it was now acceptable for adults too. American comics at the time primarily had a huge audience of young boys idolizing superheroes whose sole mission was to defeat crime, but the Japanese community developed its own audience of both male and female groups, ranging from children to adults.

From 1980 to 2000, manga saw not only an evolvement of genre and style, but also the introduction of sophisticated techniques specifically geared toward enhancing its looks and effects. Techniques like *screen tones* (a series of adhesive, stylized, design patterns used to suggest color) gave new sleek looks to the finished pages. Story lines became more complex and widespread to include more audience interests, such as science fiction (mostly for males), sports, politics, religion, sex, and romance (pulling in more female readers and artists). Thanks to professional computer graphics software, such as Adobe Photoshop and Illustrator, manga artists (referred to as *manga-ka*) throughout Japan can put in more detail and all sorts of cool effects in less time. Along with the growing market appeal, scores of new artists are coming up with original ideas of their own in hopes of making it big in Japan and worldwide. At the same time, the number of talented female artists has skyrocketed; many of these artists are housewives who saw the opportunity of launching their manga career in drawing manga catering to female readers. This manga is now referred to as shōjo (young girl) manga.

Today, many successful artists, such as Fujiko Fujio *(Doraemon)*, Matsumoto Leiji *(Starblazers)*, Toriyama Akira *(Dragon Ball)*, Rumiko Takahashi *(Ranma ½)*, Takehiko Inoue *(Slam Dunk)*, and Masashi Kishimoto *(Naruto)*, have followed in the footsteps of Tezuka to contribute to the lucrative and popular entertainment industry.

All Manga Is Not Created Equal: Looking At the Different Genres

Just *how* diverse is the manga world? Any major publisher has at least three types of manga magazines catering to different groups of people. Following is a list of the recognized types of manga being published in Japan:

- ✔ **Kodomo Manga:** Comics for little kids

- ✔ **Shōnen Manga:** Comics for teenage boys

- ✔ **Shōjo Manga:** Comics for teenage girls

- ✔ **Seinen Manga:** Comics for young adult males

- ✔ **Redisu Manga:** Comics for young adult females

- ✔ **Shōjo-ai Manga:** Romantic comics for teenage girls

- ✔ **Shōjo-ai Yuri Manga:** Romantic comics for lesbians

- ✔ **Shōnen-ai Manga:** Romantic comics for men

- ✔ **Shōnen-yaoi Manga:** Romantic comics for homosexual men

- ✔ **Seijin Manga:** Comics for adult males

- ✔ **Redikomi Manga:** Comics written by women for late teen to adult women, depicting more realistic, everyday accounts; literal translation: lady's comics

- ✔ **Dōjinshi Manga:** Comics written and illustrated by amateurs (usually circulated among a close group of other manga amateurs)

- ✔ **Yonkoma Manga:** Four-panel comics, usually published in newspapers

- ✔ **Gekiga Manga:** Comics focusing on serious topics; geared toward mature audiences

- ✔ **Ecchi Manga:** Comics focusing on heterosexual/lesbian erotic themes (softcore pornography) read by men

- ✔ **Hentai Manga:** Comics focusing on hardcore pornography

For those of you who are already seasoned manga fans, some of these genres may be unfamiliar to you because publishers have a tendency to simplify everything into either the boy (shōnen) manga or girl (shōjo) manga category, regardless of the specific subcontents. With the exception of the yonkoma, redisu, and redikomi manga genres, most of the genres are available in the United States. For the purpose of this book, I base my example characters mostly on the shōnen and shōjo manga genres.

This long list testifies to the immense and diverse popularity, interests, and tastes of Japanese manga readers. As time progresses, no doubt the genre will shift to include other topics.

Looking over this list, you may notice the number of comics that are geared toward the female audience. A large number of girls read comics in Japan, and a large number of publishers specialize in comics geared toward women readers only. (In comparison, the number of females who casually read American comics is, to say the least, small.)

The Key Components of Manga

You find several key components in most popular manga. For example, weekly magazines are restricted to 16 pages. These titles are designed to quickly satisfy the reader's short attention span, because many readers are busy commuters who don't have time to sit down for hours to read through a long book. Those magazines are eventually compiled into books that can be collected as a multivolume series. Not all magazines have those crazy weekly deadlines. Some magazines release their titles on a biweekly or monthly schedule.

Most mainstream manga features certain archetypes. For example, you'll see the main lead character (who is often androgynous), a sidekick, a single attractive female character (who is either a lover or nurturer), and a wise old man (depending on whether the manga is action oriented). The villains usually have the charmingly evil leader accompanied by his strong henchman.

Manga versus American Comics

When you pick up and open a manga book for the first time, you're no doubt confused. "Wait a minute," you say, "I'm looking at the end of this book?" Exactly. In Japan, you open and read manga (as well as all books in the country) from right to left and back to front. Reversed reading isn't the only difference between manga and American comics, though. In Table 1-1, I list some additional differences between the two.

Table 1-1	First-Glance Differences between Manga and American Comics
Manga	*American Comics*
Most manga is printed in black and white (occasionally the first several pages are in color, depending on the success of the title).	Most comics are printed in full color. Comic book retailers often fail to receive black-and-white titles well.
All weekly manga magazines and compiled titles are printed on economical recycled paper.	More and more printers are now using recycled paper. However, until the recent past, elaborate variant issues used high-cost paper for covers and interiors (which attracted retailers and collectors).

Manga	*American Comics*
Manga is first published in thick weekly or monthly magazines before finally being compiled into a single series of issues.	American publishers publish titles as stand-alone issues. Depending on the sales, the publisher may opt to compile the single issues to form a "graphic novel."
Most competitive publishers release manga magazines on a weekly basis — deadlines are never, never, *neeeeeeever* missed. Publishers would never want to upset their 1 million plus regular weekly readers.	American publishers try to release titles on a monthly basis. Occasionally, some titles miss deadlines, upsetting retailers and readers who must order them through distribution catalogues. Best titles average 40,000 to 50,000 copies in monthly sales.
Manga and manga magazines can be bought at newsstands, bookstores, candy shops, gift shops, train stations, and almost anywhere else. If you miss out on those weekly issues, the compiled series (usually 180 pages) appears on your local bookstore shelf, and you can easily order it if you don't see it.	If you want to find your favorite title selection and it isn't a superhero title, you have to visit your "local" comic book store where they *might* have it. If they don't, good luck getting the store to re-order the issue listed in last month's distribution catalogue. Time to test your luck on eBay.

Besides these at-a-glance differences (like physical look and accessibility), do these two forms of comics have other *big* differences? You may be thinking, comics are comics, right? Not really. Both forms share a sequential format and have a story to tell. However, if you examine not only the national but also the international impact, you definitely find differences.

In the following sections, I compare American comics' and manga's demography and distribution.

Broader readership than American comics

Popular mainstream American comics have traditionally been geared toward children (mostly teenage boys) and collectors. Mention you're a comic book artist at any social gathering and you're guaranteed to get a weird look (especially from the women) that says, "Excuse me, how *old* are you?" Chances are good that the general public doesn't take your job seriously. Although the genre has expanded (thanks to the independent and manga publishers), comics in America are still dominated by Marvel, DC, and Image Comics, which still rely upon their superhero titles to survive. At major comic book conventions, these top three publishers usually take center stage among the smaller independent publishers. Smaller publishers put up a good fight to present the readers with their own original, independent titles, but many of them usually last no longer than a few seasons due to either poor management or the harsh market.

In contrast, manga has a wider genre and audience. Being a comic book artist, or *manga-ka,* in Japan is no laughing matter! If you ever visit Japan, you see manga pretty much everywhere you go. For example, if you're riding the subway to work, you commonly see a lot of people (a diverse range in age, sex, and occupation) engrossed in reading their favorite title in the latest manga magazine. From waiting rooms at doctors' offices to small cafés, you're guaranteed to see a stack of these manga magazines. Picture a high school student on his way to school reading the latest *Shōnen Jump* while a businessman next to him in his 40s is totally engrossed in the latest *Business Jump* magazine.

Availability differences

As I mention in Table 1-1, major differences between American comics and manga are the distribution and availability. Currently, you can find American comics mostly in comic book stores. Depending on where you live, you may have to drive miles and miles before finally getting to your "local" comic book store to buy your favorite book. Then, depending on how large that store is, the selection or choices you see may be very disappointingly limited. Sure, you may see comic titles in the form of graphic novels at major bookstores, but they usually consist of mainstream superhero comics. The space they occupy may be only a shelf or two.

In contrast, the Japanese market for manga grosses a whopping $4.7 billion a year. For those of you manga fans thinking that the manga market is huge in America, it amounts only to a $100 million industry. While manga artists and their teams of skilled assistants (ranging from 5 to 15 artists per title) constantly struggle to meet weekly deadlines, the publishers are using their much larger budgets to promote to a large, diverse audience. Unlike American comics, you rarely see manga published in book format without first being serialized in chapters or segments in weekly or monthly manga magazines. Among the many magazines, some claim 1 million readers *per week.*

But that's not the end. After a certain number of publications, the works of manga artists are compiled and sold at bookstores nationwide. Seeing up to ⅓ of any bookstore's sections devoted to manga titles isn't unusual (compared to maybe a shelf or two in bookstores in the United States). In addition, larger distributors, such as Broccoli International, have contributed to the increased sales of manga and *animé* (Japanese animation) products in the United States.

The guts and glory: Differences in workload and credit for artists

Many comic book artists and manga-ka go into the market for the love of the sequential art rather than for the money. However, the two have different processes by which they execute their work, and they're glorified in different ways.

If you work for either Marvel or DC Comics, chances are you're under a "work for hire" clause. This clause basically means that you don't own the rights to the artwork, characters, or story. Depending on the terms of your contract, you may own the actual artwork itself (which is why you see artists at conventions displaying the original pages for sale), but you technically don't have permission to reproduce the work or claim the characters you draw as your own creation. After you're paid a page rate depending upon your specialization, the publisher owes you nothing more. Many freelance illustrators (myself included) cringe at the thought of losing the rights to the work they spend so many hours to complete. But these jobs give artists better chances to get additional work from other publishers. Here I list some of the main specialized jobs that complete a comic book in America:

- **Penciler:** This artist lays down the frames and images based upon the script he receives from the writer. Usually, the penciler gets paid the most because his responsibility takes the most time and usually dictates the overall look of the book.

- **Writer:** The writer is responsible for writing the story of the comic book. She makes sure that the story not only flows well from page to page (without cramming too many frames into one page), but also ends within 22 pages, which is the usual comic book page count. Many successful comic book writers have gone on to write their own novels.

- **Inker:** The inker goes over the pencils and enhances or "interprets" the quality of the line work before sending the illustrations to the colorist. Traditionally, pencil drawings were more difficult to reproduce, so the inkers were in charge of making sure that the lines were clear. However, thanks to rapid scanners being pumped out at increasingly more affordable prices, more and more comic book projects are foregoing the inking process and moving straight to color.

- **Colorist:** Traditionally, colorists colored the pages by hand. However, again, thanks to powerful technology, colorists all (and I do mean *all*) use graphics software such as Photoshop and Painter to pump out pages at a faster pace while inventing new special effects.

- **Letterer:** In the past, lettering was a craft that required the special skill of making sure that words were legible and easy to read. The process took care but also cost time and money. Thanks to computers, almost all comic book lettering is now done digitally. Only a few titles still use a specialist to handle such a task.

In the manga world, a manga-ka is expected to do the creating, writing, penciling, and inking (even though he relies on his assistants to help him make the tight deadlines). Coloring isn't a huge factor in the equation because most manga is published in black and white. Although an increasing number of artists work with writers (especially with publishers with monthly or bimonthly deadlines), most published manga stories are each created and illustrated by one person. The publisher types in the lettering inside of the balloons (with the exception of editorial yonkoma manga, which is hand-lettered by the artist to match the simplicity of the art style).

Although the publisher retains the rights to publish the work exclusively, the manga-ka retains the rights to the creation and also receives royalties and overseas exposure. As I mention earlier in this chapter, the publishers also compile the artist's work after a number of magazine appearances. The compilation is in graphic novel form and distributed nationwide. In the end, the manga-ka is forever credited exclusively with his work, as opposed to the American comic book artist who may draw a Marvel comic book character for her entire career, but never get an iota of credit for its design or creation.

"Making It" in the Manga World

So how does a Japanese aspiring artist "make it" in the professional manga industry? Typically, an artist starts as an apprentice to a manga professional (referred to as teacher, or *sensei*). After honing his craft under the sensei's wings, the fledgling builds his own works and submits them to the sensei's publisher.

Most manga-ka (such as Rumiko Takahashi) who made it were assistants at some point in their career. Interestingly enough, you can actually tell who studied under a specific manga-ka by the similarity in style.

Becoming an apprentice isn't the only way of getting into the business in Japan. Some aspiring artists use the direct approach of bringing in and dropping off their work to the publisher — an approach known as *genkō mochikomi*. Artists can also submit their works to a competition sponsored by publishers and judged by a selected group of famous manga-ka. These competitions tend to be more competitive, because judges must choose a winner out of the thousands of works submitted. This competition's winner, however, shines above others as the "chosen one" and receives more publicity.

In Chapter 21, I talk about different methods of shopping your portfolio, exposing your work to the public at conventions, and establishing a working network with professional artists. Entering competitions and working with other artists are great ways of opening up opportunities and breaking in, but they don't substitute for the importance of networking at professional gatherings.

Chapter 2

Gearing Up and Getting Ready

In This Chapter

- Collecting the materials you need to get started
- Discovering how to use the materials
- Taking care of your investment

It's time to lock and load — with art supplies, that is. Manga is so popular that an entire product line is geared specifically to accommodating the manga artist's (or *manga-ka*'s) needs and demands. From inks to paper to pens, most major art stores in Japan have an entire section devoted exclusively to selling manga materials. Obtaining these materials if you live in America used to be extremely difficult, unless you wanted to make a trip to Japan. Thanks to Internet shopping and growing demand due to manga-mania, you can easily attain materials today. I personally recommend visiting Wet Paint Art (`www.wetpaintart.com`). They carry an impressive array of manga materials, including major brands that aren't easy to find in the United States.

In this chapter, I explain the various types of materials used by manga-ka and how to use and properly maintain them. I also talk about the importance of setting up your studio and environment. After reading this chapter and gathering the necessary gear, you'll be ready to get down to business.

Materials You Need to Get Started

Despite the different brands, types of pencils and brushes, and sizes of papers on the manga market, the basics you need to start drawing manga are quite simple. All you need is a pencil, pen, eraser, and paper. Pretty simple, eh? That doesn't necessarily mean that you can rely solely on whatever you have in your first grade pencil case. Sometimes you may need some of those professional-looking materials you see on the market.

Starting off with the correct paper size is helpful, as is working with materials that a typical manga-ka uses. But although I give advice and information on specific materials that are readily available, don't despair if you can't find every single tool I mention. Many artists have gone on to become successful without using them. However, if you can afford these materials and have access to them, I recommend trying them out to see whether you like working with them. If not, you can always go back to the materials that you're used to working with.

The advantage, of course, of trying out these materials is that comparing and sharing techniques with other manga buddies is easier when everyone is using the same tools. Another reason I recommend looking into some of the materials is that many of them are manufactured with you, the artist, in mind. For example, although certain cheap and generic inks may be easier to find, they may discolor and smudge easily.

The same thing applies to paper quality. You can't draw or ink on cheap toilet paper and expect to get decent results no matter how good you are. Working with quality materials is important. Although you don't need brushes that are made out of gold, going that extra mile to find and obtain materials that don't cause unnecessary problems doesn't hurt (and it isn't expensive).

In the following sections, I give you more details about various manga supplies.

Paper (genkō yōshi)

If you're drawing manga for the first time, don't worry about the type or size of paper you're using (after all, paper is paper). I don't see anything wrong with using regular photocopy paper to practice your characters. If you're thinking of self-publishing or presenting your works to editors and publishers, consider working with the standard manga paper (referred to as *genkō yōshi*). Printers and editors sometimes expect to see a certain paper size from artists and young prospects. You don't want to submit your best work on, say, a crumpled receipt! If you're already experienced, seriously consider paper size and paper quality issues. After all, if you draw your manga using paper that's too big, publishers can't fit all the content within the allotted space. As a result, your image runs off the page and gets cut off. Major publishers often provide their artists with company paper to ensure that the size is correct.

A manga-ka uses smaller, thinner paper sizes than the standard American comic book artist. For example, American comic book artists draw on 11-x-17 inch, quality paper known as *smooth Bristol paper*. Although many American comic book artists may opt to buy large sheets of Bristol paper and later measure and cut the sheets down to a specific size (usually to save cost), a manga-ka has her own specific high-quality paper that she buys precut, measured, and treated for the exclusive purpose of drawing manga. These sheets are B4 size, which measure 180-x-270 mm. Although many companies sell this type of paper, I recommend buying from a Japan-based manufacturer called Deleter (www.deleter.com). Deleter sells different paper sizes for different purposes and at the same price or cheaper than the Bristol pad.

Protecting your borders

Line frames, known as *borders,* tell you how much of the paper space you can use for your manga images. Artists rely on these boundary lines to contain their drawings and avoid having their work cropped out when it's published. Both American comic book artists and Japanese manga artists incorporate their own standard measurement sizes. You need to be aware of several border measurements, and you should indicate them on your paper even before you pick up your pencil to draw (if you get the official genkō yōshi, the measurement guides are marked). Here are the terms you need to know:

✔ **Safe Area:** All images within this area are guaranteed to be printed without any threat of being cropped out.

✔ **Trim Area:** Basically, this area signifies the "end" of the paper. The closer an image runs to the border, the better its chances of being cropped by the printing machine.

✔ **Bleed (Expendable) Area:** Cutting machines are imperfect. Sometimes you want to extend an image all the way to the end of the paper, but unfortunately, the cutting machines don't always cut right at the trim line — sometimes they go past the area. Therefore, if your image stops right at the trim line and you want it to go all the way to the edge, it may be cut too short due to the overshot of the cutting blade. To ensure that the edge of the image doesn't end before the printed image does, use the bleed area. The printing company considers this area expendable. Art must extend past the trim line all the way to the bleed line.

If you're waiting to get your hands on the manga genkō yōshi, using 8-x-10 inch, smooth Bristol paper is perfectly fine, and you can find it at any art store.

If you decide to stick with the 8-x-10 pad, I recommend getting the Strathmore 300 Series brand. It generally stands the test of time, unlike other, cheaper Bristol paper brands, which bleed. However, even with this type of paper, I find some drafting markers I use still bleed. For this reason, I recommend eventually working with the smoother, lighter manga paper even if you have to go through the hassle of ordering it online. Companies sell these sheets in packets, and the paper is a delight to work on.

Drawing supplies

Drawing supplies differ depending upon an artist's personal choice. Try different types of pencils, erasers, and inking methods until you find what you like best. The good news is that pencils are generally inexpensive and affordable. If you don't like one, getting another one is cheap.

In this section, I explore different types of pencils and drawing tools that artists commonly use today. If you're just starting out, pick up any pencil, as long as you feel comfortable drawing with it. However, if you're interested in either publishing or showing your work around, consider investing in a variety of pencils and drawing tools.

Choosing your drawing pencil

Art supply companies sell drawing pencils in different degrees of hardness or softness. Ultimately, rather than just choosing a pencil at any generic stationery store, I recommend going to your local art supply store where you have a diverse range of selection. There, you can find pencils with varying degrees of lead hardness and softness. Some brands range from extra hard (5H) to extra soft (8B). You can find the degree of hardness or softness by looking at the ends of the handles.

I recommend getting at least three different pencils with contrasting levels of hardness to get a "feel" for the different lines you can draw. Beginners should try using leads HB, B, and 2B. Not many pros go past 2H or 2B. The harder the lead is (higher H level), the more accurate your lines are. This accuracy means you can easily erase the lines after you're done inking over them. The trade-off is that you lose a certain degree of feel or sensitivity of the line. Drawing with harder leads also damages the paper if you apply too much pressure. If you're drawing carefully and lightly, this isn't a problem. Most American comic book pencilers opt for harder lead because it facilitates the inker's job of erasing and gives the penciler more accurate lines, which minimizes any misinterpretations during the inking process. In contrast, the softer the lead (higher B level), the looser and wider the range of line quality. Like the harder leads, softer leads have their own trade-offs. The lines you draw with high B pencils tend to be messier and much harder to erase.

Unlike the American comic book world, where you may have to worry about inkers misunderstanding your pencil lines, in the manga world, you're responsible for inking your own work (unless you have an assistant), so you don't need to worry about someone misinterpreting your penciled lines.

Adding a couple mechanical pencils

Take a look at mechanical pencils. They're cheap and easy to use, and you're always guaranteed a sharp point. You can find a lot of fancy brands on the market, but you don't need to shell out big bucks to get one that works. Make sure you get the right size lead to go with your mechanical pencil. Most mechanical pencils come in 0.5 mm standard size. To refill them, pop open the cap and load the lead. In addition to the 0.5 mm lead size, the mechanical pencils come in sizes 0.3 mm, 0.7 mm, and 0.9 mm (the thickest). With a thicker mechanical pencil, you have more choices of lead softness because thinner leads are more brittle and break too easily if the lead is too soft.

If money's no object: Lead holders

Lead holders are another alternative to pencils, but they're pricier than mechanical pencils because you also need a barrel-shaped sharpener. Like the mechanical pencil, you load or refill the lead by removing the end cap and inserting the lead from the top. After you replace the end cap, press down on it while holding the pencil right-side up. This causes the metal contraption at the front opening of the pencil to release the lead. The advantage of using a lead holder is that you can get a very fine line detail when you need it. The leads come in a package of a dozen with a wide range of softness and hardness.

French curves

These plastic transparent templates have edges that are molded into various shaped curves. They come in a set of three different sizes and are great for drawing speed lines (see Chapter 17). Handle them carefully as they tend to break and scratch easily.

Templates

Templates, which are plastic semitransparent sheets with various cutout shapes, are great for drawing geometric objects that are difficult to draw freehand.

Screentones

Screentones are thin acetate sheets consisting of a wide range of design patterns. The most common types used by manga-ka are gray scale patterns and speed lines.

Inking materials

You have many options to consider when selecting your inking materials. My advice to beginners is to try out as many as you can and see which ones work the best. Be patient with this process, and don't be afraid to experiment with different techniques. I always tell my students that I'm much happier seeing them take risks rather than just attempting to get good grades. Try different inking techniques even if it means not always getting the desired results.

Markers

Artist's markers are useful when you want to draw mechanical objects, border frames, and small details. The ones I like to use are the Staedtler Pigment Liner and the more popular Sakura Microns. Either brand is excellent for starters. Like pencil leads, markers come in various thicknesses. They range from as thin as 0.1 mm to as thick as 0.8 mm. Although they're fairly expensive compared to cheap kid's markers, they're certainly worth every cent. Three sizes I recommend for starters are 0.3, 0.5, and 0.8 mm.

Be careful if you use low-grade markers that aren't waterproof — they fade and discolor over time. Cost is a huge factor for my beginning students when they're purchasing quality markers. Although they're not ideal for inking smaller details, I recommend getting Sharpie or Bic permanent markers. Both are waterproof, cheap, and widely used among American comic book artists to sometimes ink frames around the images. To ensure as much longevity as possible, always remember to put the cap back on the marker when you're not using it.

The advantage of using markers is that they're fast and easy to use. If you want a wider range of thickness, certain brands have brush pens that work just like markers but have a brushlike, flexible tip. The disadvantage to using these markers is that they tend to fade after erasing the pencil marks underneath. The life span of calligraphy brush pens isn't that great, either. Most markers (except for the more expensive synthetic brush pens) wear down fairly quickly, depending upon the amount of usage. Therefore, I recommend choosing another inking tool to supplement the markers.

Brushes

Despite popular use by American comic artists, a typical manga-ka doesn't use much brushwork in his work (maybe due to the smaller size of paper — see "Paper [genkō yōshi]" earlier in this chapter for details on paper size). Manga studios are more likely to rely on pen nibs to get the work done (as I discuss in the next section). However, several brushes in varying sizes are worth mentioning. Sable brushes make excellent lines. Good ones can be expensive, but they last longer than markers when you properly clean and maintain them. In addition, you get more expressive and diverse line work with brushes. To ensure longevity, always wash them with soap under warm water and store them upside down to prevent any debris from getting into the base where the hairs of the brush meet with the cylindrical, metal part of the brush (known as the *feral*). One way to store them is to tape the brushes to a slanted drawing table.

Many artists favor Windsor Newton's flagship brush, Series 7. Because these brushes are rather expensive, start with the most widely-used size, the number 2.

In addition to brushes for inks, I advise getting a couple thin brushes for correcting mistakes with the white manga correction fluid only (never use your art brush for applying the white correction fluid you find in regular office stationery stores).

Nibs

A *nib* resembles a sharp pointed dart when fitted into its nib holder, and is the heart and soul of inking in today's manga world. Companies such as Zebra, Nikko, Tachikawa, and Deleter have created and marketed many nibs exclusively for manga inking. When you use a brush, the quality and length of the hair strands determine the thickness of the stroke, but a nib has the flexibility of two metallic sharp prongs, which pinch tightly together. Dip the nib in ink and it stores and dispenses the ink from between the two tightly compressed metal tips. By transferring the pressure from your hand to the tip of the pen, you control the thinness or thickness of the line. The difference from one pen nib to another is the flexibility of the two prongs. The softer the metal is, the easier it is to draw wider lines. When you have harder, more resistant metal, you get thinner, more tightly controlled lines. Although nibs may be difficult to find at your local art store (depending upon its size and location), you should have no problem finding and ordering them online. I recommend starting off with the G-Pen. It's the most popular nib used among pros and amateurs because its metal is well balanced and allows artists to draw both wide and narrow lines with equal flexibility.

Following are the most common nibs used in manga:

- G-Pen (most widely used)
- Maru (Circle) Pen
- Spoon Pen
- Kabura Pen
- School Pen
- Nihon-ji Pen
- Brauze Pen

Don't forget to get the nib holder that corresponds to the nib. Not all holders accommodate all nibs. Make sure you check for the matching size.

Inks

As I mention earlier in this chapter, using waterproof ink is imperative. My personal favorite is the Japanese Kuretake Sumi Ink (green bottle). It's not only waterproof, but it also delivers excellent deep blacks and has a nice texture. If you visit the Deleter online store (www.deleter.com), you'll see plenty of other choices marketed as "manga ink," which are also waterproof. If you're on a tighter budget, I recommend getting the Higgins India Ink, which is the popular waterproof ink used by American comic book artists.

Miscellaneous items

Following are other types of tools you should have in your manga arsenal. You can find these items in most art stores or even a grocery store:

- Kneaded and plastic erasers
- Paper towels (for cleaning any ink spills)
- Rulers (triangle and straight edge)

✔ Plastic or Styrofoam cup (for rinsing brushes)

✔ Thumbtacks (for securing your ruler or French curve)

✔ White correction fluid (for correcting ink mistakes)

Setting Up Your Studio

When you have the materials you need, set up a proper environment so that you can work productively. The basics of setting up a place to work in the beginning are quite simple. You need a chair, a table to draw on, and a light source bright enough that you don't strain your eyes. It's actually that simple.

"Okay," you say, "So what's the catch?" I'm glad you asked; the catch is that the place you choose to work needs to be a place where you can be productive without everyday distractions. This task is actually a lot more challenging than you may imagine. Small distractions add up and can throw an artist off focus. So from time to time, take a walk or temporarily change working locations. Speaking from my own experiences, you need to try different places because everyone has different working habits. For example, I enjoy occasionally working while drinking a latte at my local coffee shop, but some of my colleagues need complete solitude in order to work effectively.

Finding a quiet place to draw

Although no single right solution works for everybody, try to identify some distractions that prevent you from concentrating on your work. For example, do you have chatty friends who keep calling your cell phone? If so, set the phone to silent mode when you work and let your voice mail pick up. Does your neighbor blast the radio so loud that you can hear it all the way across the street? I usually wear ear plugs or listen to my favorite music on my iPod to combat this problem. How about any siblings or roommates who watch TV or play video games all the time in the same room you draw? Move to a different room with a door or designate a quiet time when the TV stays off. Bottom line: Be proactive in getting the most out of your working environment. You may find the best place for you to work is as simple as the kitchen table or the coffee table in your living room.

When looking around for a good place to work, keep track of your time to see how much you can accomplish in 30 minutes without having to stand up or leave your drawing table. Are you able to do it? Good! Next, try to work for 45 minutes and then for a full hour. This exercise helps you to gauge your work productivity.

Using the right equipment

As I mention at the beginning of this section, all you really need to start your first manga studio is a drawing table, a comfortable chair, and a lamp. You don't have to have several thousand dollars worth of equipment for your studio to be an effective working environment from the start. My first setup was a ping-pong table, an old toddler's bar stool, and a 15-year-old lamp.

If you plan on working for more than an hour, I recommend getting a good lamp that reduces strain on (and ultimately prevents damage to) your eyes. You should also take a moment from time to time to stand up and stretch your body. As I mention in the nearby sidebar "The ultimate studio makeover," some chairs come with adjustable height levels so your neck doesn't strain from supporting the weight of your head leaning over the artwork. In the next section, I give you some advice on upgrading your work equipment if you plan on working for an extended period of time.

Upgrading your basic studio

If you ever decide that you want to upgrade from the basic table, chair, and lamp, the following list can help you decide what you need:

- ✔ **Drafting table:** Your drafting table should be slightly tilted toward you, which minimizes the strain on your back and neck from your head weight. Back pain occurs when you constantly bend too far forward over your work. Aside from the ergonomic issue, a tilted table can improve your work. Having your work more or less parallel to your body minimizes the amount of distortion perceived by your eye. You should also get a side tray to hold your pencils, brushes, inks, and nibs (see "Materials You Need to Get Started" earlier in this chapter for more info). Your side tray should be sturdy and have enough compartments to accommodate your wide range of materials. Because your table is on an incline, your tools slide off if you don't have this tray.

- ✔ **Lights:** Lights are an essential tool in reducing the strain on your eyes. Working long hours without proper lighting can hurt your vision. If you're drawing for long hours on an everyday basis, I recommend getting clamp lights that have a socket for a regular bulb in addition to a separate socket for a halogen tube. When you simultaneously switch both lights on, you get a natural-looking light color that looks like the outside, natural daylight. Although these lights aren't cheap, my eyes are less strained after gazing at my work for a long period of time.

- ✔ **Chair:** Choose a solid ergonomic studio chair for your work space if you find yourself sitting at your drawing table for more than an hour at a time. Make sure you get a chance to sit in and try out a chair before you buy one. You may visit different art stores and try out several chairs before making a decision. You'll potentially be sitting in this chair for a very long time, so make sure you get adequate cushion and back support. Your drafting chair should come with a lever to adjust its height, and it should give your feet the option of touching the ground for support. Finally, should you need to stretch your back or move away from your drafting table, the back section of the chair should tilt and the legs should have ball bearing coasters that enable you to move around without having to get up.

✔ **Side table:** Your side table can be anything that's stable that you can use to place extra stuff on that can't stay on the drawing table. Actually, it doesn't even need to be a table. It can be your dresser, a mini-bookshelf, or even a trunk or case that happens to be lying close to your drawing table. If it has a place in which you can store additional items, that's an even bigger plus! In my case, I keep my oil painting materials for my illustration work in my side table. On the top, I have my most treasured equipment of all — my coffee maker!

✔ **Light box:** This item comes in handy when I need to copy or transfer a drawing from one paper to another. The construction of a light box is quite rudimentary and simple. It's basically a box with a couple of halogen tubes inside. The top lid is semitransparent, milky plastic, where I place my original drawings. On top of the original, I place the paper onto which I want to transfer the drawing. When I switch on the lights inside the box, they shine through both sheets of paper and reveal the original image. Using the image as my guide, I trace over the lines to get an accurate reproduction. As I demonstrate in Chapter 18, I use a light box to transfer my thumbnail sketches to my final manga drawing paper.

If you can't afford a light box, you can easily get the same effect by placing your sheets of paper over a glass window during the day. The natural sunlight helps you see the original drawing from behind the sheet of paper you want to transfer the image onto.

You don't need to get everything at once, but if you're serious about drawing manga, this equipment may improve not only your working environment but also your final product.

The ultimate studio makeover

Because my artwork is my lifestyle, I invest in an even more extensive setup. I have two drafting tables that are ergonomically tilted to reduce the neck strain from the long hours I spend drawing. I use an adjustable drafting chair and adjust the height to my liking. Keeping good posture and drawing habits are important to me because I'm usually working 12–14 hours a day.

For my light sources, I have two studio lamps attached to both sides of my table (because it's larger than a normal drafting table), so that my entire view is evenly lit. In addition, because a lot of my clients have tight deadlines, I have two separate digital work stations (one Mac and one PC). I also carry a laptop and scanner when I work on-site (and during my vacations). Basically, I have a live, eat, breathe, and sleep art lifestyle.

Although I don't think investing so much money and energy when you're just starting is necessary (or practical), you may want to eventually think about getting an affordable digital work station (computer, scanner, and printer) to aid you with your manga projects.

Chapter 3

Drawing: Starting with the Basics

In This Chapter

- Becoming familiar with basic drawing tools
- Discovering basic drawing techniques
- Trying out different types of lines and shading

After you gather all the tools you need (take a look at Chapter 2 for more info), it's time to use them. In this chapter, I demonstrate how different types of inking and drawing materials produce different types of lines. You can use these techniques and tools when you begin drawing your manga characters.

Note: As you go through the exercises in this chapter, you may find that some materials work better for you than others. That's okay. Finding the tools you like is similar to trying on different shoes to find a pair that fits comfortably. But don't return materials or get rid of them just because they don't work for you at first. Be patient; some of these tools take some getting used to.

Making Your First Moves with the Pencil

Making a series of scribbles is a good way to get used to using your pencils. When selecting a pencil's hardness, look for something that glides comfortably on the paper. If you're going to be at your drawing table for a long period of time, you want to make sure your hand doesn't cramp up, so a comfortable glide is especially important. In this section, I show you several simple exercises you can do to loosen up.

For the first simple exercise, follow these directions:

Create a series of swirls using different types of pencils, as shown in Figure 3-1.

Explore the various types of line quality (thinness versus thickness) you create when you apply pressure to the strokes. In Figure 3-1, I use a 3H lead to get lighter, thinner strokes and gradually switch to a softer 4B lead to achieve the darker, wider strokes that are typically created with softer leads.

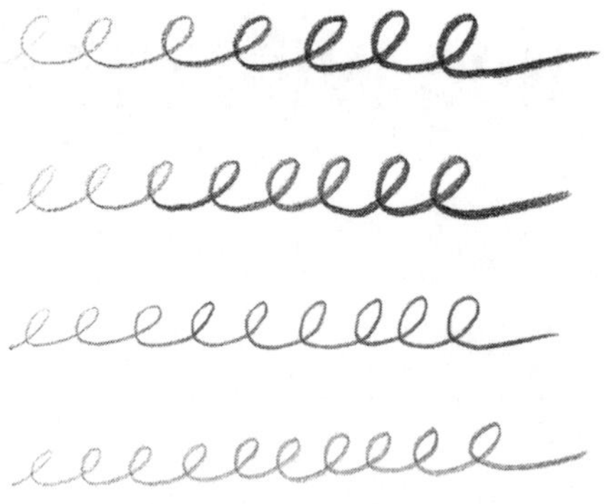

Figure 3-1: Warming up by drawing loose swirls using different types of leads.

You'll notice pros and cons to using harder versus softer leads. Although harder leads take time to get used to because their lines are so light, you get more control of details and you can more easily erase the final lines after inking over them. Unfortunately, you also scratch the paper if you press down too hard. Softer leads produce darker, thicker lines, but they can get a bit messy and you have more difficulty erasing them. I recommend trying both extremes just to get a feel for what you can do.

When you're ready, move on to the next exercise:

Draw a small circle, and then use it as your center core as you continue to draw slightly larger circles around it, as shown in Figure 3-2.

Don't rush through this one. Take your time, making sure that you're making the circles as round and symmetrical as possible as you build up the series of "rings" to form a large circle.

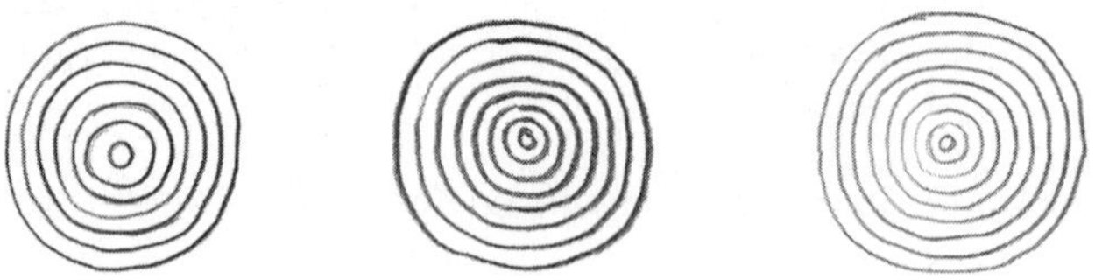

Figure 3-2: Warming up by drawing circular "ring" marks around a smaller circle.

Finish warming up with the last exercise in this section:

Use your wrist as a *fulcrum* (the point of support) to create a series of rapid zig zag shading marks, increasing the pressure gradually from soft to hard, as shown in Figure 3-3.

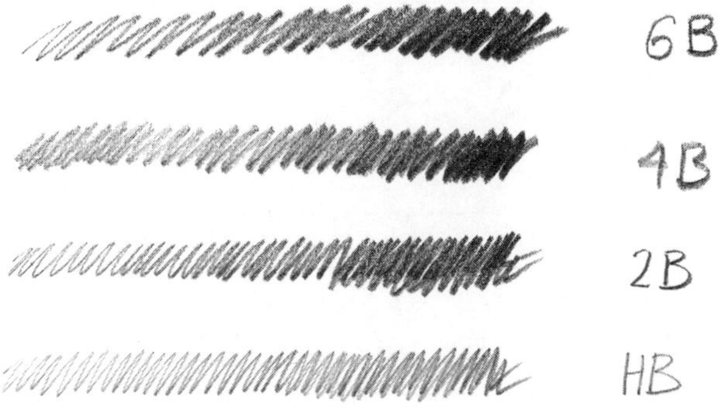
6B
4B
2B
HB

Figure 3-3: Loosening the wrist using a rapid back and forth motion.

TIP

The key is to keep your wrist loose through this exercise. You should experience a "flicking of the wrist" motion as you rapidly go from left to right. As the pressure you put on the pencil gets harder, you find the shades get darker (depending on which pencil level you choose, you may get less or more depth of contrast).

REMEMBER

Nothing is more refreshing than shaking your wrist from time to time during long drawing sessions. Too much pressure building up on your fingers and wrist from holding the pencil tightly for a long period of time can result in pain and pinched nerves. Refer to Chapter 2 for more ergonomic tips for working comfortably and effectively at your drafting table.

Exercises Using Your Ruler

A ruler appears to be a simple, straight, plastic bar, but you'll find no limit to its importance in creating cool effects. Make sure you have a transparent ruler for these exercises. Here are some tips to using the ruler effectively:

- Make sure the pencil point rests securely against the edge of the ruler when you're drawing straight lines, as shown in Figure 3-4.
- As shown in Figure 3-5a, ink tends to seep underneath the ruler when you use it right side up. Flipping the ruler upside down solves this problem, as shown in Figure 3-5b.

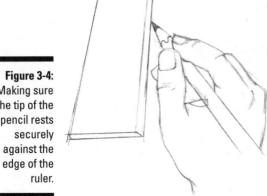

Figure 3-4:
Making sure
the tip of the
pencil rests
securely
against the
edge of the
ruler.

Some rulers come with a beveled edge so that the ink doesn't bleed underneath. If you can, shell out a few extra bucks and invest in a nice one. If you're using pen nibs or quills, make sure to wipe the ruler clean with a tissue or rag after every couple of lines you ink, or the collected ink will drip down and bleed on the paper.

Figure 3-5:
Avoid ink
seeping
under your
ruler by
flipping it
upside
down.

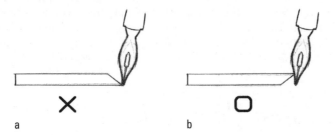

a   b

✔ If you find your ruler slipping while you use it, wrap a small rubber band on both sides of the ruler to prevent it from sliding under pressure (as shown in Figure 3-6a) or use paper-safe tape to secure the ruler to the paper without damaging the drawing underneath (as shown in Figure 3-6b).

Drawing and inking basic straight lines

Now, try your hand at the following exercise:

1. **With a pencil, draw a series of lines equidistant from each other while going from right to left (as shown in Figure 3-7a).**

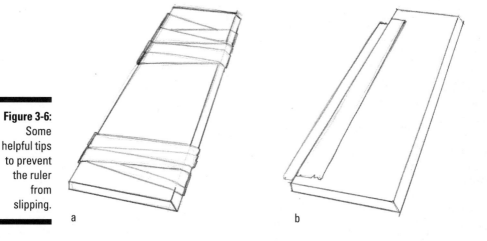

Figure 3-6:
Some helpful tips to prevent the ruler from slipping.

a   b

Don't rush through this one — try to be as accurate as possible.

2. **Draw another series of lines, slightly increasing the distance between them (as shown in Figure 3-7b).**

3. **Draw another set of lines, alternating between the narrower and wider gaps between the lines (as shown in Figure 3-7c).**

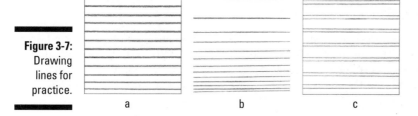

Figure 3-7:
Drawing lines for practice.

a   b   c

4. **Practice your inking by going over the pencil lines with a 0.5 mm marker while keeping the distance between the lines accurate (see Figure 3-8).**

Don't forget to flip over the ruler (you don't want to let any of the ink seep underneath the ruler and create smudges between the lines).

The width of your pencil lines may not perfectly match the thickness of your markers. That's normal — the objective of inking is getting used to seeing the pencil lines as guides rather than becoming obsessed with tracing over them perfectly. Your challenge is to stick to your pencil lines as closely as possible. However, if the difference is so extreme that your ink lines begin to overlap the neighboring pencil lines, consider switching to a thinner marker.

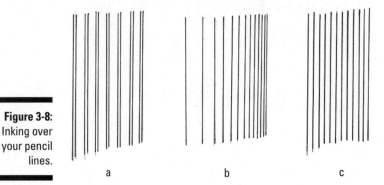

Figure 3-8:
Inking over
your pencil
lines.

a   b   c

As you become used to inking over your own drawings, in the future you may find that you don't need to put so much detail or work into your pencil drawings because you know how to ink them in the final product.

Inking from thick to thin

In this section, you get to try your hand at using the popular *G-Pen* (the widely used inking pen nib in the manga-ka industry). As I mention in Chapter 2, Deleter, Nikko, Tachikawa, and Zebra are among the big company suppliers of this pen nib. If you're looking for an American comic inking pen nib substitute, check out the Hunts 102.

Figure 3-9a shows how you "feed" ink into the pen nib by dipping the tip into an ink jar. Try not to get too much ink (see Figure 3-9b) into the pen nib; if you do, the excess spills over onto the paper. To get rid of the excess ink, simply tap the sides of the pen nib against the inside of the ink bottle opening.

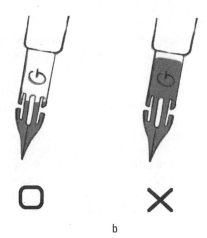

Figure 3-9:
"Feeding"
your pen.

a   b

Unlike a marker, the G-Pen can take some time getting used to, because its metallic tip doesn't glide as smoothly across the paper. Some of the paper bits get wedged between the two pointed prongs. To get them out, gently press and drag the pen tip against a smooth, hard surface to separate the two prongs and release the paper.

Try the following to get familiar with inking:

Starting from the top and going down, draw a series of equidistant lines going from thin to thick to thin (as shown in Figure 3-10).

Remember to flip the ruler upside down.

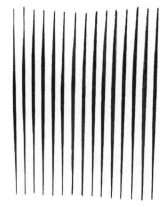

Figure 3-10:
Using the G-Pen nib to draw thin-to-thick-to-thin lines.

Start off by applying very little pressure to the pen holder, using the weight of your index finger. These pen nibs make great, crisp lines by merely touching the surface of the paper. The key to getting solid control of the lines' thickness or thinness is to apply gradual pressure from your index finger over the pen holder. For thicker lines, let the weight of your hand transfer to the pen holder. Don't use your body weight or force pressure onto the pen holder — you'll damage or shorten the life span of the pen nib.

These pen nibs are *very* sharp and can easily puncture your skin with little force. Be careful using this tool (especially when little children are around). The pen nibs are small and can be a choking hazard to children and pets.

Splattering

Rulers aren't just for drawing. You can use the edge of a ruler to create what's called a "splattering" effect with a brush. This technique works with either white ink or regular black ink. If the white ink is dry, you can revive the solution by adding water and letting it sit before stirring it up (you can't revive the black ink because it's waterproof after it dries). To create the spattering effect, follow these steps:

1. **Dip a stiff brush into the ink, as shown in Figure 3-11.**

    If you don't have a brush handy, an old toothbrush is okay to use.

Figure 3-11:
Dipping a
brush into
black or
white ink.

2. **Hold the edge of the ruler over the specified area and let the brush flick over the edge, creating a splatter over your work (see Figure 3-12).**

    In Figure 3-12a, I show the flicking motion of the brush against the ruler. If you're using a toothbrush, you can also use your thumb. In Figure 3-12b, I show the result.

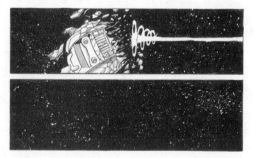

Figure 3-12:
Splattering
a black
panel to
create the
start of a
galaxy.

a

b

This technique works best on contrasting values (black ink on a white background or white ink on a black background). In Figure 3-12, I use the white ink splattering technique on a black panel to create a star constellation effect.

You can use the black splattering technique to show blood splattering or dirt being kicked around.

The trick to getting this technique right is angling the edge of the ruler slightly away from the paper (toward you). I recommend practicing this technique on different paper before trying it on your original work.

Creating Patterns

Just like an athlete warming up with a series of stretching exercises, a *manga-ka* (or manga artist) also has a series of standard drills. These drills are fun because you can use any tool to do them at any time.

In this section, I show some drills for creating different types of hatchings and line work. For beginners, I recommend starting with either a pencil or a fine (0.3 mm or 0.5 mm) marker. Later on, as you become more comfortable drawing lines with the pen nib, you can use that as well.

When you're really advanced, check out some of the excellent manga graphics software. You can use this software to digitally paste in some cool pattern effects and other designs for your backgrounds. The software also includes different shades and tones, which you can use to give your characters shadow, ethnicity, and personality. Although getting used to these tools may take time, they can save you a lot of time, frustration, and money down the road.

Trailing pattern

Try your hand at following these instructions to create a trailing pattern. This manga technique is known as *Nawa-ami:*

1. **Draw five small, short, parallel, equidistant lines, as shown in Figure 3-13.**

2. **From each line, draw another line, creating another series of segments in an alternate direction. Repeat, changing directions again.**

   In Figure 3-14a, I keep the angles rather narrow so that the overall weaving pattern curves smoothly. In Figure 3-14b, I switch the direction of patterns.

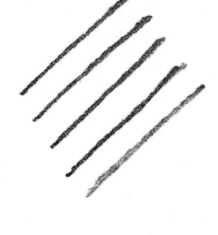

Figure 3-13:
Starting off
the weaving
pattern with
parallel
lines.

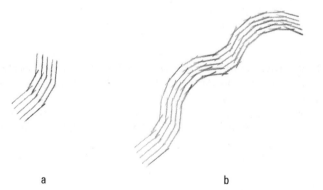

Figure 3-14:
Alternating
the direction
of lines to
complete
the overall
weaving
pattern.

a   b

Half-tone patterns

A manga-ka often uses half-tone patterns (or modified variations of them) in her background as an alternative for a solid black background. Because manga is printed in black and white, manga-ka have come up with creative ways of representing a wide range of in-between shades, known as *half-tones*.

Drawing hito-keta (one-digit) half-tone patterns

Hito-keta is a shading technique used to darken in shadows and backgrounds. It's clean, fun, and relatively easy to create. Its direct translation is "one digit," and it's lighter than the futa-keta (two-digit) half-tone pattern (see the next section).

To master the technique, start with these steps:

1. **Draw a 3-x-3-inch manga frame (referred to as *koma*).**

2. **Start from the center of your koma, and draw five to seven small, short, parallel, equidistant lines, as shown in Figure 3-15.**

Figure 3-15:
Starting the
hito-keta
pattern.

3. **Add another set of five to seven lines perpendicular to the first set, and then repeat, as shown in Figure 3-16.**

Figure 3-16:
Adding the
next sets of
lines to the
hito-keta
pattern.

As you follow the instruction to repeat Step 3, keep adding more sets of lines randomly — just make sure each set is physically attached to the set of lines you drew previously, and fill any empty gaps (see Figure 3-17).

The lines aren't all the same length because you have to fill all white spaces. These patterns continue on until your entire koma is filled. Some of the lines may fall perpendicularly, while others simply exist to fill a gap.

Figure 3-17:
Completing
the rest of
the hito-keta
pattern.

Going a bit darker with futa-keta (two-digit) half-tone patterns

If you want to go a shade darker than the hito-keta pattern, you don't have to start all over again. Instead, take the completed hito-keta pattern (see the previous section) and apply the *futa-keta* concept by following these steps:

1. **For every set of parallel lines, add the same number of lines crossing over perpendicularly (see Figure 3-18).**

   By adding this second set of lines, your overall pattern is darker.

Figure 3-18:
Starting the
futa-keta
based upon
the hito-keta
pattern.

2. **Continue to repeat, adding the lines throughout the rest of the patterns to get a darker background, as shown in Figure 3-19.**

Figure 3-19:
Completing
the futa-
keta pattern.

Fixing Mistakes

Every professional or amateur manga-ka makes mistakes — it comes with the territory of being human. For every wrong line or ink spill, you can usually find a solution to fix it. As you get used to using your tools, you learn to minimize the careless mistakes and deal with the unavoidable accidents. Regardless of the kind of mistake, don't fret or panic when you make it. In this section, I introduce some techniques for correcting common mistakes.

Brushing it out

As I mention in Chapter 2, you should have two thin brushes set aside for just correcting mistakes. Don't use the same brushes for inking purposes because the ink can come off the brush and create a mess in the white correction fluid jar. The advantage of using a brush to correct your mistakes is that you have excellent control over where you want to apply the white correction fluid.

The most common lines that you need to erase are the lines that overextend the *koma* (manga frame borders) — see Figure 3-20a. In Figure 3-20b, I show an example of ink smudges or splotches, which are also frequent occurrences.

You can easily fix mistakes by dipping your brush into white correction solution and thinly applying it to the desired area. Figure 3-21 shows how the images should look when the koma and smudges have been corrected.

Figure 3-20:
Just a few examples among many typical inking mistakes.

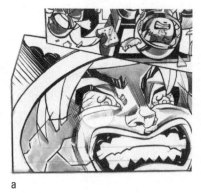
a

b

In reality, I find the lines sometimes *do* end up showing through the correction fluid despite the "bleed-proof" label. In such cases, simply wait until the solution dries before applying another thin coat.

Figure 3-21:
Inking mistakes corrected with white correction fluid.

a

b

Some correction fluids are *not* waterproof. If you go over non-waterproof correction fluid with ink, you may smear the applied correction. If this happens, use either the pen nib or brush-based office correction fluid that I mention in Chapter 2.

Although you may run into difficulty at art stores (even the larger chain stores), try to get the waterproof correction fluid to begin with. The one I use is manufactured by Deleter. It's great because you can smoothly ink right on top of your corrected mistakes.

Cutting it out

Sometimes you need to redraw an entire frame. Because applying correction fluid takes time (and looks messy when you apply it excessively to any certain area), you may want to consider cutting out the original frame and replacing it with a freshly redrawn frame. Follow these steps to cut and replace an image:

1. **Place the original image over your light box (see Chapter 2 for details on the light box) and draw the corrected image that will replace it.**

   When drawing the replacement image (like the one in Figure 3-22), make sure you draw the image right up to the border of the koma. Don't draw the border itself.

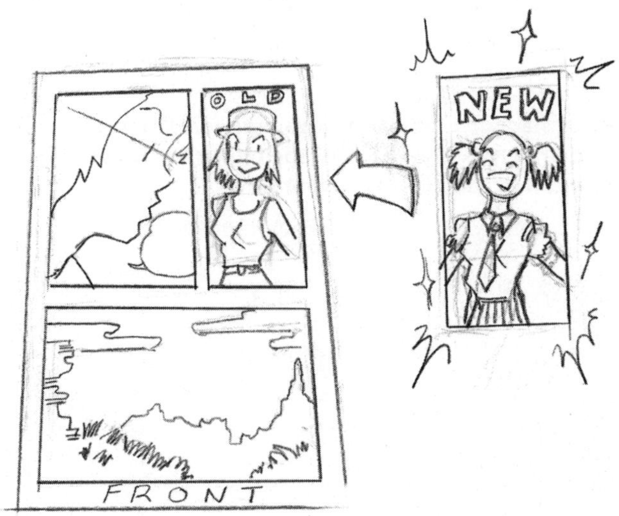
OLD
NEW
FRONT

Figure 3-22: Drawing the image to be used as a replacement.

2. **Cut out the original image with a blade and ruler, as shown in Figure 3-23.**

   The key to getting this technique right is to cut right inside the koma line so that you cut out just the image itself.

   REMEMBER: Don't forget to place a cutting mat underneath the image you're cutting out. Blades can damage the surface of your drafting table. If you don't have a cutting mat available, a thick piece of cardboard will do just fine.

3. **Cut out the replacement image with a blade and ruler.**

BLADE
OLD

Figure 3-23: Cutting out the original image you want to replace.

4. **Fit the replacement image in the hole left from the original image and use scotch tape on the back of the paper to secure the replacement image in place (see Figure 3-24a).**

   In Figure 3-24b, you see the corrected image from the front.

BACK SIDE
NEW
FRONT

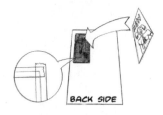

a

Figure 3-24: Fitting and securing the corrected image in place with scotch tape.

b

If you have the computer resources available, I *strongly* recommend using graphics software such as Adobe Photoshop to perform your cut-and-replace operation. Scan in both the original page and the corrected image, crop out the image from the original page that you want to replace or resize, and fit the corrected image right over the original frame. This software saves lots of time, it's very clean, and above all, it's practical.

Part II
To the Drawing Board

The 5th Wave By Rich Tennant

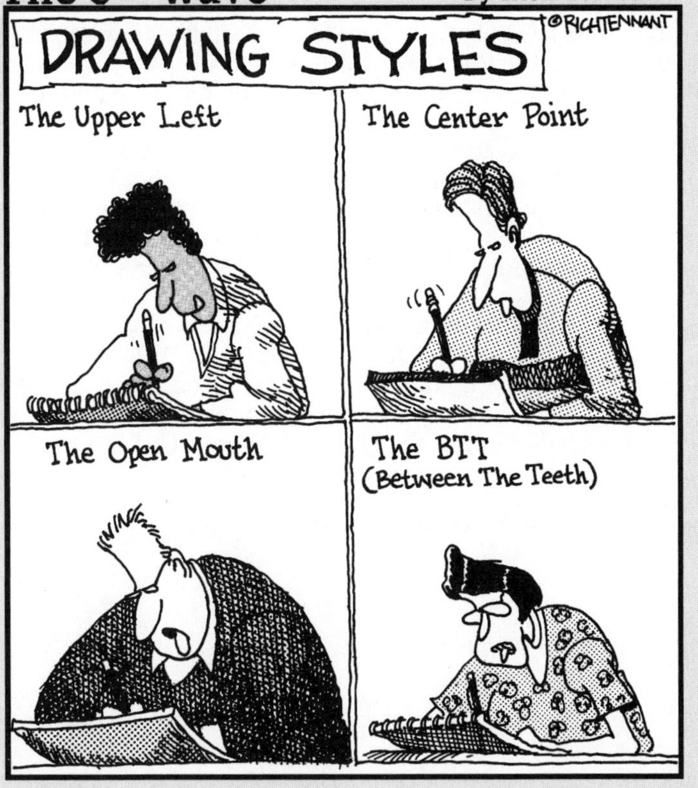
©RICHTENNANT
DRAWING STYLES
The Upper Left
The Center Point
The Open Mouth
The BTT
(Between The Teeth)

In this part . . .

By now, you've collected all the materials you need — maybe you're sitting at your drafting table with a fresh piece of white Bristol paper, a sharpened pencil, and a kneaded eraser. If you're also wondering "So, where do I start?" you've come to the right place.

In this part, I show you where to start, whether you're drawing for the first time or you're an experienced comic book artist trying something new. If you want to get off to a head start, I say start with the head. More specifically, I show you how to start by drawing one of the most distinguishing features of manga — those sweet Bambi eyes. You see them on a great many manga characters, and they look so cool! Personally, I love how they communicate such a wide range of expressions despite their simplicity.

After you master the eye, I show you how to tackle the rest of the unique facial features, and then I explore the rest of the figure. By the end of this part, you'll be drawing all sorts of characters and making them your own. Sharpen your pencils and head to the drawing board to kick-start your first manga experience.

Chapter 4

Taking It from the Top with the Head

In This Chapter

- Discovering the basics of manga faces
- Exploring the differences between male and female facial features
- Communicating a number of expressions the manga way

The head and its features are probably the most distinguishable traits that classify a character as "manga." Most manga faces have trademark Bambi eyes and cute little noses and mouths. American comic characters generally have more realistic features than manga characters. On the other hand, many of my students prefer manga because of its effectiveness in achieving a wide range of facial expressions with fewer lines and realism. They all say manga is so much fun to draw. You will too! In this chapter, I demonstrate how to draw your first manga head and facial features from scratch.

Heading Out on a Manga Mission

In this section, I show you how to face off in the right direction by drawing both male and female head structures.

In today's mainstream manga, most features appear to be unisex (especially with teenage characters). Some distinct differences, however, separate the male and female characters. For the purpose of diversity, I use a full-grown adult male head to show the contrast in structure between that and the young adult/teen female head. First, I show you how to draw the female head (note that you can also use this head shape for androgynous male characters).

Drawing the female head

To draw the basic female (or androgynous) head from three different angles (front, side, and ¾), follow these steps:

1. **Draw a round oval and two slightly wider ovals, side by side (see Figure 4-1).**

   Be sure to place the ovals approximately 1 inch apart. Although the shapes in Figures 4-1b and 4-1c are wider than Figure 4-1a, all three shapes should be the same height.

2. **Draw four guidelines across all three shapes.**

   As shown in Figure 4-1, divide the ovals into approximate thirds by drawing straight horizontal lines across each oval, starting from the top. From top to bottom, draw four guidelines. These guidelines help you block in the rest of the basic head features. From the top, label these guidelines A through D.

3. **Draw another guideline under D and label it E.**

   The distance between DE is roughly equal to the distance between BC and CD. Finish up the guidelines by drawing a center line down the ovals in Figure 4-2a and Figure 4-2b.

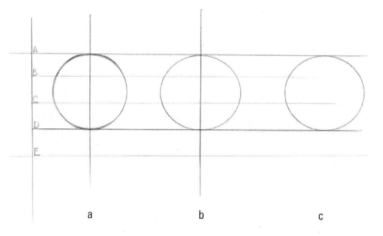

Figure 4-1:
These ovals represent the front, side, and ¾ views of your character's head.

4. **Lightly sketch in the jaw, chin, ears, and neck for the front view of the head (as shown in Figure 4-2a).**

   Draw two lines starting from opposite sides of the oval to form the sides of the face from C heading down to D. From guideline D, draw the lower jaw lines angling down to converge where E meets the center guideline. Draw the ear shapes to fall approximately between C and D (the top of the ear shape is slightly higher than C for all three views.

To draw the neck, mark the midpoint between the center guideline and the left side of the oval. Repeat the process to find the midpoint between the center guideline and the right side of the oval. Use the distance between the two midpoints to determine the width of the neck. From both points, draw the sides of the neck below the chin.

5. **Draw the jaw, chin, ears, and neck for the side view of the head (as shown in Figure 4-2b).**

   Start with the jaw line, which begins on guideline C. From the midpoint of the center guideline and the left side of the oval, draw the upper jaw line at an angle until it connects with guideline D. From D, the lower jaw angles to connect with guideline E at approximately the halfway mark between the center guideline and the right side of the oval. The front of the face slightly curves from C down to meet with the end of the jaw line on guideline E.

   Start the ear behind the upper jaw line, ending at the midpoint of the center guideline and the left edge of the oval. Start the front of the neck from the midpoint of the lower jaw line. The back of the neck starts right behind the ears.

   I draw the side view of the ear shape tilted to match the angle of the upper jaw line. Most beginners make the mistake of drawing the ears completely vertical. I tell students to look at the ears on other people's profiles to get an idea of how the ear should look. Another common mistake is to draw the neck straight rather than slightly angled. Profiles of characters with straight necks look stiff and unnatural. A slightly angled position makes the overall stature and balance flow naturally.

6. **Create the shapes for the jaw, chin, ears, and neck for the ¾ view of the head (as shown in Figure 4-2c).**

   Think of the ¾ view as the front view and side view of the head rolled into one. Off the left of the oval, sketch a slightly curved guideline to indicate the center of the face from this angle. Draw the left side of the face dropping down slightly below guideline D before making a sharp turn toward the bottom of the chin at guideline E. Complete the other side of this view by drawing the upper and lower jaw line down to join the chin at E. Draw the ear behind the upper jaw line.

   Make sure the bottom of the chin lines up with the curved center guideline.

Drawing the male head

In this section, I show you how to map out the head for the mature, heroic, male character. Lead characters with this head shape are typically in their late 20s to late 30s. Although the process of drawing this head is virtually identical to drawing the female head in the previous section, pay attention to the change in the shape of the jaw line. For the following steps, you need to draw the three oval shapes and guidelines from Steps 1-3 in the previous section.

Draw the three oval shapes and guidelines you see in Figure 4-1, but make a couple changes. Guidelines A through D divide the male oval shapes in *exact* thirds (the distance between all guidelines are equally spaced out). And the distance between D and E is 50 percent longer than the distance between guidelines A through D. Sketch that out, and then try your hand at completing the rest of the basic head shapes for male characters:

1. **Draw the jaw, chin, ears, and neck for the front view of the head (as shown in Figure 4-3a).**

   Extend two lines starting from the left and right side edges of the oval to form the sides of the face from C heading down past D. Think of the side face length as 50 percent longer than the female's. Draw the lower jaw angling down to form the bottom of the chin along guideline E.

   The trick to making the male head shape look older and more masculine is to draw the jaw line so that it hits guideline E well to the left or to the right (depending on which side of the face you're drawing) of the center guideline. When I connect the bottom left and right jaw lines, I get a flat chin instead of a pointed one. If you want to increase the masculinity, increase the distance between the bottom jaw lines along guideline E so that he has a wider chin.

   The placement of the male ear shape is no different than that of the female, but the width is narrower and more angled (as you can see in Figure 4-3b and Figure 4-3c).

   Stronger masculine male characters have thicker and shorter necks than females. In Figure 4-3a, I draw the neck starting from the point where the side of the face and lower jaw line meet. That makes the width of the neck just as wide as the entire head!

2. **Draw the jaw, chin, ears, and neck for the side view of the head (as shown in Figure 4-3b).**

   Draw the upper jaw line from guideline C, extending past D by 50 percent.

   If you want to make sure the length and shape of your upper and lower jaw matches consistently with the other two angles in Figure 4-3, draw a line from the top of the lower jaw in Figure 4-3a and extend it across Figures 4-3b and 4-3c. Use this as a guideline to make sure you're not drawing the jaw lines too short or too long.

   Draw the lower jaw by connecting from guideline E to the right side edge of the oval at approximately the midpoint of the center guideline. The front of the face drops at a slight angle to meet with guideline E. Complete the square chin by connecting the gap between the bottom of the lower jar with the bottom of the front of the face.

   Ears sit behind the upper jaw line. Don't forget to draw the side view of the ear shape tilted to match the angle of the upper jaw line.

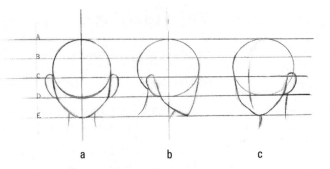

Figure 4-2:
Mapping out the basic head shape for a young adult or teen female.

3. **Draw the jaw, chin, ears, and neck for the ¾ view of the head (as shown in Figure 4-3c).**

   Sketch a slightly curved guideline to indicate the center of the face from the ¾ angle. The left side of the face extends past guideline D before slightly turning to connect at guideline E (off to the left of the center guideline). Draw the upper and lower jaw line down to guideline E (off to the right of the center guideline). Complete the wide chin by connecting the bottom of the face with the bottom of the lower jaw line. Finally, draw the ear behind the upper jaw line. Make sure that the center guideline aligns with the midpoint of the flat chin.

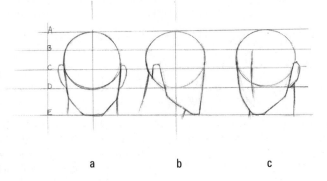

Figure 4-3:
Drawing the basic male head shapes.

The Eyes Have It!

In manga art, the eyes draw you in. You can use them to convey various emotions in your characters. Sad eyes look very different from happy or frightened eyes. In this section, I show you how to draw eyes the manga way. I also explore different types of eyes that you commonly find in today's manga world.

Beginning with the basic eye structure

When constructing eyes, you want to use the basic structure of the eyeball and eyelid as a template. The eyeball itself consists of the pupil and the iris. As you become used to drawing the eye over and over again, you may find that drawing the eyeball each time you draw your character is no longer essential. However, for the purposes of this chapter, humor me and draw the eye from the start. Keep in mind that a solid foundational structure underlies everything, even cuteness.

Large manga eyes are cute and feminine looking, but a *manga-ka* (or manga artist) also uses them for male characters, especially the young, lead male character. Having said that, some differences do separate the male eye from the female eye:

- Male characters don't have exaggerated eyelashes.
- Artists sometimes choose to draw the male characters with thicker eyebrows.

Follow these steps to draw a basic manga eye:

1. **At the center of your paper, draw two identical circles next to each other.**

   These circles represent the front view and the side view of the eye. My circles are around 1 inch in diameter and approximately 1 inch apart.

   For consistency, I recommend using a circle template (refer to Chapter 2) to draw these round objects. Most templates have diameter measurements marked next to each shape.

2. **Draw two ovals (one inside the other) inside each of the circles to represent the iris and pupil (see Figure 4-4).**

   Draw the large oval slightly narrower than the oval that's nested inside. The outer, larger oval is known as the *iris,* which is the most visible and colorful part of the eye. The smaller, rounder oval located at the center of the iris is the *pupil,* which expands and contracts to control the amount of light that enters the eye. Shade the pupil in black, as I do in Figures 4-4a and 4-4b. For the iris, I randomly draw a series of lines starting from the outside edge of the oval heading toward the center of the iris.

   In the manga world, both the iris and pupil are exaggerated in size so that they take up more space in the eyeball than they do in real life. When your character shifts her gaze from the front (where the iris and pupil are rounder; see Figure 4-4a) to the side, the iris and pupil shapes become narrower (as shown in Figure 4-4b).

Figure 4-4:
Drawing the two separate views of the eyeball, pupil, and iris.

a   b

3. **Draw the lower lid of the eyeball, keeping in mind that the lower lid represents a "flab" of flesh wrapping around the spherical eyeball form (see Figure 4-5).**

4. **Now, draw the upper lid of the eye (shown in Figure 4-5), forming an arc from the left edge of the eyeball to the right edge.**

5. **Add the final touches with eyelashes on the corner of the top lid and dark shadows over the iris and pupil.**

From the front view in Figure 4-5a, I draw three pointed eyelashes that get thicker and longer as the eyelid hugs around the eyeball. For the side view, I draw an additional set of eyelashes that curl up at the front (as shown in Figure 4-5b).

Draw the dark shadow of the eye in a form of an arc crossing over the middle of the iris and pupil. This shadow is cast by the upper lid. The darkness of the shadow blends in with the darkness of the iris, so they appear to be one shape.

Note: Don't add thick or too many eyelashes for a male character unless you want to emphasize his *yaoi* (androgynous) personality.

6. **Give the eye a highlight toward the upper left of the pupil and erase the edges of the eyeball sphere.**

Adding the highlight is the fun part — like adding the icing to the cake. The effect makes the eye sparkle and look realistic. With a clean eraser, erase the area you want highlighted. You can use many shapes and sizes for your highlights, but I choose an elongated oval. If you want to show your character on the verge of tears, increase the size of the highlight or draw additional smaller highlights that overlap the iris and pupil.

7. **Draw in the eyebrow (as shown in Figure 4-6).**

The eyebrow is an elongated shape that curves around right above the eye socket and dips slightly downward as it approaches the center of the forehead. Be sure to erase any parts of the oval eyeball shape that are hidden behind the eyelids.

Figure 4-5:
The bottom
and top lids
wrap over
the eyeball.

a   b

Figure 4-6:
Drawing the
eyebrow.

a   b

One secret to getting the eyes to fit your character's personality is to pay attention to the eyebrows. Thicker, angled eyebrows suggest strength and confidence. Thinner and more rounded eyebrows convey gentleness and grace.

Seeing eye to eye

When you're placing the left and right eyes together, side by side, the distance between them when they're facing forward is roughly one manga eye apart (see Figure 4-7).

If you're not sure whether your eye measurements are accurate, lightly draw a generic eye symbol between the right and left eyes with a pencil.

One of the biggest challenges of drawing both eyes from the front view is making sure that they're close to symmetrical to each other. To make the character's eyes symmetrical to each other, try the following suggestions:

✔ **After drawing both eyes, put the drawing in front of a mirror.** Check to see whether both eyes look accurate when you view them backwards. If either one of them looks off, pick the eye that you don't like and adjust it to fit the other.

✔ **Take tracing paper and trace one eye with a soft pencil.** Then, flip the tracing and position the flipped image where the other eye should be. With a sharp pencil, trace over the flipped tracing. A perfectly mirrored eye should transfer onto the paper.

✔ **Flip the drawing of both eyes over and hold it up against the light.** You then see the backward mirror image of the drawing. See where any part of the image is asymmetrical before turning it back over and making the necessary corrections.

Figure 4-7:
Picturing an imaginary eye to measure the distance between two manga eyes.

Drawing all shapes and sizes

Not all manga eyes are drawn in the same style or size. In mainstream manga, eyes range from large to larger. But other manga genres have eyes that are much smaller and closer to looking real. In this section, I show you some of the various types of manga eyes.

Mega manga eyes

There is almost no limit as to how big you can make those mega manga eyes. In fact, because big eyes are the symbol of innocence, some young, female manga characters have eyes so large that there just isn't enough space to fit the rest of the face! I include the character's entire head in Figure 4-8 just to show you the enormity of the eyes.

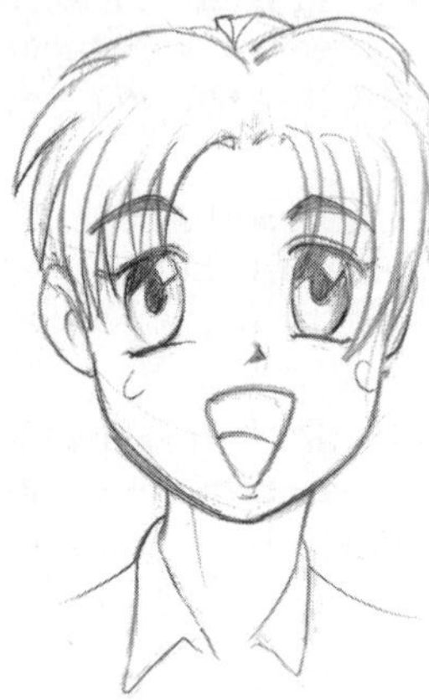

Figure 4-8: Check out the popular big eyes.

Sometimes, what makes *shōjo manga* (comics geared toward teenage girls) uniquely different from other manga genres is not only the size of the eyes, but also the thickness of the eyelashes (see Figure 4-9).

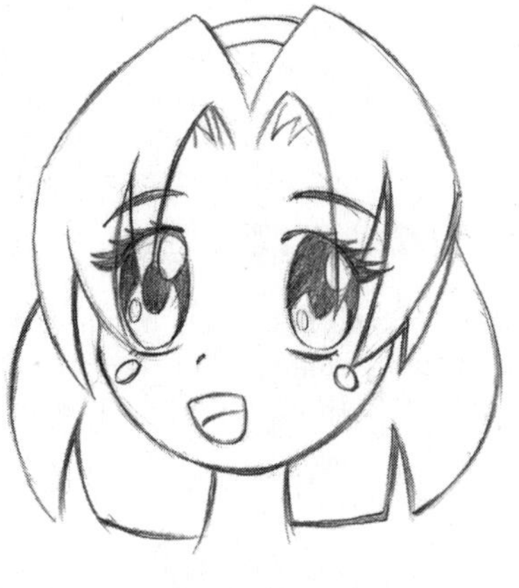

Figure 4-9: Can the eyes get any bigger? Sure!

TIP

The rule of thumb is the larger the eyes get, the more exaggerated the hair becomes in shape and size to match the eyes.

More realistic eyes

Characters don't need big eyes in order to be classified as manga. If you read the more serious, action-oriented manga, you find that the eyes are smaller and more realistic (see Figure 4-10).

Figure 4-10:
Smaller
eyes, with
the same
manga
structure.

The eyes in which the eyelids angle upward (as in Figure 4-11) usually indicate aloofness or coldness. Picture these eyes on a cold-hearted female who has no problem telling the protagonist that she just cheated on him simply because he scored poorly on his test. These eyes commonly appear in *shōnen manga* (comics geared toward teenage boys).

Figure 4-11:
Some
eyelids are
angled
rather than
smooth.

Stories focusing on more serious topics geared toward adults have even more realistic eyes (see Figure 4-12).

Figure 4-12:
These
eyebrows
are so
detailed that
they come
close to
being
realistic!

Generally speaking, the wider or bigger the eyes are, the more pure, young, and innocent the character appears. The narrower or smaller the eyes are, the more wise, cunning, or sometimes evil the character seems to be.

Incredibly simple eyes

If you're not into realism, manga does offer other options. Manga eyes can go the opposite way to complete simplicity. Many *yonkoma manga* (editorial comics) in Japanese newspapers have simple eyes, yet they communicate emotions and personality just as effectively as the more typical manga eyes. Although these eyes may not be the most artistically elaborate or ornate, they can communicate complex emotions that would take longer to express if you were drawing more realistic manga eyes.

Check out Figure 4-13 for examples of yonkoma manga characters that I created. In Figure 4-13a, simplicity is a powerful way of getting the attention of busy commuters reading their morning papers; showing "doubt" took just three lines with the pencil. Figure 4-13b is simple, but the structure of the eyes is still there.

Figure 4-13:
Simplicity gets the job done in the yonkoma manga style.

a   b

Filling In the Features

In this section, I show you how to draw the nose and mouth shapes to accompany the eyes. Just as eyes are big in mainstream manga, noses and mouths are commonly small. As I show, however, you can draw these features in more than just one style. Like the eyes, you can draw these features traditionally or realistically in today's manga world.

Being nosy

Noses are one of the most fun parts of the face to draw. A manga-ka often selects nose sizes and shapes based upon the personality of the characters. Smaller noses generally imply cuteness, innocence, and youth, and you see them on cute girls and young boys. Bigger noses, on the other hand, show a character's maturity, complexity, and age. Read on to find out how to draw some of the basic manga nose shapes and when each is most appropriate.

Ski jump nose

I refer to this nose type as a ski jump nose (see Figure 4-14). You generally use this nose on younger characters (especially the main lead girls). Try your hand at drawing the ski jump nose by checking out these steps:

1. **Draw a slightly curved line, as shown in Figure 4-14a.**
2. **Curve the line back under to complete the bottom side of the nose (see Figure 4-14b).**

   The end point should be vertically aligned to the top of the first line, where you started in Step 1.
3. **Add several lines above the bridge of the nose, as shown in Figure 4-14c.**

   These lines show the flat surface of the bridge of the nose.

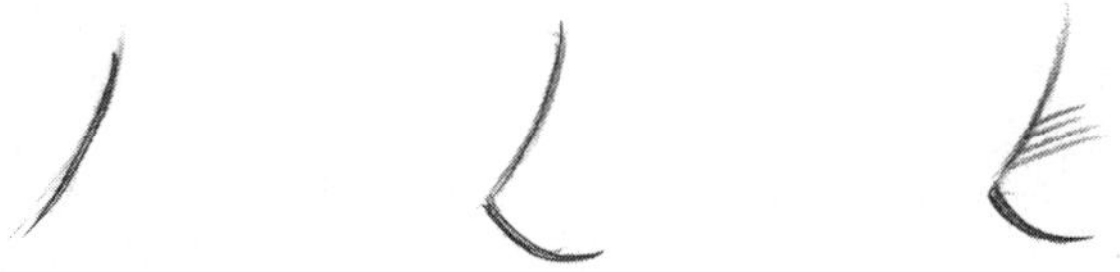

a b c

Figure 4-14: Ski jump noses are simple and cute.

TIP

Here are some things to keep in mind when you sketch out ski jump noses:

- They need to be cute — keep 'em short!
- Never draw in the nostrils. Suggesting that the character can be seen with her nostrils pointing right toward the reader's face would be inappropriate. When in doubt, leave them out.
- Keep the lines short and thin. If you draw the lines too long or thick, the nose stands out. You can't have that on an adorable princess face!
- The tip of the nose should have a blunt tip pointing toward the sky. From the side profile, it should resemble a cute slope.

✔ Make sure you include the thin lines on the bridge of the nose right before the nose starts turning up. Those lines help push the top part of the nose forward and add more dimension to the overall structure.

Shadow nose

You may want to consider using what I call the shadow nose (I show you two types in Figure 4-15 and Figure 4-16). You see these noses mostly on older teen and young adult characters. The manga-ka usually draws a thin outline suggesting the outside shape of the nose and adds an outline of the shadow shape caused by the light source. In Figure 4-15, the shadow shape comes across the opposite side of the nose. In Figure 4-16, I draw the shadow shape falling below the nose.

Follow the steps to drawing both types of the shadow nose, starting with Figure 4-15:

1. **Draw a curved segment for the nose bridge as shown in Figure 4-15a.**

   The nose bridge consists of a vertical line with the midsection slightly curving toward the right before returning back to its original course.

2. **Add a shadow shape to the right of the nose bridge to complete the shadow nose as shown in Figure 4-15b.**

   Starting from the top of the nose bridge, draw the shadow shape using a wider arc so that the overall nose shape appears dimensional. Finish the shadow shape by connecting the bottom of the shadow shape line to the bottom of the nose bridge.

Figure 4-15:
The vertical shadow nose.

a

b

Now try the other shadow nose in Figure 4-16:

1. **At the center of the paper, draw a small ½-inch curve to represent the front tip of the nose as shown in Figure 4-16a.**

2. **Draw the four-sided shadow shape as shown in Figure 4-16b.**

   Starting from both ends of the arc line, draw sides of the shadows by sketching two short lines angling away from the arc.

   Complete the shadow shape by drawing two more lines that angle back to meet at the center.

Figure 4-16:
The wider
shadow
nose.

a   b

Here are some helpful tips for this type of nose, its shadow shapes, and its placements:

✔ Never draw in the nostrils. As with the ski jump nose (see the previous section), showing the character's nostrils pointing toward the reader is inappropriate.

✔ The nose should be a little longer with a sharper point toward the top before it turns inward toward the mouth.

✔ Depending on the desired effect, you can shade in the shadow with screentone (refer to Chapter 2) for normal lighting and environment, or you can fill in the shadow with black to exaggerate the emotional state or situation of that character. When dealing with a very neutral situation, you can even leave the shadow blank.

✔ If you want just the shadow to define the nose, draw the nose first with the shadow. When you have the shadow the way you want it, erase the nose. Without actually knowing where the nose is, you run the risk of guessing where the shadow should fall.

Realistic nose

You commonly find the realistic nose (see Figure 4-17) on adult characters who don't have extreme, exaggerated features. You see noses like this one usually in shōnen and business manga. Check out the following steps on drawing the realistic nose:

1. **Draw a straight line at a 45 degree angle as shown in Figure 4-17a.**

   Observe that the bridge doesn't curve upward like the ski jump nose does (see "Ski jump nose" earlier in this chapter for details).

2. **Draw the underside of the nose as shown in Figure 4-17b.**

   From the tip of the bridge, I sketch a short arc for the bottom of the nose that curves back toward the face. Draw the arc at a 45 degree angle. For this nose to work, the short arc should *not* extend to align with the base of the nose.

3. Add a small curve for the nostril as shown in Figure 4-17c.

Figure 4-17:
The realistic
nose has
more detail
than other
manga
noses.

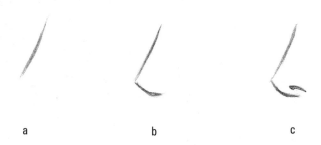

a   b   c

Following are some tips for drawing great realistic noses:

- Draw the nostrils as small arcs. Never draw nostrils as round objects shaded in with black ink — that's just gross!
- The top of the nose can be rounded instead of blunt or sharp. Male characters should have a slightly more rounded nose than females.
- Elegant females should have a straighter nose bridge than males.

Lend me your ear

Most manga characters with exaggerated features have very small ears with very little detail. In fact, you never see the ears of some manga characters (often the females). If you don't like drawing those awkward shapes, this is good news. However, I want to demystify this feature in the following sections. Drawing ears is actually fun after you get to know them!

Figure-6 ear

You see the figure-6 ear mostly on young, innocent characters, often in conjunction with big eyes, smaller noses, and smaller mouths. The figure-6 is basically the ear in its most simple form. Besides the outline of the outer tube and outer ear shape, a simplified inner ear completes this type of form — all you do is draw a figure "6." Follow these steps to draw the figure-6 ear:

1. Draw the outside ear shape as shown in Figure 4-18a.

Think of the outside ear shape as a modified semicircle. Make sure that the bottom end of the semicircle extends to align slightly further than the top of the semicircle. This ensures that the ear position properly aligns with the jaw line of the basic head shape.

For a "macho" style, simplify the outside ear into a five-sided shape (see Figure 4-18c).

2. **Create a figure "6" shape in the middle as shown in Figure 4-18b.**

   I place my figure "6" shape so that left edge aligns with the top end of the outer ear. This shape is a simplified version of the inner ear structure.

   To complete the "macho" style, make the figure "6" less rounded (see Figure 4-18d).

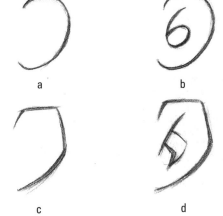

a   b

Figure 4-18:
Drawing the
side view of
two types
of the
figure-6 ear.

c   d

When you draw the front view of the figure-6 ear, you still see a little of the inside ear. To draw this ear from the front, use these steps:

1. **Draw the outside of the ear as shown in Figure 4-19a.**

   The front view of the outer shape of the ear looks identical to the side view, only it's horizontally compressed to become vertically thinner. Drawing this view is like taking a clay hemisphere shape between the palms of your hand and slightly flattening it.

   Figure 4-19d shows the outer ear in a more masculine style.

2. **Draw a curve to show the front shape of the ear at an angle at the center of the outer ear (see Figure 4-19b).**

   Picture the ear as a circular tube (like a doughnut or onion ring — but not as delicious). When drawing the curve, keep in mind that the space to the left is the side of the ear that's facing toward you. Everything to the right is facing away, toward the side.

   Check out Figure 4-19e for the squared-off version of the same thing.

3. **Complete the shape of the inner ear with a smaller curve as shown in Figure 4-19c.**

Toward the bottom of the original curve, draw a smaller rounded curve going in the opposite direction. This shape represents the inside section of the ear and is approximately half the height of the front shape curve.

Figure 4-19f shows the completed "macho" ear from the front.

a
b
c
d
e
f

Figure 4-19: Drawing the front view of the figure-6 ear.

TIP

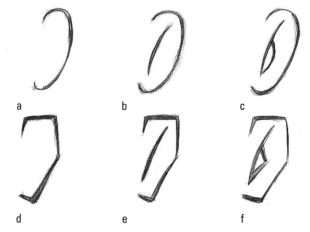

Following are some tips for drawing a figure-6 ear:

- Restrict the ear to two lines when drawing the "6" shape.
- When drawing an infant whose head and facial features have yet to fully develop, simplify the shape by erasing the lower part of the front shape curve.
- For the more "macho" looking boys, you can get rid of the curves and replace them with angled lines for an edgier feel.

Shadow ear

You see the shadow ear mostly with more realistically drawn high school characters. The inner ear is basically simplified with a shadow shape. You can shade in the shadow with screentone (see Chapter 2 for more) for normal lighting and environment, or you can fill in the shadow with black to exaggerate the emotional state or situation of your character.

Try your hand at drawing the side view of the shadow ear (as shown in Figure 4-20) by using these steps:

1. **Draw a modified hemisphere for the outer ear as shown in Figure 4-20a.**

   Observe the small dip at the bottom and to the right of the ear. This gives the overall shape more detail and realism than the figure-6 ear in the previous section.

2. **Draw the curve for the front shape of the ear as shown in Figure 4-20b.**

   Toward the bottom of the curve, add a new "tab" shape. This small shape functions as a shield to cover the ear tunnel inside the inner ear from dust and debris. The tab shape is rather abstract; think of it as a modified rectangle that's been sliced in half.

3. **Draw the shadow shape of the inner ear (see Figure 4-20c).**

   Start from the front curve shape of the ear, and leave a thin space between the top of the shadow and the outer ear shape. The top shadow angles slightly upward before angling back down and back toward the front curve. Draw another shadow shape below the top shadow. This square shape doesn't extend past the upper shadow.

   The bottom shadow shape mimics the shape of the ear "tab." The only difference is that the lower portion of the shadow dips down.

Figure 4-20:
The shadow shape resembles the head of a monkey wrench from the side.

a   b   c

When drawing the front view, make sure you see the shadow shape (as shown in Figure 4-21). Follow these instructions:

1. **Draw the outer ear so that it resembles a figure "6," but with edges that are more angular and less round (see Figure 4-21a).**

   I draw the bottom part of the ear turning upward (like a fishing hook).

2. **Draw the front curve shape of the ear as shown in Figure 4-21b.**

   I draw the front curve shape straighter to give the ear shape a more angular look than a rounder one like the figure-6 ear. The tab shape is the same shape as the tab of the figure-6 ear (see the previous section for details).

3. **Draw the shadow shape for the inner ear (see Figure 4-21c).**

   From the top of the front curve shape, draw the top shadow shape angling down (almost level to the top of the ear tab) before angling back up toward the front curve shape. Note that the distance between the overall inner ear shape and the outer ear shape is consistent. Go on to complete the rest of the shadow shape around the ear tab. The overall shape mimics the shape of the tab it surrounds. Avoid the mistake most beginners make by leaving enough space between the bottom of the shadow and bottom of the ear.

Figure 4-21:
The shadow
ear from
the front.

    a   b   c

Here are some tips to keep in mind when drawing the shadow ear:

- ✔ Make sure the outer tube of the ear is more narrow than the figure-6 ear.
- ✔ The top shadow shape of the inner ear angles sharply to resemble the tip of an arrow.
- ✔ Notice the slight droop at the bottom of the outer ear. Be sure to include this droop in addition to space between the bottom of the droop and the bottom of the shadow because your character may want to wear earrings.

Realistic ear

The realistic ear takes drawing ears to a higher level. You draw the inner ear more accurately and see a clear distinction in form that separates the inner ear from the ear tunnel. Follow these steps to draw the realistic ear in Figure 4-22:

1. **Draw a modified hemisphere for the outer ear shape as shown in Figure 4-22a.**

   This shape is rounder than the shadow ear from the previous section. In addition, the lower end of the ear doesn't curl up as much.

2. **Draw the front curve of the realistic ear as shown in Figure 4-22b.**

   Instead of drawing the curve at an angle, I extend the curve to loop around the inside of the outer ear shape. Don't connect the looping line; keep the shape open. The top edge of the ear is a tube shape. In addition to extending the front shape curve of the ear, I simplify the tab at the bottom of the front curve shape. Unlike the rectangular form in the shadow ear, the tab of the realistic ear resembles the shape of the ski jump nose from earlier in this chapter.

3. **Render in the inner portion of the realistic ear (see Figure 4-22c).**

Draw the dark shadow shape next to the ear tab, making sure the top end is pointed. The rest of the shadow shape mimics the shape of the tab. I draw a short curve starting from the top of the ear and ending at the right side of the ear. Look at your own ear as a reference to fill in the shading details.

Figure 4-22: The inside of the realistic ear — the more detailed the better.

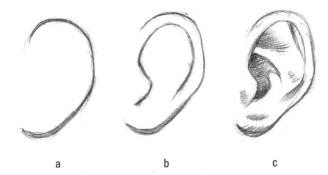

a   b   c

Now, I show you how to draw the front view of the realistic ear. The more realistic the ear becomes, the more detail you need to add. The larger shapes are broken up into smaller, more complicated pieces, as you see in Figure 4-23. Use these steps to draw your own realistic ear from the front:

1. **Draw the front portion of the outer ear shape as shown in Figure 4-23a.**

   This part resembles the butt end of a cigarette drawn at a slanted angle. You draw the back portion to complete the outer ear shape in Step 4.

2. **Starting at the right, bottom side of the outer ear shape, draw the ear tab (see Figure 4-23b).**

   In this case, it protrudes out like the ski jump nose. Note that the size of the tab is slightly larger and rounder when you're drawing realistically.

3. **Start from the side of the outer ear shape, and sketch the inner portion of the ear curving around to connect to the bottom of the ear tab (see Figure 4-23c).**

4. **Complete the lower portion of the outer ear as shown in Figure 4-23d.**

   This is a two-fold process. In the first stage, draw a line from the top corner of the outer ear shape down to the inner ear shape. Keep in mind that this line doesn't stop there, but continues to run behind the inner ear shape. Start the second stage by drawing the outer ear shape line coming out from behind the inner ear shape. As you complete the shape, remember to leave space between the bottom of the outer ear shape and the tab.

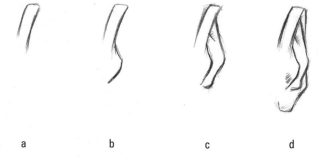

a b c d

Figure 4-23: Constructing the front of the realistic ear, shape by shape.

TIP

Here are some tips to keep in mind when drawing the realistic ear:

- The more detail you can add, the better.
- Make sure that some lines overlap others. That way, the ear becomes dimensional.
- Look at your own ear in the mirror or take a close-up picture of your friend's ears with your digital camera for reference.

Speak your mind: Drawing the mouth

Overall, manga mouths are very simple. At times, the lines that represent the mouth are so minimalist that their existence is suggested by a small dot or a short line. Depending upon the genre, you may not even see them at all. That's right; the artist may not even draw the mouth. Rather, he may let those big eyes do all the talking. So if drawing mouths isn't the thing for you, and you want to draw the manga way, you're in luck!

Despite its simplicity, the manga mouth is expressive — the smallest twitch can make a huge difference to the delicate, subtle expression on a face. If you're creating characters with mouths, you may be wondering what makes a successful manga mouth if it's nothing more than a simple line. Believe it or not, an accomplished manga artist has a solid understanding of the anatomy of the human mouth. So, first I give you a quick background of the basic structure of the mouth.

Drawing the basic mouth structure

The mouth is made up of two sections — the lower lip and the upper lip. Don't view either the lower or upper jaws as two-dimensional, flat objects. As you can tell by feeling your own jaws, they have a rounded structure going from the front of the teeth heading back toward the neck. Follow these steps and look at Figure 4-24 to draw the manga mouth structure:

1. **Draw a short cylinder as shown in Figure 4-24a.**

   This cylinder is your basic jaw shape.

2. **Draw a center line going across the cylinder (see Figure 4-24b).**

   This line is the top of the lower lip.

3. **Draw the lower portion of the lower lip as I do in Figure 4-24c.**

   I draw the lower portion of the lower lip by sketching a curve that stretches below the top line from left to right.

   If you want to draw fuller lips, draw the bottom part of the curve lower, or lower the entire curve altogether.

4. **Draw the upper lip wrapping over the lower lip as I demonstrate in Figure 4-24d.**

   Start by drawing the bottom of the upper lip *over* the top of the bottom lip. The center shape at the middle of the upper lip protrudes forward and curves down to cover part of the lower lip.

   Next, I draw the top of the upper lip. Both sides of the upper lip begin from the end corners of the mouth and angle up toward the center, above the mouth. Instead of joining the two lines at the center, draw an arc that's similar to the center arc that overlaps the lower lip but slightly wider to give balance to the overall mouth shape. Connect the line of the upper lip to each side of the arc.

   The top and the bottom of the upper lip both resemble an "M" as they dip down in the center.

5. **Erase any part of the lower lip that you cover with the top lip (see Figure 4-24d).**

6. **Highlight the lower lip to give the illusion that it has a shiny or moist surface (as shown in Figure 4-24e).**

   As a rule of thumb, surfaces that are more perpendicular to the light source catch more light (and therefore have larger highlights). As I later show in Figure 4-25, the lower lip has more direct contact with the light than the upper lip.

Do the best you can to match the center of the upper lip's "M" with the center of the lower lip. Also make sure that a portion of the "M" overlaps the top of the lower lip. If it doesn't, the lips will appear flat.

Drawing objects or shapes overlapping one another helps create the perception of three-dimensionality. This rule is simple but it works wonders when you apply it.

Here, I show the lips at two different angles. In Figure 4-25a, the top portion of the lip curves slightly up before angling down to meet the center of the lower lip. Also notice how the upper lip protrudes farther than the lower lip.

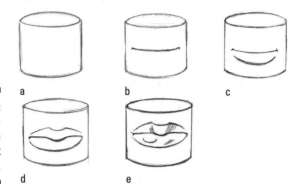

Figure 4-24:
Demonstrating how to construct the lips.

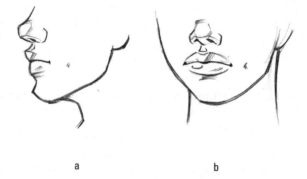

In the ¾ view of the face in Figure 4-25b, you see how the highlight shape on the lower lip and the thick-to-thin lines help create dimension and the appearance of realism on a flat, two-dimensional surface.

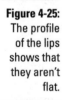

Figure 4-25:
The profile of the lips shows that they aren't flat.

Primping up the androgynous mouth

It's time to explore the more simplified manga mouth. Most manga-ka draw their characters' mouths and expressions using short lines, dots, and circles. Conveniently, as a result, the manga mouth is, for the most part, unisex.

When you start off with a generic, simplified manga mouth that's smiling toward you, only two lines are visible (one for the bottom of the mouth and the other for the top). As I show you in Figure 4-26, you can make the lips look sexier with a couple of simple tricks. In Figure 4-26a, I add an outline around the mouth and shade the space between to indicate that the character has luscious lips and is wearing red lipstick. In many cases where the character in the frame is drawn smaller, the mouth and lips are too small to go into detail. In that case, I forego the outline and shading and just darken the top and bottom parts of the lips with a dark thin line.

The second method, which I use in Figure 4-26b, is creating fuller lips around the mouth by adding two lines above and below the mouth (one represents the top of the upper lip and the other represents the bottom of the lower lip). Even without shading in the lipstick, the two lines show that the mouth belongs to a female as opposed to a male.

Figure 4-26:
Adding lipstick and creating thicker lips to boost the sex appeal.

a   b

Further exploring the simplified manga mouth

After you draw and understand what goes on with the realistic version of the mouth, drawing the simplified manga mouth is easier. To elaborate further on the previous section, most of the time, you don't have specific methods, steps, or techniques when drawing a simplified manga mouth because of its very simplicity. If your character's mouth is closed, you can use just simple lines, dots, or ovals (see Figures 4-27d, 4-27e, and 4-27f). At times, your character's mouth may not show at all (letting those big eyes do the talking).

When you're drawing a mouth in an open position (screaming or laughing; check out Figures 4-27a, 4-27b, and 4-27c for examples), the common mistake is to draw the upper lip too high or too low. The lower jaw usually does all the big movement while the upper mouth is immobile (after all, that whole section of the jaw is fused with the skull, so it doesn't move as freely). I recommend drawing the top of the mouth before drawing the lower lip and jaw that are wide open.

Because cute is king in manga, here are some tips that you can use to keep your mouth as cute as ever:

✔ Add small dimples next to both sides of the corners of the mouth. I like to draw small arrow marks that resemble > and < signs on each side of the mouth for my dimples. This works especially well with a smiling mouth.

✔ Curve the ends of the mouth upward when drawing a smile. Even the slightest, most subtle upward turn works miracles.

✔ Never draw individual teeth. Rather, draw each upper and lower set of teeth as a single strip. I draw a simple horizontal line beyond the lips when the character opens his mouth (as shown in Figure 4-27c). In cases where the teeth are clinched together, I like to show both upper and lower sets of teeth as a single object (as shown in Figure 4-27a).

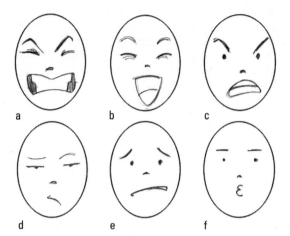

Figure 4-27:
Having fun
mouthing off
with
simplified
manga
mouth
expressions.

✔ Try experimenting with both symmetrical and asymmetrical shapes in your expressions.

✔ Use the images in Figure 4-27 as a basis to combine different types of lines, dots, and other simple curves to come up with your own set of basic expressions. For now, don't worry about trying to make the face look realistic or bothering to make it look finished. What happens when you raise an eyebrow higher than the other? How about skewing the triangle shape so that one end is sharper than the other?

Capping it off with hair

The hairstyle you choose describes a lot about your character's attributes and personality, as well as the nature of the manga story. The shapes, and even colors, you choose can present your character as a rebel with a cause, a loner, an intellect, or a bully.

The androgynous yaoi culture plays a major role in the men's manga fashion world, especially when it comes to hair. As I show you in this section, yaoi hairstyles (accompanied by the huge manga eyes) have made gender appearances indistinguishable at times.

In Figure 4-28, you can see just some of the many versions of the yaoi hairstyles. Generally speaking, the smoother and rounder-edged hair shapes suggest tidiness and a higher level of intelligence. The hair can be as long as the shoulders. The hair shapes with sharper and jagged edges usually suggest a disheveled youth who spends most of his day on cloud nine. This type of hair is usually short.

Figure 4-28:
Different
types of
androgy-
nous
hairstyles.

To make the most of this section, you need the complete head shapes I show you in the beginning of this chapter. If you've never drawn a manga head before, read through the section "Heading Out on a Manga Mission."

In Figure 4-29, I show the steps you take to draw the hair on top of the basic head shape. Start with the ¾ angle of the basic androgynous head shape, and then follow these steps to draw the jagged "Rugged Yaoi" hairstyle:

1. **Locate and mark with an "X" the spot where the hair shapes will begin (you can call it your "bald spot"); Figure 4-29a shows you how to do this.**

   The spot usually begins just past the peak of the skull. About ¼ inch above the X, I make my first hair shape, which resembles a checkmark.

2. **Starting from that origin, draw in the jagged sections of the left and right sides of the hair as shown in Figure 4-29b.**

   Starting from the left side of the checkmark and drawing left toward the front of the head, I first draw a couple of curvy lines with pointed edges. As the hair approaches the front of the head, I draw more sharp points and fewer curvy lines. The direction of the points curve toward the head.

Next, I return to the top of the right side of the checkmark and draw the hair toward the back of the head. My first curvy line is the longest one; it ends at a sharp point right above the ear. Three more sharp points curve toward the head. Be sure to place enough space between the scalp and the hair.

I find that the distance between the head and the hair increases toward the front of the head. The distance decreases at the point right above the X.

3. **Draw the jagged bangs as shown in Figure 4-29c.**

   From left to right, I draw a series of sharp pointed shapes for the bangs. These shapes are thinner and longer than the rest of the hair. When drawing these shapes, I use my wrist as a pivot point to draw the sharp angles going in an up-and-down motion. A couple shapes overlap the eye region.

Here are some tips to getting the overall jagged hair shape to look right:

- ✔ Start at the top with smaller jagged shapes.
- ✔ Alternate the ends of the shapes facing up with shapes facing down.
- ✔ Toward the bottom, the shapes should get longer and narrower.
- ✔ Try rotating the paper sideways to complete the bangs.
- ✔ The entire hairstyle's overall shape should be round or slightly oval.

Figure 4-29:
Drawing the jagged yaoi style; working along the outsides of the hair first.

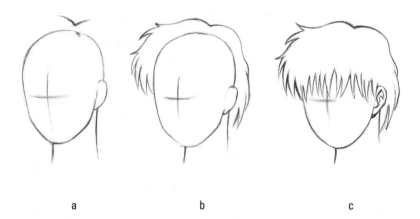

a   b   c

Start with a head, like the one I use in Figure 4-30a, and turn your attention to these steps to draw the rounder, "Smooth Yaoi" style:

1. **Start just to the left of the vertical center line, and draw the parted bangs first.**

The parted bangs should be fairly long. In Figure 4-30b, the bangs on each side of the part are clearly visible. For the left side of the bangs, I draw what I refer to as "ribbon hair." I start by drawing a short pointed hair shape. At the end of the sharp point, I draw a similar shape that's shorter and going the opposite direction. I follow up with one long and one very short wave. Before continuing on to finish the right side of the bangs, I add short lines beneath the first short, pointed hair shape. These lines represent the base of the hairline shape.

The shape of the right side of the bangs resembles the tail of a horse. Toward the bottom of the bangs, draw a series of short sharp points clustered together to form a larger, rounder shape. Finish this side by drawing the pointed hairline shapes underneath.

2. **Draw and complete both sides of the hair (see Figure 4-30c).**

Start at the part where the two sides of the bangs meet. Here, I draw four to five lines stretching toward the back of the head. The back of the hair is smooth with several subtle bumps. For the most part, the hair shape sticks flat against the head shape (unlike the "Jagged Yaoi," where the hair is further from the head). The only place where the hair lifts away from the head is behind the ears. I finish the back of the hair by extending the smooth curve down the back of the neck, ending right at the level with the chin.

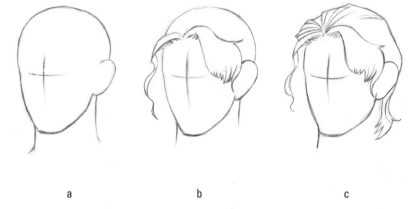

Figure 4-30:
Drawing the "Smooth Yaoi" hairstyle.

a   b   c

The Emotions Tell All

After you have a basic character put together, set her in motion by putting her on the acting stage. In this section, I look at several physical characteristics that help bring out the right emotions in your character. So get into your Director's Chair and get ready to take charge. Camera, Lights, and Action!

Before you examine some popular emotions, try this simple visual exercise: Take 15 minutes in front of a mirror and act out an emotion. Observe what happens. In some extreme emotions, such as rage or fear, an eye may appear to be higher than the other. See how the mouth and nostrils contort into twisted shapes that would make your mother scream. Have fun, and then get back to the drawing board!

Neutral face

Imagine the face of a young girl who has just walked outside of her apartment to face another day at work. She appears neither happy nor sad. Although readers don't know the exact emotion going through her head, her neutral face tells them that she's in touch with society or at least with her surrounding environment.

Follow these steps to draw the neutral expression in Figure 4-31:

1. **Draw the androgynous head shape for your character.**

2. **Draw the eyes staring straight forward with the eyebrows forming an arc around the eyes.**

   Keep the eyebrows perfectly arched as if to mirror the shape of the eye itself.

3. **Draw the ski jump nose.**

4. **Draw the simplified mouth slightly upturned into a subtle smile.**

   I draw an arc shape for the mouth with a smaller arc shape underneath to show the bottom of the lower lip. Adding the lower lip gives more dimension to the mouth.

5. **Draw the figure-6 ears.**

6. **Draw bangs and pigtails.**

   Pigtails are fun and relatively simple to draw. The hair shape sticks close to the head shape. The pigtails emerge from the back of her head. I draw the long pointed hair shapes for the bangs. Where the bangs extend down toward her chin, I incorporate some of the wavy patterns I use in the "Smooth Yaoi" hairstyle. To give the back of the head dimension, I draw lines starting from the sides of the head going toward the rectangle shape I draw for the hair band.

Serious face

Suppose your character enters her office but senses that something is awry. Her friends are hesitant about breaking bad news to her. Unlike the neutral expression she has in the previous section, emotion is more apparent when she puts on her serious face. Readers get a feeling of tension. With the smile completely gone, the character's features begin communicating that something isn't right. The expression on her face isn't subtle.

Figure 4-31:
Drawing the
neutral face.

Follow these steps to change the neutral face into the serious face in Figure 4-32:

1. **Slightly curve her eyebrows down to create a little frown just above her eyes.**

2. **Curve the mouth upside down.**

   The mouth should resemble the upside down version of the subtle smile in the neutral face (see the previous section). Observe how I even flip the smaller arc to mirror the longer mouth shape.

Figure 4-32:
Drawing the
serious
face.

Mad face

You're about to find out the source of your character's anger as she puts on her mad face. She didn't get a promotion she was promised at work! Follow these steps to turn the serious face into the mad face in Figure 4-33:

1. **Draw her eyebrows so that they're straighter and digging even closer to the center of her forehead.**

   Note that the eyebrows angle higher up toward her hairline as they move away from the center of her face.

2. **Add a series of hatch marks going across above the nose to suggest temperature change (in this case, the color red).**

   Don't put too many lines in at this stage (we need to save that for the even more intense emotions that are yet to follow this one). For now, I draw just five short, diagonal lines.

3. **Alter the mouth by dropping the top center of the lip's dip down a bit and raising both sides of the upper corners of the mouth.**

   In addition, I raise the center of the bottom lip or lower the edges of the bottom lip to expose the gnarling lower teeth.

Figure 4-33: Drawing the mad face.

Psycho mad

Okay, your character has gone from mad to psycho mad. She finds out that the co-worker who got the promotion she wanted just happens to be the CEO's son! And to make things worse, he used to be her boyfriend! She's now yelling and screaming at the ex-boyfriend as he prances off happily toward his new private office and sits down in his expensive leather chair.

Follow these steps to go from the mad face to the psycho mad face in Figure 4-34:

1. **Draw her eyebrows down even farther than they were in the mad face.**

   When characters get this mad, the eyebrows obscure part of the eyes.

2. **Arch the lower lids of the eyes to show the raised and taut cheek muscles.**

   Take the lower eyelids and flip them so that the curves are parallel to the top eyelid curve. Now, she's so mad that the lower part of her vision is obscured.

3. **Draw a series of hatch marks reaching underneath both eyes.**

4. **Draw the open mouth with the center of the upper lip dipped down so that she's baring her teeth.**

   TIP

   When drawing an angry mouth, draw the lower portion of the open mouth wider than the top. Adding small fangs on the top and bottom of the teeth makes for a cool effect.

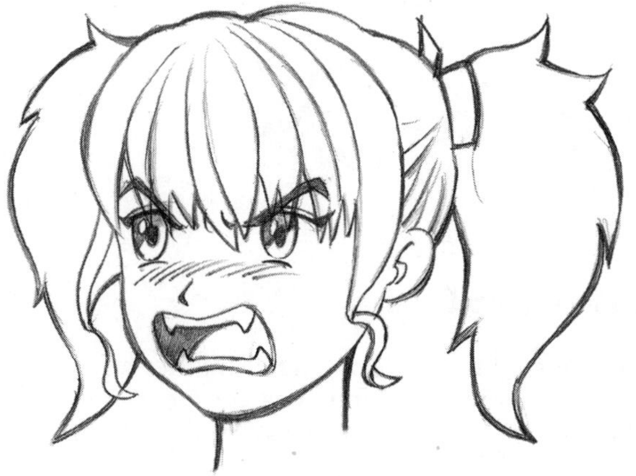

Figure 4-34: Drawing the psycho mad face.

Sad face

Reality starts to kick in as your character slumps into the old, tiny chair in her crammed cubicle at work — her dream position is now gone. Follow these steps to turn the neutral face into the sad face in Figure 4-35:

1. **Draw big eyes and keep 'em big.**

Draw a large highlight at the upper-left corner of the eye and draw another smaller one off to the lower right of the eye to show that she's getting teary-eyed.

2. **Draw straight eyebrows, angled up at 45 degrees.**

3. **Add faint hatch marks underneath each eye to show that she's becoming bloated and ready to shed some tears.**

4. **Add the sad mouth by drawing an arc that looks like a boomerang.**

   Draw a short line right below the mouth to help emphasize the pouting.

Figure 4-35:
Drawing the
sad face.

Even sadder face

Your character just got off the phone with her mother after telling her that she isn't coming home for the weekend because she isn't getting a raise or the job she had hoped to get. Follow these steps to go from the sad face to the even sadder face in Figure 4-36:

1. **Draw small tears forming at the lower corner of her eyes.**

   When drawing the eyes, raise the lower lid to heighten the effect that she can no longer hold in her tears.

2. **Draw slightly crooked eyebrows close to the eyes.**

3. **Draw even more hatch marks under her eyes.**

4. **Draw the mouth shape turned down (like an upside down hot dog) with a narrower width than the mouth in the sad face.**

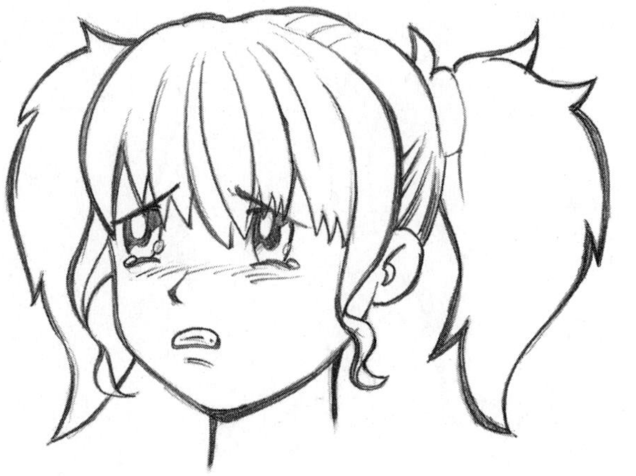

Figure 4-36: Drawing the even sadder face.

Total devastation

Adding insult to injury, your character has just been ordered to go get coffee by the ex-boyfriend co-worker who got the promotion she wanted. Oh, the humiliation and the shame! Take advantage of your character's total devastation as she dashes out of the office building, bawling as she heads toward the nearest coffee shop. Follow these steps to turn the even sadder face into the total devastation face in Figure 4-37:

1. **Clamp the eyes shut by drawing them in a half-moon shape like a bracket.**
2. **Add tears streaming down both cheeks.**

   Start from the end of the closed eyes, and make sure the tear streams curve as they follow the contour of her round cheeks.

   TIP: Make the closed eyes look innocent by thickening the bracket eyelid shape (especially if you're drawing a shōjo lead character).
3. **Draw the bawling mouth elongated and wide open.**

   The center of the upper lip angles to a sharp point. When drawing the open mouth from this angle, make sure that the curved sides of the mouth are parallel to each other. Finally, I draw the upper teeth and the tongue.

REMEMBER: Some things to keep in mind when drawing this mouth:

- Draw the upper lip curving down.
- Show the upper teeth.
- Add in the tongue.
- Make sure that the lower part of the mouth is wider than the top.

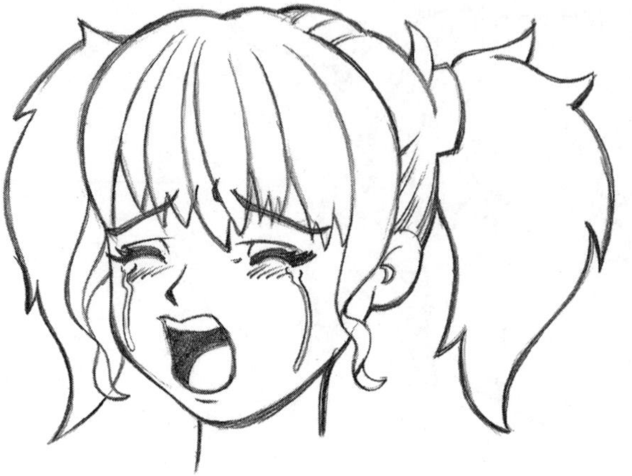

Figure 4-37: Drawing the total devastation face.

Surprise or shock

Your character finds out from her co-worker friend that her slime-bucket, ex-boyfriend, job-stealing co-worker has just been caught taking illegal bribes from investors. He's been arrested and now the position she wants is potentially in her grasp! When drawing an expression of surprise or shock, make the eyes the main focus.

Follow these steps to go from the total devastation face to the surprised or shocked face in Figure 4-38:

1. **Draw the eyes wide open.**

   Observe that the eyes are smaller than usual and they don't touch either the top or bottom of the eyelids. Draw the eyebrows thin and raised high so that your reader's attention goes to the pupils.

2. **Draw the mouth wide open.**

REMEMBER

Some things to keep in mind when drawing this mouth:

- Draw the top of the lip's curve going down slightly while extending past the width of the lower mouth.
- The lower mouth shape should arc and come down narrower to form the smile.
- Draw the tongue large enough so that it takes up most of the mouth.

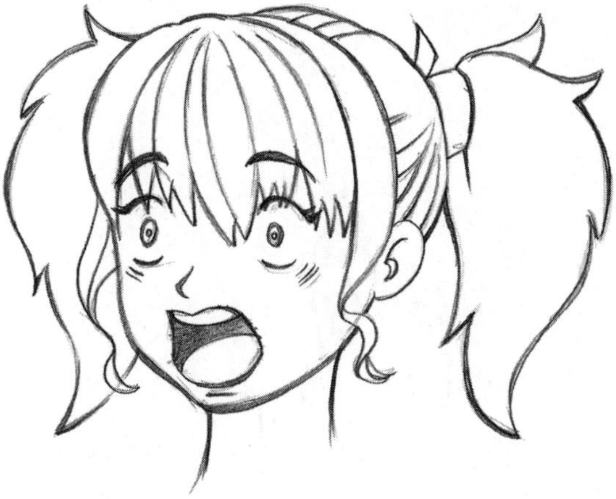

Figure 4-38: Drawing the surprised or shocked face.

Happy face

Looks like things are finally shaping up for your princess character; she was informed that the position she wants has just been reassigned to her. Follow these steps to turn the neutral face into the happy face in Figure 4-39:

1. **Draw the eyes, making sure the eyebrows are raised high.**

   Observe how the lower lid of the eye is raised up in this expression.

2. **Add the happy mouth.**

REMEMBER

Some things to keep in mind when drawing this mouth:

- Avoid drawing individual teeth. Always draw teeth as a group.
- When drawing a jubilant face, make the cheeks slightly curved outward.

Super happy face

When your character's emotions turn ecstatic, the eyes squeeze shut, indicating that she's so happy that she can't see. Her eyebrows peak up to form a high arc position. As with the sad and angry faces earlier in this chapter, most artists draw at least several light marks on each cheek to show a shift in color or temperature when they draw this super happy face. Finally, the top of the mouth curves toward the cheeks more than before so that the smile becomes broader. Readers get a sense that her emotions are of such extreme joy that she's about to burst out with laughter. She should be — she just got a glimpse of her first paycheck after her new promotion!

Figure 4-39:
Drawing the
happy face.

Follow these steps to transition from the happy face to the super happy face in Figure 4-40:

1. **Draw the arcs for the super happy eyes.**

   Be sure to arch the eyes higher than those of the total devastation face, earlier in this chapter.

2. **When drawing the mouth, the upper lip should curve up even higher than it does in the happy face.**

   Also the upper lip of the smiling mouth should be slightly wider so that you have more room to show the teeth and tongue.

Figure 4-40:
Drawing the
super happy
face.

Chapter 5

Nice Bod: Manga Body Basics

In This Chapter

- Understanding basic body proportions
- Building body structure using basic geometric shapes
- Bending and twisting figures into poses you like

If you're ready to draw your first manga body, you've come to the right place.

First things first: You need to understand how to apply basic proportions to your characters. A solid *manga-ka* (or manga artist) knows how to create not only a good-looking face, but also a body to go with it. How tall, short, fat, or thin your character is doesn't matter. He or she needs to look consistent and natural throughout your manga story. Create your skeletal structure first, and adding the muscles and curves will come more easily.

In this chapter, I demonstrate how to build up your characters in three stages. In the first stage, I show you how to achieve accurate proportions using a skeletal wire frame figure. In the second stage, I show you how to add structure to your character using basic geometric shapes. Finally, I show you how to add muscular definition to the body.

How Many Heads? Setting Up Your Character's Proportions

So what are proportions? Simply put, a *proportion* is the head-to-body ratio of your character. Measuring proportions means using individual body parts (usually the head) as a ruler to measure how tall the character needs to be.

Measuring someone's proportion usually begins by taking what's called a *head count* — taking the height measurement of the head (from the top of the head to the bottom of the chin) and using that as your measuring stick for the height of the entire human body. If you attend a live figure-drawing course, your peers likely take a pencil and hold it up toward the posing model with their arm fully extended and with one eye shut. They're measuring out the proportions of the body. After using the pencil to gauge how tall the head is, the artist uses that length to measure the size of the rest of the body.

Take a field trip if you live near an art museum that has figure sculptures or small figurines. Choose a specific sculpture and, using a pencil to measure it, see whether you can determine the proportions of that object. I recommend observing works from different cultures and periods.

In the manga world, the characters of simple manga are usually 2 to 4 heads tall, as shown in Figure 5-1a. By contrast, lead characters in action manga are drawn a whopping 10 to 15 heads tall, as shown in Figure 5-1b. Depending upon the proportion scale you use, you can achieve either a simplified or more realistic figure. Traditionally, the human figure is 7 to 8½ heads tall.

Throughout this book, when addressing the proper length and width of specific body parts, I use the size of the head as the standard measuring unit for that particular figure. Writing down how tall and wide the head of my character is means that I don't have to keep remeasuring.

Figure 5-1:
Simple manga and action manga use different head-proportion scales.

a   b

When you're dealing with proportions, here are a few things to keep in mind:

- ✔ The more simplified your proportions are, the more your features are exaggerated.
- ✔ Simpler characters have larger symbolic props (such as hair, clothing, jewelry, and so on).
- ✔ The more realistic your proportions are, the more precisely you have to draw the physical features.

If you're drawing manga for the first time, or if you haven't taken any figure-drawing courses yet, I recommend not attempting to draw realistic manga until you get comfortable drawing the more typical, exaggerated style. Drawing realistically usually entails spending more time doing research for references (clothing, advanced anatomy, and so on). Getting caught up with the details can get in the way of the big picture (no pun intended).

Whichever manga genre you choose to illustrate, determining how many heads tall your average characters are going to be is crucial. Successful manga artists make a point of fleshing out their characters from different angles in their *character design sheets*. In Figure 5-2, I show you an example of a character design sheet for my character, Java, and her sidekick, La-Té. The purpose of this study is to make sure that I know how to draw my character from different angles using the same proportion measurements. Note the head measurements on the side figures. Starting from left to right, from my series, *JAVA!,* are Swizz Mizz, Astronomus, Java, La-Té, and Mickey. Having this chart gives me a better idea of how my characters measure up against each other in strength and size in their next encounter.

Start by drawing the front view of one of your characters, and then go on to create your own character design sheet by drawing each character side by side like I do in Figure 5-2. Don't worry about drawing the details for a finished look — you just want to get a feel for how your characters look next to each other. Drawing just the outline of the character is enough for now.

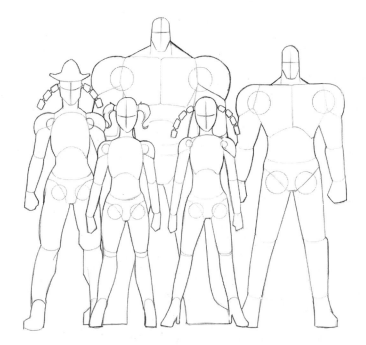

Figure 5-2:
An example
of a
character
design
sheet.

Taking a top-down approach

So where's the best place to start when drawing your first manga body? In my opinion, it's "from the top" for a couple of good reasons:

- First, manga places a huge emphasis on the face — so much so that if the face doesn't look right, it can zap your inspiration to do well on the rest of the body.

- The second reason can be summed up in one word: gravity. Your hands and eyes

work better when you're working with nature's gravitational pull. I can prove it to you: Select a simple object in the room. On your sketch pad, begin drawing that object, but work from the bottom to the top (rather than from the top down). Notice how awkward and tight your wrists feel when drawing this way. Working against gravity's pull makes your arm tired at a faster pace than normal.

Drawing a Wire Frame

After you set your character's proportions (refer to the previous section), your next step is to create a skeletal *wire frame.* A wire frame is best described as a simplified skeletal structure. As I show you in this section, it's a quick and accurate tool that helps you get the pose you want from your character with proportional accuracy.

One advantage of a wire frame figure is its flexibility to represent both sexes. In addition, getting a desired action pose is easier when you use a wire frame before getting into the heavier anatomy session. In this chapter, I draw the front and the side at the same time so that you can compare what the wire figure looks like from different angles.

Note: If you haven't read the previous chapter on drawing the manga face, you don't have to backtrack, because you aren't filling in the actual facial features yet. However, you should definitely spend time going over Chapter 4 before attempting to create your own characters from scratch.

Drawing a body isn't a skill you can master overnight. For most people, it takes practice and patience. Although I provide examples and tips, you have to practice to become accustomed to using and controlling the tools to get the feel and the accuracy of the lines and shapes that you make.

So, are you ready to get wired-up? Follow these steps to draw your wire frame figure, which serves as the basic foundational skeleton for your character:

1. **Draw a slightly egg-shaped oval for the head.**

    You're drawing the front view, as shown in Figure 5-3a. You use this oval to measure the rest of the proportions of the body.

Patience, Grasshopper!

I can't stress enough the importance of being patient while learning to draw. I always encourage my students to stick with the class they're in. Unlike some academic courses, you can't cram to learn an art project or skill. Pacing yourself is important, as is practicing on a daily, consistent basis. If your schedule isn't flexible, you should still make a point to draw for just 15 minutes a day. If you don't have time to sit at a drawing table, carry a small sketch pad and mechanical pencil with you. During a break or some time off, create some sketches or doodles!

Be sure to give yourself plenty of room below the head for the entire body to fit. If you draw a head with too little space for the rest of the body to fall under, you may find yourself subconsciously distorting the body to fit the space.

2. **Draw cross hairs on the front of the face to indicate roughly where the features will be.**

Drawing cross hairs helps you decide which way the face is pointing.

3. **Next to the head, draw another head that's looking sideways in a profile (you can see this head in Figure 5-3b).**

Make sure you put plenty of distance between the two heads. Draw the same oval shape for each head, but for the profile, drop a slightly curved line from the right side of the circle (which is the front of the face) going down and angling back into the circle to indicate the jaw. Refer to Chapter 4 for more on drawing the head.

4. **Draw the neck. Starting from the base of the head, draw a line indicating the length of the neck.**

Use longer necks for the female characters and shorter necks for males and teenagers. I choose a shorter neck as my default in both drawings in Figure 5-3.

Don't extend the neck too much. If the neck is too long, it throws off the balance of the rest of the body.

5. **Draw a horizontal line indicating the shoulder.**

The wider the shoulder is, the more a character appears to be masculine and bulky. Stick to more narrow shoulder frames for female characters. The default is 2½ heads wide (see Figure 5-4a). The shoulder frame is indicated in the side view (as shown in Figure 5-4b) with a shorter line because you're looking at it from a different angle.

6. **From the center of the neck, draw the spine.**

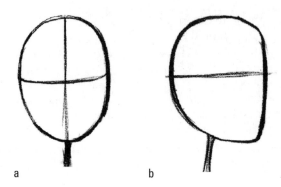

Figure 5-3:
Drawing the
head and
neck of the
wire frame
figure.

a   b

Looking from the front (see Figure 5-4a), the spine is drawn as a straight line. However, as you can see in the side view drawing in Figure 5-4b, the spine has a slight "S" curve as it travels from the head and into the crotch at a slanted angle. *Note:* In females, the angle of the profile "S" curve is a little more tilted.

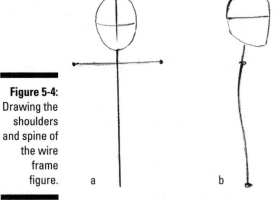

Figure 5-4:
Drawing the
shoulders
and spine of
the wire
frame
figure.   a   b

For the default wire figure, the length of the spine should be 2½ heads down from the shoulder line. The younger the character is, the shorter the length should be. Adolescents, for example, may measure only 1½ heads.

7. From the bottom of the spine, draw a line for the hip.

This line is parallel to the shoulder line but slightly shorter. Draw the line slightly above the end of the spine as shown in Figure 5-5a.

8. **From both sides of the hip line, draw down both legs (see Figure 5-5a and b).**

   Here's a good way to determine the right leg-length for your default figure: The length should be roughly the same as the measurement from the top of the head to the bottom of the spine. The crotch (intersection point of the spine and the hip line) should be the midpoint of the figure.

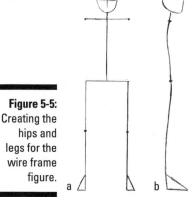

Figure 5-5: Creating the hips and legs for the wire frame figure.

9. **Draw the knee joints and add the feet.**

   As I show you in Figure 5-5, use circles to indicate where the joints are. You can determine where to place the knee joints by measuring 1½ heads from the hip. As for the feet, use the simple triangle shape that I draw in Figure 5-5. The triangle is slightly skewed — the side facing inside should be flatter than the outside.

10. **Draw the arms.**

    They should be 2 head lengths (see Figure 5-6a). The upper arm and lower arm are both 1 head length long.

    When you place the arms tightly against the body without the hands (see Figure 5-6b), they should end right at the end of the spine.

11. **Finally, draw the hands.**

    For the wire figure, use the same triangles you use for the feet (see Figure 5-6). The side facing outside should be flatter than the inside edge facing the body. A good way of determining the size of the hand is by checking the size of the face. With your pencil, estimate how much space (height) the face will take up on the head. Then take that measurement and apply it to the hands.

After you finish your skeleton stick figure, add some flesh and muscle by heading to the gym to get in shape — geometric shape, to be more precise. Read on for more.

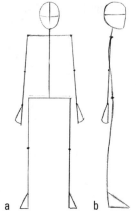

Figure 5-6:
Completing the legs and drawing the arms and hands for the wire frame figure.

a   b

Getting in Shape with Geometry

When you look around at your surroundings, objects appear quite complex and loaded with detail. Take the human body, for example. Did you know that you're packing 206 bones inside of you? An infant has even more bones — 350 (the bones fuse together as you mature). Yes, it's a bone-chilling world indeed. But despite all that detail, complex objects such as your body structure can be generalized into simple yet versatile geometric shapes. In this section I show you how to create the individual body parts using larger geometric shapes.

In this world of complexity, visual simplification is key. All you need to know are some basics from geometry class. The four basic geometric shapes that you need to familiarize yourself with are the cylinder, cube, sphere, and cone (see Figure 5-7).

Figure 5-7:
Cylinders, cubes, spheres, and cones are your best friends!

Using these shapes, you can create any character, animal, hi-tech prop, or background. You name it, you can make it!

Practice drawing the geometric forms in Figure 5-7. Try drawing them at different heights and widths. For example, what would a sphere look like if it were, say, a rubber ball being squished? What about a tall cylinder bending forward like a slinky? Also try drawing shapes, such as the cone, upside down or rotated at different angles.

While practicing these shapes, I show you two types of shadows that make the shapes look dimensional and real; *form shadows* (the shading that curves around an object based on the light source near it) and *cast shadows* (the shadow the object casts on the floor or wall behind it) create the look of three-dimensionality. See Figure 5-8 for an example of these shadows.

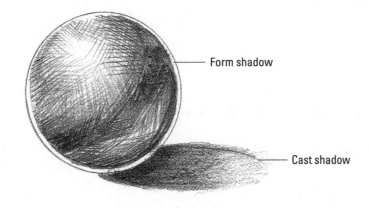

Form shadow

Cast shadow

Figure 5-8:
Exploring
the form and
cast
shadows.

Throughout this book, I use the term *bearing sphere* to describe the object that serves as a joint between movable body parts. The purpose for introducing this feature is to help simplify the complexity of the joint/ligament structure that actually exists. This section could get really long and boring if I approached it from a pure anatomical perspective.

Defining the head

I talk about the head structure in depth in Chapter 4. Keep in mind that the head is a three-dimensional sphere and not just a circle. This concept is critical when you're drawing poses where the character has her head in a twisted or tilted position. In three dimensions, the cross hairs run around the spherical head and give readers a better sense of which way the character is looking.

Start with the head and draw three elongated oval shapes, as shown in Figure 5-9.

I make the bottom of the oval more pointed to describe the chin. I wrap the cross hairs around the round form of the head in the ¾ angle view.

If you have a clear sense of how the cross hairs fall on the form, you also have a good idea of how the features rest. At this stage, don't add the details of the features to the head yet; leave everything in its basic geometric form.

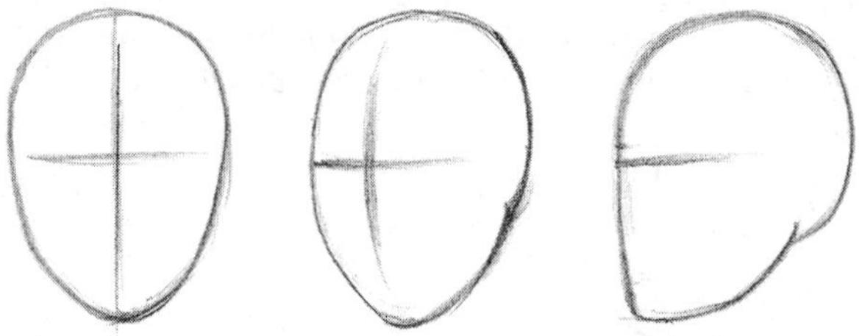

Figure 5-9: Drawing the sphere for the head — front, side, and ¾ views.

Taking on the torso

The *torso* is essentially the upper body or general ribcage area. It measures approximately 1½ heads tall and 2 heads wide, and it's a slightly egg-shaped sphere.

TIP

Similar to the shoulder line in the wire figure, the torso's width expands to fit the proportions of a bulkier, broader character. Likewise, it's narrower for female and teen characters.

Follow the steps for drawing the torso from several different angles:

1. **Draw three separate, slightly egg-shaped spheres, as shown in Figure 5-10.**

   Although I draw the front view of the torso (the first drawing on the left in Figure 5-10) as if it's positioned upright, by observing the ¾ view (in the center) and side view of the torso (on the right), you can see that all three are a little tilted to reflect the "S" curve of the wire figure spine (see "Drawing a Wire Frame" earlier in this chapter for details on the wire figure).

2. **Cut a half-moon arc shape at the center bottom of all three spheres, as shown in Figure 5-11.**

Figure 5-10:
The tilting of the torso from different angles — front, ¾, and side views.

This cut has two purposes. First, it mimics the indentation of the structure of the actual rib cage. Second, it makes room for the stomach structure to snap in. Note that on the side view (third drawing in Figure 5-11), the cut is there, but it isn't visible.

Figure 5-11:
Cutting into the torso from the front, ¾, and side views.

3. **Cut a hole on the upper left and right of the torso and fit in a bearing sphere for each shoulder.**

   Be careful not to place the arm holes too high on the torso. Also, make sure they're level with each other (see Figure 5-12).

Figure 5-12:
Creating the opening for the arms to fit in.

Can you stomach this?

The stomach is essentially a sphere — and that's it (no strings attached)! Don't let its simplicity fool you, though — the stomach plays a very crucial role in making your character's poses work. It functions as a large *bearing sphere* (joint) between the torso and the hip so that your character can bend forward, backward, and sideways. In Figure 5-13, you see how the stomach fits into the torso from the front, ¾, and side views.

Figure 5-13: Fitting the stomach sphere snuggly into the torso opening.

It's all in the hips

The hip is basically half of a sphere that looks like a pair of underwear when completed. Follow these steps to get your shorts:

1. **Draw three separate spheres.**

   Figures 5-14a, b, and c show these spheres from the front, ¾, and side views.

2. **Erase the top half of each sphere, leaving the remaining portion for the hip (as shown in Figures 5-14d, e, and f).**

3. **Cut holes in the lower portion of each half-sphere for the legs to fit in.**

4. **Draw a bearing sphere in both sides, as shown in Figures 5-14g, h, and i.**

   Think of each bearing sphere as a hip joint to which your leg bones attach. Draw the bearing spheres smaller than the hole openings.

Forging the arms

Think of the arms as cylinders. You have the upper arm *(biceps)* running from your shoulder to the elbow. Next, you have the lower arm *(forearm),* which runs from the elbow down to the end of the wrists. I show you how to take these two shapes and attach them together.

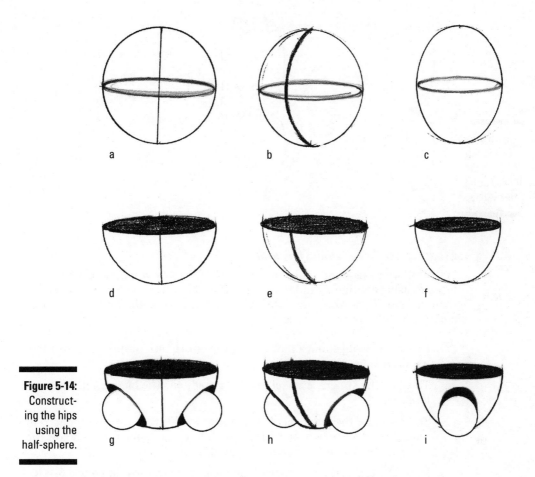

Figure 5-14: Constructing the hips using the half-sphere.

Drawing the upper arm (biceps)

Follow these instructions to draw the upper arm in Figure 5-15:

1. **Draw two narrow ovals 1⅓ of a head length apart from each other (as shown to the right in Figure 5-15a).**

   Both ovals are the same size. To make sure they're the right amount of space apart, I draw two head shapes to the left of the narrow ovals to use as a measurement guide.

2. **Connect the two ovals with slightly curved lines to complete the cylinder for the upper arm (as shown in Figure 5-15b).**

   Make sure both lines are parallel to each other.

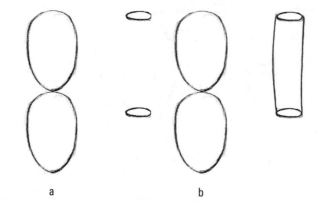

Figure 5-15:
Construct-
ing the
biceps using
the cylinder.

a   b

Creating the lower arm (forearm)

In the following sequence shown in Figure 5-16, I show you how to draw a forearm using another cylinder. Observe that the top of the forearm is wider than the end of the wrist. Start with the upper arm from the previous section, and then check out these steps:

1. **Draw a bearing sphere that covers the entire end of the bottom of the upper arm (as shown on the right in Figure 5-16a).**

   This bearing sphere is the elbow joint that joins the biceps with the forearm.

   To make sure the two ovals for the lower forearm are properly spaced in relation to the upper arm, I attach two additional head shapes below the first two head shape measurement guides on the left.

2. **Draw the top of the cylinder of the forearm (as shown in Figure 5-16b).**

   The width of the oval is the exact same width as the opening of the biceps. This cylinder overlaps the sphere representing the elbow and creates the perception that the two forms are securely joined.

3. **Draw the bottom of the cylinder for the lower arm approximately 1 head length apart from the top (as shown in Figure 5-16c).**

   The bottom of the cylinder is narrower than the top.

4. **Connect both sides of the cylinder with slightly curved lines (as shown in Figure 5-16c).**

   The inside line curves in at a slightly steeper angle than the outside line. This angle aids the overall balance and design of the arm.

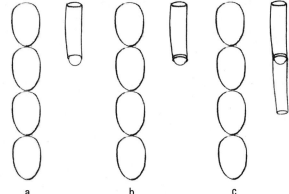

Figure 5-16:
Building and
connecting
the forearm
to the
biceps.

a   b   c

On to the legs

Like the arms, the legs are also divided into two sections — the upper leg and
the lower leg. The upper leg is much bulkier than the lower leg because it
contains larger and more powerful muscles.

Legs are probably one of the most important and most overlooked parts of
the body. Most people forget that without the legs placed in the proper position, the body may not be able to support a pose. In the section, "Getting off
on the right feet," later in this chapter, I talk about the importance of keeping
track of where one leg rests in relationship to the other leg. Also, with all the
exaggerated proportions you see in manga, you may easily discount the fact
that the legs and feet count for half the human proportion.

Upper legs

Time to get some good leg-work done! Bring out the hip structure that I discuss in the earlier section, "It's all in the hips." This structure gives you a
more accurate shape and overall better proportion as you draw the upper
leg. Refer to the set of demonstrations in Figure 5-17 as you follow these steps
to draw the front, ¾, and side views:

1. **Draw the top of a cylinder partially covering the bearing sphere on
   the hips for both the left and right legs.**

2. **Draw the bottom side of the cylinder for the upper leg 1¾ head
   lengths down from the top.**

   The width of the bottom of the upper leg should be about half the width
   of the top. The bottom of the cylinder shouldn't be parallel to the wider
   top side. The top is angled 45 degrees higher.

In order to avoid drawing body parts colliding into each other, draw limbs branching slightly out to angle *away* from the body. Poses look more stable and stronger when the legs and arms angle away to form a more triangular-shaped composition. A good way to start is by drawing the ovals for the knees slightly separated.

3. **Draw both sides of the cylinder to complete the upper leg.**

    You can see how the outer edge of the upper leg is higher than the opposite, inner side.

Lower leg

Next in order is the lower leg. In Figure 5-18, look at how narrow the cylinder structure is compared to the upper leg. Before starting to draw the lower leg, make sure you construct the hips and attach the upper leg with a bearing sphere as I show you in the previous section.

To continue constructing the lower leg, just follow these steps, keeping in mind that I show you the front, ¾, and side views, left to right:

1. **Draw a bearing sphere into the bottom of the upper leg (as shown in Figure 5-18a).**

    This bearing sphere fits snuggly into the lower end of the upper leg to create the kneecap.

2. **Draw the top of the cylinder around the lower half of the bearing sphere (see Figure 5-18b).**

3. **Draw the bottom of the cylinder for the lower leg 1½ heads from the top.**

    As shown in Figure 5-18b, the bottom side of the cylinder is narrower than the top.

4. **Draw both sides of the cylinder to complete the lower leg (see Figure 5-18c).**

    The lower leg is slightly longer than the upper leg. Most beginners make the false assumption that the upper and lower legs are the same length.

All hands on deck

The hands are probably the most sophisticated part of the body. I show you in Figure 5-19 how to break down the hand structure into a simpler object, but the best way of achieving success in drawing hands is to practice. Sometimes the importance is not on what you practice, but on how you practice. In this case, conceptualize the hand into geometrical shapes. Carry around a small sketchbook wherever you go. You never know when you're going to get the urge to sit and draw.

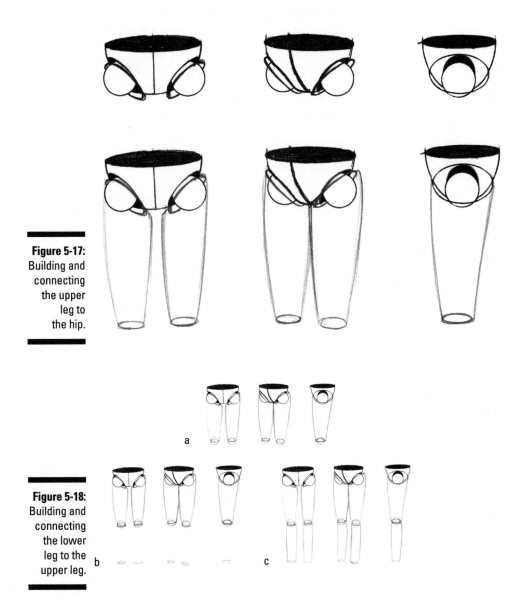

Figure 5-17: Building and connecting the upper leg to the hip.

Figure 5-18: Building and connecting the lower leg to the upper leg.

Another reason to practice getting better at drawing hands is that they convey a wide range of emotions. For example, clenched fists may show anger. When you're happy, you may clasp your hands together with thankfulness. Being comfortable drawing hands allows you to show your characters' emotions without showing their faces.

For the purpose of clarity, I divide this section into two parts: the palm and the fingers. In each section, I give you the chance to draw step by step the subject at hand (no pun intended).

Let me tell you a secret. The hand is used to moving and functioning in only so many patterns — no more than ten, by my book. Any other positions are uncommon, impractical, or simply unappealing. The more you draw the hands, the more you begin to identify these patterns on your own and add them to your repertoire of things you comfortably can draw from memory or without having any reference.

The palm

Although the palm (like the entire hand) contains a very detailed anatomical structure, you can simplify it into three basic sections. Take time to get to know these sections to help you understand how the rest of the hand works. Each section in Figure 5-19a has its own specific function:

✔ **Section A:** Aids the thumb's lateral and vertical movement

✔ **Section B:** Groups the index and middle fingers

✔ **Section C:** Groups the fourth and fifth fingers

Note the "curving" change in shape and movement that the three sections of the palm make from the front view (as shown in Figure 5-19b).

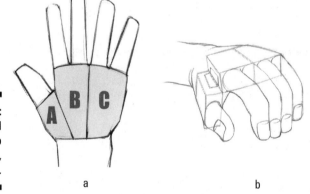

Figure 5-19:
The hand divided into sections A, B, and C.

a   b

Start at the upper-left corner of your sketch pad (if you're left-handed, you start at the upper right), and follow these steps:

1. **Draw the basic palm outline (as shown Figure 5-20a).**

2. **Draw a straight, vertical line to divide the center of the palm (as shown in Figure 5-20b).**

   The divided sections are as follows: B on the left and C on the right.

3. **Divide Section B with a diagonal line as shown in Figure 5-20c.**

   The new section on the far left is section A.

Figure 5-20:
Drawing
the hand,
sections A
through C.

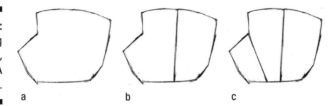

a   b   c

The fingers

The key to understanding the fingers is to see how they group and move in relation to one another. Most beginners are intimidated by the number of intricate gestures associated with the fingers. One student told me that she hated drawing hands because there are simply "too many fingers to draw." In this section, I show you how to draw the fingers without becoming overwhelmed by the sheer number of them.

Observe how the fingers move in sync with their respective sections of the palm. Consistent with the letter codes in the section on the palm, each finger naturally mimics or follows the movement of the other finger in the same section. The thumb rests by itself in Section A.

Look at your hands in motion. Run through normal gestures such as pointing, holding a coffee cup, waving a casual hello, and so on. Keep the gestures simple and relaxed. Observe the motions that happen between the index finger and middle finger (both attached to section B) and the motions that happen between the fourth and fifth fingers (both attached to section C).

Figure 5-21a shows how the finger joints follow the "curving" movement of the three sections of the palm. (I note the joints of the fingers so the arc is clear.) In Figure 5-21b, you see how the index and middle fingers rise in accordance to the higher arcing of section B. Relax your hand in front of you. Then, looking from the side, lift up either the index or middle finger and watch what happens. You should find that depending upon which finger you moved, the other followed. Even when fingers from one section are higher than the fingers of the other, the arc shape is still there.

This arc shape helps create a well-balanced and well-designed hand. Without this balance, the hand you draw looks awkward and poorly contrived.

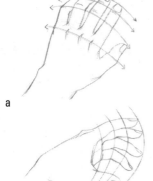

a

Figure 5-21:
Tracking
the finger
movements.

b

The hand is a lot bigger than you may give it credit for. Most beginners make the mistake of drawing the hands on their characters way too small. Don't let that narrow wrist and the small bones in your hand fool you. The hand is as big as the face of the character, which mimics real life. Don't believe me? Stand in front of the mirror with your open hand in front of your face.

Now, try your hand at drawing the fingers. You need the palm of the hand that I show you in the previous section. Use it as your starting point and follow these steps:

1. **Draw a vertical line extending from the center of the division of sections B and C (as shown in Figure 5-22a).**

2. **Mark the midpoints of sections B and C with small notches, and extend two segments from them, as shown in Figure 5-22b.**

3. **From each midpoint, draw an elongated cylinder to represent the middle and fourth fingers (see Figure 5-22c).**

   Make the middle finger slightly longer than the fourth finger. Use the division marks you made on sections B and C to determine the width of the fingers.

4. **Add the index finger to the left of the middle finger and the fifth finger to the right of the fourth finger (see Figure 5-22d).**

   Both fingers are shorter than the middle and fourth fingers. The fifth finger is the shortest of the four. The width of the fingers should start from the middle of sections B and C and extend to the edge of the top of the palm.

5. **Draw the cylinder for the thumb (Figure 5-22e).**

The width of the base of the thumb is the same width as the top of section A. I draw the right of the thumb (facing the palm) by extending the diagonal line of the right side of section A upward and away from the palm. The outer side of the thumb (facing away from the palm) angles inward, almost perpendicular, toward the sky. Complete the top of the thumb by connecting the outside and inside lines of the thumb with a short segment that's parallel to the bottom base of the thumb. The length of the thumb is approximately the same as the length of its base.

6. **Draw four arcs (as shown in Figure 5-22f) to determine the placement of the finger joints.**

   The first arc goes over the first joint of the thumb and top of the palm. The second wave crosses over the second joints of all the fingers. The third wave goes through the second joint of the index, middle, and fourth fingers and over the top of the fifth finger. The fourth and final arc travels over the finger tips of the four fingers. This final arc shape is slightly higher than the first three.

   These arcs help the overall design and balance of the hand. Whenever you're in doubt, use these arcs to check your hands.

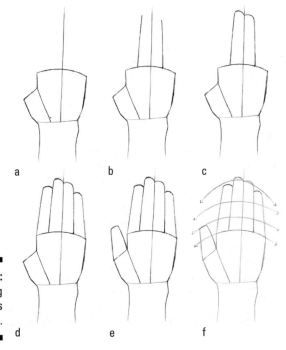

a   b   c

d   e   f

Figure 5-22: Connecting the fingers to the palm.

Covering your foot tracks — bad idea!

In many comic books, I've seen instances of artists adding a lot of smoke and mist on the ground to cover up the feet. Luckily for them, battle scenes are abundant! But when a fan at a comic book convention asks you to do a full sketch of a character and you can't draw the feet, you may end up ruining your reputation. That's just one important reason why every artist should continue to draw from life. Keep practicing and get out there to see what kind of shoes are in the fashion world that you want to use for your characters.

Getting off on the right feet

Feet are essential to drawing a solid manga pose for your character. Most beginners and even professionals hate drawing feet because they can be such an awkward shape depending on the angle from which you're looking at your character.

Go ahead, take a stand!

Having a solid footing helps establish your character's relation to her surroundings. Without feet, your characters can't stand. Your character's feet support the weight of the pose. A cool manga pose may require the body to lean more one way than the other. As a result, you need to adjust the feet of the character to compensate for the weight shift. If you're not used to drawing feet, you have problems guessing where to position them.

Your feet have to be in sync with each other in order for you to stand confidently and comfortably. Check out sports magazines or watch any athletic event on television. Note the placement of the athletes' feet when they strike an action pose. How does a pitcher, for example, place his feet to keep his balance after throwing a 99-mile-per-hour fastball? How does a ballet dancer arrange her toes to keep the center balance of her body from spilling over when she pirouettes?

The structure of the sole

Start drawing the foot from the source of its origin — the lower leg. Start with the front view of the foot. Check out the section on the lower leg earlier in this chapter and then follow these steps to draw the foot:

1. **Attach a bearing sphere to the bottom of the lower leg (as shown in Figure 5-23a).**

   This is the ankle, which secures the foot in place.

2. **Draw a short necktie shape over the lower portion of the bearing sphere (as shown in Figure 5-23b).**

This necktie shape is the front view of the foot. The bottom tip of the shape is off to the right side. Because the big toe fits in that top section, you can see that I'm drawing the character's right foot. Consequently, if you want to draw the left foot, you skew the necktie shape so that the tip is off to the left.

Be careful not to make the necktie shape of the foot too long. The only exception is for a character wearing high heels.

3. **Draw a single arc toward the bottom of the foot (see Figure 5-23c).**

    Similar to marking the knuckle joints of the fingers (see "The fingers," earlier in this chapter), this arc is the guideline for the front portion of the foot, right before the toes extend out.

4. **Map out each toe, starting with the big toe right at the end of the corner of the foot (see Figure 5-23d).**

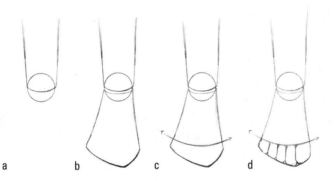

Figure 5-23: Attaching the front view of the foot to the lower leg.

a   b   c   d

Next up is the side view of the foot. Use the front view as your reference point. As you do with the front view, start with the lower leg. I show you both side views of the foot, so you need two lower legs to start. Take the lower leg and glance at these steps:

1. **Attach a bearing sphere to the bottom of each lower leg (as shown in Figure 5-24a).**

    This is the ankle, which secures the foot in place.

2. **Draw a right triangle shape (with the top end cut off), as shown in Figure 5-24b.**

3. **Smooth out the details of the curves in the foot (see Figure 5-24c).**

I fine-tune the foot by rounding off the edge on the bottom of the heels and creating an arch in the midsection. Also, I like to add a subtle slope leading down from the top of the ankle to the end of the toes in the front. The foot is approximately the same length as the forearm.

4. **Select one side-view foot, and draw its big toe (as shown in Figure 5-24d) to show the inside view of the foot.**

   You don't see the rest of the toes because they're all hidden behind the big toe. You're done with the inside view!

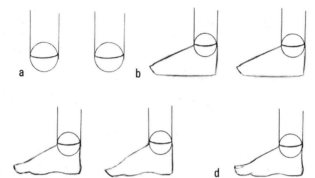

Figure 5-24:
Attaching the side view of the foot to the lower leg.

5. **For the outside view of the foot, use the other side view foot and draw a guideline arc as shown in Figure 5-25a.**

6. **Draw the toes, starting from the smallest "little piggy" (as shown in Figure 5-25b), and continuing to the big toe.**

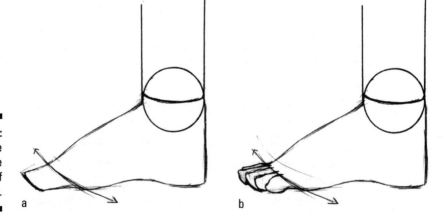

Figure 5-25:
Drawing the opposite side of the foot.

Toes have joints as well. Although they don't get as much attention as finger joints (mostly due to the fact that characters wear shoes and socks all the time), the joints in your toes allow them to curl.

TIP

Whenever I'm drawing overlapping shapes, I start with the largest object closest to me. There certainly isn't one "right" way of drawing, but try to find the "smartest" way of working.

Merging the shapes to the wire figure

The second stage of building your character starts here. In this section, you use the wire frame figure (from "Drawing a Wire Frame," earlier in this chapter) and piece all the individual geometric parts together. This process is like snapping clothes onto an action figure or doll. I show you how to go about drawing your manga character from the start:

1. **Pose your wire frame figure (see Figure 5-26).**

   Start with a simple pose. Avoid complex action poses that have foreshortening or distortion. I lay out a standard pose with the character's arms pretty much straight.

2. **Fit in the neck and torso/stomach (see Figure 5-27).**

3. **Snap in the hips, legs, and feet (see Figure 5-28).**

4. **Fit in the left and right arms and hands (see Figure 5-29).**

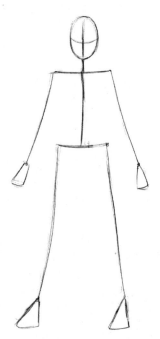

Figure 5-26:
A standard pose for the wire frame figure.

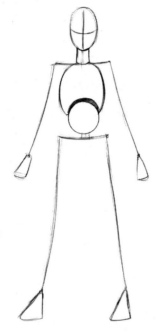

Figure 5-27:
Attaching
the neck
and torso/
stomach.

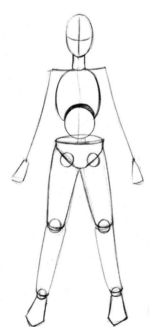

Figure 5-28:
Adding the
lower body.

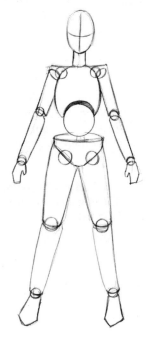

Figure 5-29:
Including
the left and
right arms
and hands.

And that's it! By keeping the pose straightforward and simple, you can work out the drawing proportion issues before tackling more challenging poses.

Beefing up with muscles and rhythm

In the third stage of building up your character, you define the specific physical profile with basic muscle structure. Is your character strong? Slender? You get to choose his or her appearance!

Throughout this section, I show you the basic muscle structure, which I believe is the key to understanding the dynamics and rhythm of the figure. Whichever part of the body you choose to exaggerate should communicate the character's essence. Not every muscle is accentuated. I certainly encourage all artists (students and professionals) to study human anatomy and physiology and draw from life, but don't overwhelm yourself with information overload to the point that you lose sight of the objective of your studies.

Be careful not to overdo the muscle detail if you're drawing manga characters for the first time. Start off drawing the simple shapes that are closer to real life proportions rather than overwhelming your readers with all the busy muscle structure details.

In this section I show you how to add definition, and I note the differences between the male and female figures. Males and females share the same basic anatomical structure, but you need to be aware of major, obvious differences. I list some major muscle groups that you can use, starting from the neck.

The neck

Adjusting the width of the *sternomastoid* and the *trapezius* muscles in the neck is the key to showing strength in men. Including the shape of these muscles in female characters can also suggest elegance and beauty. You have more room for play with the size of these muscles when you're drawing male characters. Check out these steps to draw the neck:

1. **As shown in Figure 5-30a, draw two muscle bands (the sternomastoid) coming from behind the jaw and under the ear down to the center of the character, right above the middle of the torso.**

2. **From each band, draw a curving line (as shown in Figure 5-30b) to create the trapezius muscle form.**

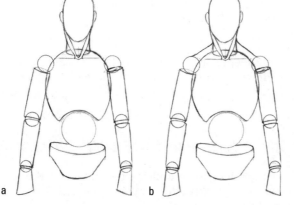

Figure 5-30: Drawing the sterno-mastoid and the trapezius.

a   b

The chest

Shōnen action manga characters often have bulging muscles in their upper torsos. These muscles are the *pectoralis* muscle group — they just aren't as big in real life. As you see in Figure 5-31, this muscle group joins from the center of the rib cage and connects underneath the shoulder muscle where a bearing sphere is located. The stronger the character is, the more prominent the bulge is. Use these steps to draw the chest:

1. **Draw a line to divide the center of the torso into left and right pectoralis muscle groups (see Figure 5-31a).**

2. **Add the pectoral muscles to complete the upper torso (see Figure 5-31b).**

   When drawing the left and right pectoral muscle group, make sure they stretch to slightly overlap the upper arms. It's important that the outer top and bottom sections of both groups angle inward toward each other before connecting with the upper arm.

3. **As a finishing touch, add a couple of marks just below the torso or ribcage to give definition to the overall structure.**

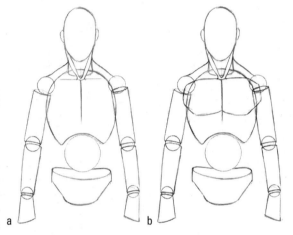

Figure 5-31: Stretching the pectoralis muscles over the torso.

a   b

The stomach

The stomach consists of a pair of muscles groups *(rectus abdominis)* in the shape of a wide band, running side by side. As I show in Figure 5-32, the pectoralis muscle overlaps the very top of the stomach muscles. That's why you see six-pack abs rather than eight-pack abs on those fitness magazine models. To draw the rectus abdominis, try these steps:

1. **Lightly sketch three lines going from the center of the torso down to the bottom center of the hip (as shown in Figure 5-32a).**

2. **Lightly draw three cross-division lines hinting at the individual muscle divisions (as shown in Figure 5-32b).**

3. **Decide which lines to keep and which ones to erase.**

   In Figure 5-32c, I erase some lines to avoid including too much detail. Otherwise, the overall anatomy is too busy and distracts the readers. Sometimes less is more!

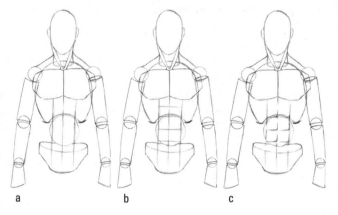

Figure 5-32:
Stretching
the rectus
abdominis
over the
stomach.

a   b   c

The hips

Include three body landmarks when you're defining the hip. First, fit on the
external oblique. Don't let the name intimidate you. As shown in Figure 5-33,
it's just two small bumps on both sides above the hips. Keep them small and
subtle. The second landmark, *iliac crest,* includes the two lines marking the
front of the hipbone, slightly protruding from the skin. The final landmark is
the curve for the groin area, *symphysis pubis.* Use these steps to draw the hips:

1. **Draw two lines to connect both sides of the torso to the hips (as shown
   in Figure 5-33a).**

2. **Add two bumps for the external oblique (as shown in Figure 5-33b).**

   If you make these bumps too big, they end up looking like love handles,
   and you don't want that (unless, of course, your character has a massive
   beer belly).

3. **Create two marks in front of the hips (as shown in Figure 5-33c).**

4. **Draw the curve for the groin area (as shown in Figure 5-33d).**

A good way to see whether you're placing the hipbones correctly is to compare them to the lines and markings of the torso/stomach area. The overall
markings of the torso and stomach muscle groups should resemble the
bottom of a turtle shell.

The legs and feet

In my opinion, legs are one of the more fun and rhythmical parts of the entire
body. As I show you in the following steps, a distinct rhythmical flow starts
from the hips and continues down to the feet. Draw this part of the body with
the aid of these steps:

1. **Draw an outline of the muscle form *(vastus lateralis/medialis)* from the upper leg crossing over diagonally from the outside of the lower hip to the inside of the leg where the knee cap is (see Figure 5-34a).**

   Observe the way the overlapping shape slightly extends past the cylinder of the upper leg as it travels down to the knees. This is the largest muscle shape of the lower leg, and it supports basically the entire upper body.

2. **On the outside of the lower leg, draw a slight curve (as shown in Figure 5-34b) to show the grouping of smaller muscles known as the *anterior* muscles.**

3. **Draw the ankles right above the feet by drawing a bump on each side (as shown in Figure 5-34c).**

   The bump on the inner side of the leg (the *medial malleolus*) is higher than the bump on the outside (the *lateral malleolus*).

Now comes the cool part. See whether you can identify the curving rhythmical lines that wind down the leg from the hip, following the structural landmarks you just created. The same mirroring curves on both legs create an "S" curving shape. See Figure 5-35.

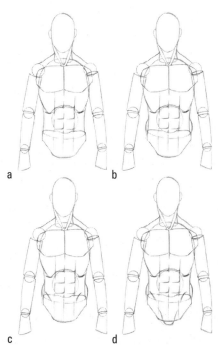

a

b

Figure 5-33:
Defining
the hips.

c

d

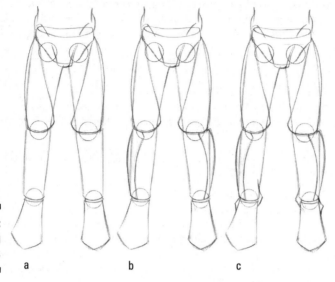

Figure 5-34:
Defining
the legs.

a   b   c

Figure 5-35:
Observe the
curving
flow,
resembling
an "S."

The arms

I save the arms for last in this particular pose because they carry the least amount of significance.

Here are some questions to ponder when posing your character:

✔ Which portion of the body is carrying the most weight?

✔ Which body part, if moved, would cause the character to lose balance?

✔ Which body part, if moved, wouldn't affect the character's balance at all?

With this particular pose, this character can be flailing his arms high up in the air without tripping or falling down.

Follow the steps and Figure 5-36 to define the arm:

1. **As shown in Figure 5-36a, cover the bearing sphere at the shoulder with a cap-like muscle structure** *(deltoid).*

   Think of the deltoid as a shoulder pad for hockey or football. Also note that the end of the deltoid is a pointed tip.

2. **Draw a line dividing the upper arm to create two muscle divisions (as shown in Figure 5-36b).**

   The back section of the upper arm is called the *triceps.* The front section of the upper arm is known as the *biceps.* Depending on which angle you draw the upper arm, either side should be drawn larger than the other.

3. **Going into the forearm, draw a dividing line from the center of the biceps down to the wrist (as shown in Figure 5-36c).**

   Observe carefully how the top of the divided forearm muscles intertwine to fit between the triceps and biceps of the upper arm.

4. **Complete the arm by drawing the hands (as shown in Figure 5-36d).**

   Be careful not to mix up the left and right hands when snapping them onto the end of the wrists. A good rule of thumb (no pun intended) is that the thumb side of the hand always faces toward the front of the body in a relaxed position.

Adding a woman's touch with curves

Rather than redrawing some of the repetitive steps over again, in this section I show you a comparison between the defined female form versus the defined male form in the earlier sections. Check out the contrast between the a and b in Figure 5-37. Here are some differences when creating definition for the female figure:

✔ **Thinner neck:** Her neck is slender. Adding the lines for the sternomastoid is okay, but keep them subtle.

✔ **Shoulders:** Keep them narrow. Notice that the trapezius is less pronounced. Also, draw the deltoids smaller.

✔ **Torso/stomach:** Note that the torso is tilted a bit more forward. The waistline is narrower and tighter. Think of the breasts as two hemispheres resting on the torso.

✔ **Hips:** Draw the hips wider. Full-grown adults should have an hourglass figure.

✔ **Legs:** Draw the legs thinner and longer (even if you have to make the torso a bit shorter). Don't draw the upper leg muscles too prominently. Draw the feet smaller.

✔ **Arms/hands:** Note how slender and less defined the arms and especially the hands are. Unless your female character is a pro wrestler on steroids, keep the figure as smooth and round as possible.

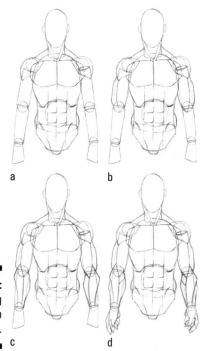

a   b

c   d

Figure 5-36:
Defining
structure in
the arm.

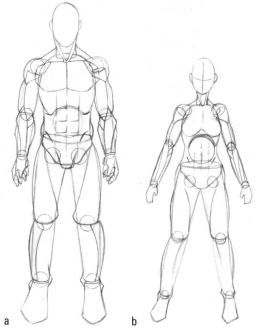

Figure 5-37:
Comparing
the male
versus the
female.

a   b

Growing Pains

As time progresses, physical changes take place before your very own eyes.
Exploring some of these changes is worth your time for a couple of reasons.
First, you may want to draw your character differently, say, ten years from
the present. When readers are hooked on your character, they want to know
everything about her (including what happens to her in the future). Second,
you need to consider drawing characters other than your main character,
and they're likely to be different ages.

In Figure 5-38, I show examples of manga characters at different ages.

Here are some helpful characteristics to keep in mind while studying proportions for children:

- Usually 3½ heads tall

- Muscles for the arms and feet aren't defined

- The forehead and the back cranium head structure are noticeably large

- Like in real life, the head is disproportionate to the body

Here are some helpful characteristics to keep in mind while studying the proportions for teenagers:

- Generally 6½ heads tall
- Muscle structure is relatively subtle
- Toward the late teens, males begin to develop muscle tone throughout their bodies (especially the torso)
- The breasts begin to form for the females relatively early in their teens

Here are some helpful characteristics to keep in mind while studying the proportions for adults:

- Males and females reach anywhere between 7½ and 11 heads tall
- Males develop a more chiseled muscle definition
- Females develop a fuller form and curves around the hips, breasts, and legs
- Females have wider hips than males
- Males develop broader shoulders and torso than females

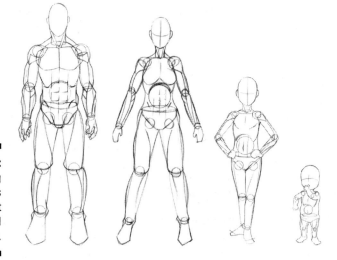

Figure 5-38:
Observing characters at different ages and stages.

Chapter 6

Customize and Accessorize Your Manga Character

In This Chapter

▶ Discovering basic fold techniques

▶ Creating your own outfits

▶ Tailoring your accessories to custom fit your character

*I*n the manga world, fashion is pivotal! It differentiates one character from another. Whether your character is the lead athlete getting ready to take on the whole world, or a regular Joe standing in the corner never to make another appearance, what he's wearing can play a huge role in whether the audience remembers your character's name or the title of your manga.

From drawing basic folds to cute hair ribbons, the choices of what your character can wear are endless. In this chapter, I give you the lowdown on how to draw basic manga clothing and accessories. Keep in mind that overloading your character with too much bling isn't always a good thing. You want to strike the right balance and make sure you dress your character appropriately for every occasion.

Know When to Fold 'Em: Drawing Fabric Folds

To get your character's clothing to look right, start with the basics — knowing your folds. In this case, folding doesn't refer to the hand you gave up at your last poker game. Instead, think of a *fold* as the kind of shape the fabric makes.

You see folds everywhere, from the simple fold in a napkin to the many folds in an elaborate wedding dress. Don't become overwhelmed, thinking that you have to draw every single fold in a character's clothing. Here are two simple rules to start with:

✔ **Softer materials create larger and rounder folds (as shown in the left-hand image of Figure 6-1).** Examples of soft materials include kimonos, pajamas, T-shirts, and cotton sweaters. Think of the characters wearing these fabrics dumping a jug of fabric softener into the washer.

✔ **Tougher materials create sharp folds (as shown in the right-hand image of Figure 6-1).** Examples of tough materials include school or military uniforms, business suits, and stiff leather. Think of the characters wearing these fabrics using up a huge can of hardcore starch before ironing.

Figure 6-1:
Rounder and sharper folds tell readers the quality of the material.

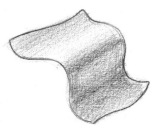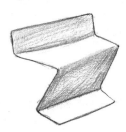

The art of the pinch, pull, and tuck: Exploring drapery folds

Folds in fabric are caused by a tug, pull, pinch, or other tension on the surface. Based on the direction and intensity of that tension (maybe due to the wind, or someone grabbing a shirt by the collar), the folds change in size and direction.

Although the clothes conceal the figure underneath, keep the figure's form while you're drawing the outfit. As I show you later in this chapter, the tensions that cause the folds can be the result of twisting, bending, or stretching motions of the body underneath. Similar to an earthquake, tension always has a source. The folds are simply pointing toward that source.

Here I give you some patterns to pay attention to when you're first drawing folds in clothing. Exceptions exist for every rule, but for the most part, the following list has withstood the test of time:

✔ As folds fall away from the source of tension, they get wider.

✔ As folds come closer to the source of tension, they get narrower.

✔ As folds fall away, they obey gravity (with the exception of folds that wrap around underneath a form).

✔ Folds angle down and away from the source of tension.

✔ Folds are almost never parallel to each other.

Building a fashion sense

Coming up with original ideas on your own is difficult without help from the outside world. Over the years, I've accumulated a bunch of images from fashion magazines to help me come up with costume ideas. Today, you can do all your research on the Internet, which makes accumulating ideas easier. You can store all your files digitally on your computer instead of buying large, heavy binders and bookshelves on which to store them. If you decide to go digital, organize your files so that images that you want or need to use are easy to retrieve. Also, store your images on a separate drive that's large enough to accommodate larger images.

Basic free-falling folds

Artists commonly draw basic free-falling folds on loose clothing hanging down, like a blanket, scarf, or towel. These folds are on fabric that's suspended or blowing loosely in the air. Starting with this fold is great, because the tension is usually caused by just one or two factors. In these examples, you can't see the form underneath these folds. Study the drawings in Figure 6-2. Try to identify the source of the tension causing the fold(s) to happen. Also, pay attention to which direction the folds are flowing.

Figure 6-2: Folds point toward the center of tension.

Overlapping folds

In Figure 6-3, I show you examples of overlapping folds. Recognize the differences between the "Z" patterns in Figure 6-3a and the "S" patterns in Figure 6-3b: The "Z" shapes suggest rapid and aggressive movement, and the "S" shapes give the sense of flowing and graceful movement. Overlapping folds show how the environment (such as wind, energy waves, or rapid movement) affects loose, large articles of clothing.

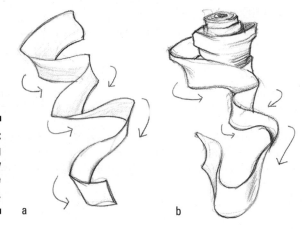

Figure 6-3:
Overlapping folds show more movement.

a   b

Folds that wrap around

In Figure 6-4, I show you folds that wrap around. These folds are commonly associated with clothing that wraps around the body it covers. When you're drawing loose clothing on a character (such as sweaters, leg warmers, or scarves), the folds get wider as they come closer to the edge of the object they cover (see Figure 6-4). If you want to draw tighter clothing (such as tight T-shirts, undergarments, or jeans), the folds should get narrower as they wrap around the edge of the object they cover (see Figure 6-5).

Folds that wrap around don't fall with gravity. Rather, the direction of the folds is dictated by the tension and the forms that lie underneath. Most of these folds travel more horizontally or diagonally than vertically.

Nesting folds

Nesting folds are more advanced; they literally fold into one another. As shown in Figure 6-6, nesting folds usually happen when clothing or drapery bunches together. Although these folds tend to be more complex in detail and design, they certainly add to the overall aesthetics of the character's appearance. (For now, just look at the examples I show and know they exist. Don't worry about drawing these advanced folds at this point; you can always iron out the wrinkles later!)

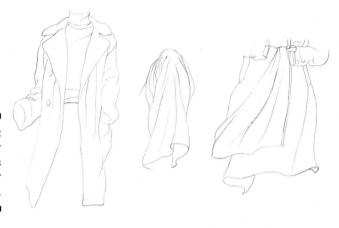

Figure 6-4:
Looser clothing has wider, softer edges.

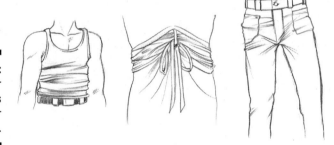

Figure 6-5:
Tighter clothing has narrower edges.

Figure 6-6:
Interesting nesting folds happen when folds overlap.

Is that leather, silk, or what?

Is your character wearing thick leather, soft wool, or paper-thin silk? By adjusting the space between the two edges of the character's uniform, the choice becomes yours (see Figure 6-7). Observe how the thickness of the decoration on the character's hat implies that it's made out of metal. In contrast, the sharp thinness of the lines in his shirt suggests that the material is made of everyday cotton. In addition to adjusting the space on the rim of the material, folds flowing down in straight lines or angles from the source of tension suggest that the material is stiff and thick. By contrast, softer materials tend to have folds coming down in wavy cascades. Often, the ends of the material flow up and down, resembling that of a bell-shaped curve.

Shadows revisited

I explain the concept of shadows in depth in Chapter 4. As you become comfortable drawing folds, you can start adding shadows to enhance depth and create texture in the fabric. As I show you in Figure 6-8a, shadows with soft edges around the rim give the illusion that the material is thick but very soft (in this case, a thick wool jacket). However, watch what happens when I replace those soft edges with a hard-lined shadow in Figure 6-8b. All of a sudden, this jacket looks like it could weigh a ton. I can't imagine any current fashion model being able to wear this jacket down the catwalk!

You can use shadows to push parts of the clothing back and forth in space as well. Look at Figure 6-8b and note how the shaded area gets pushed back behind the non-shaded area of the front. The shading gives the readers a sense of open space between the front and the back of the jacket. The moment you remove the shadow, the sense of depth is compromised.

Figure 6-7:
Adjusting
the rim
width to
show
different
material
thicknesses.

In addition to adding wider edges to the rim of the material, you can add streak marks to suggest that the material is made out of metal or glass. This technique is known as adding texture to the surface. You can easily implement these streaks by drawing several paired lines running diagonally (see Figure 6-8c).

Knowing where to place shadows takes some practice. The location of shadows shifts when the light source or direction changes drastically, but you should generally assume that the source is coming from above and to the right of the subject matter. This quick, simple project can help in figuring out where the shadows fall on the folds. Take a moment to follow these steps in creating a mock-up of the structure of a fabric fold (say you're looking at the folds of a curtain):

1. **Take a sheet of regular printer paper and draw four horizontal lines going from side to side as shown in Figure 6-9a.**

2. **Mark the letters A-B-C-B-A in the sections on the paper (see Figure 6-9b).**

3. **Fold the paper so that the sides marked A face upward, the sides marked B face the sides, and the side marked C faces upward (see Figure 6-9c).**

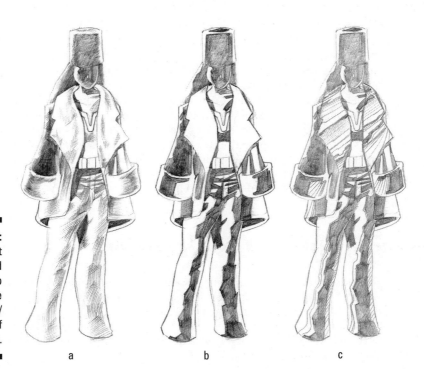

Figure 6-8:
Using soft and hard edges to create hardness/ softness of the clothing.

a   b   c

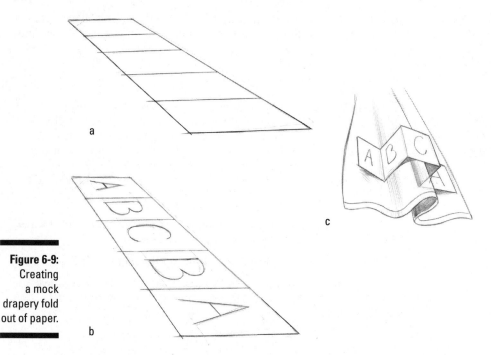

Figure 6-9:
Creating
a mock
drapery fold
out of paper.

With a mock-up of the fold, watch what happens when you put a light source (it can be a simple desk lamp or a flashlight) on either side of the model. Notice and study what happens when you place the light above and to the right of the model. Which side is the brightest and which side is the darkest? What kind of cast shadows do you see? If you push in the A sides toward side C, how does the way you perceive the light change? Finally, place this model next to a fold in a curtain and compare the two to see how the shadows on both models are similar. The goal of comparing these two models is to discover the patterns of where the light does and doesn't fall on the fold. The areas where the light doesn't fall need to be shaded in.

Dressing Up for the Occasion

For an introduction to basic shapes and how things fold together, see "Know When to Fold 'Em: Drawing Fabric Folds" earlier in this chapter. In this section, I show you how to put these concepts into action, applying these folds into drawing the actual clothing of your character. When you're getting ready to draw clothing, ask yourself whether you want your character to be wearing the following:

✔ Short or long clothing

✔ Thick or thin clothing

✔ Loose or tight clothing

When drawing a character, I usually start from the top. In this case, "top" means clothing for the upper body.

Starting from the top

You have various types of tops to consider for both sexes. In Figure 6-10, I show you some of the basic generic types of clothing that manga characters commonly wear. For the most part, girls have the fashion advantage of being able to wear most clothing that boys wear. Tops usually fall into the categories of short sleeves (such as preppy summer wear and T-shirts, like the one in Figure 6-10a), long sleeves (such as uniforms and sweatshirts; see Figure 6-10b), or no sleeves (such as evening wear or the tank top in Figure 6-10c). All you need to be aware of is maybe changing the color of the top to a warmer color (which is rarely a problem, because most manga is printed in black and white, with the exception of the cover of the trade paperback).

The differences that distinguish what the girls versus the boys wear lie within the addition of lingerie, dresses, or other skimpy outfit assortments.

Figure 6-10:
Generic, unisex tops common for manga characters.

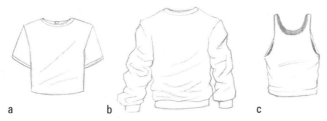

a   b   c

Collars

In this section, I get down to the specifics, exploring some of the choices and options you have when making alternations to the collar or opening of a top. Refer to the drawings I show you in Figure 6-11 to see these collars:

✔ **Raised Tube-Shaped Collar (Figure 6-11a):** You usually find this collar on school and military uniforms and on characters wearing the traditional Chinese martial arts outfit. This collar can either be connected completely or have a V-shaped opening in the front. Although you can use this type for both sexes, it's primarily associated with the boys.

✔ **V-Neck Collar (Figure 6-11b):** Boys usually have this type of opening on their sweatshirts or long-sleeved fall fashion wear. Female characters generally have the V-shape going lower to increase their sex appeal.

✔ **U-Neck Collar (Figure 6-11c):** Both boys and girls have this collar on their T-shirts and some long-sleeved shirts. Again, the U-shape should drop lower for female characters. This type is probably the most unisex collar you see today.

✔ **Dress-Shirt Collar (Figure 6-11d):** You generally see this collar on school uniforms and corporate dress uniforms. Although boys usually have a tie, the artists commonly substitute ribbons and jewelry in place of the tie for the girls. Draw this collar a little larger than you see it in real life. If the character is a rebel without a cause or a sexy girl, skip the necktie and leave the top couple of buttons open.

Sleeves

Sleeves are fun to draw because you have so much variety and liberty in how you can interpret the folds.

The key to drawing great sleeves isn't necessarily drawing them realistically. Rather than trying to draw every single wrinkle and fold that you see from your reference photo, consider taking more liberty and drawing bigger, generally abstract shapes.

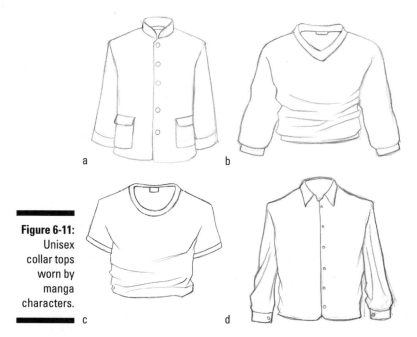

Figure 6-11:
Unisex collar tops worn by manga characters.

In Figure 6-12, I show you how to incorporate a rhythmic flow to the sleeves, similar to a rhythm I demonstrate in Chapter 5 with the human figure. The great advantage and beauty of drawing manga clothing is that you have so much freedom and room for interpretation in coming up with interesting shapes.

For the following steps, you need the arm you construct in Chapter 5 (if you haven't done that yet, flip to Chapter 5 first). Then follow these steps to draw the long sweatshirt sleeve:

1. **Draw the upper part of the outside of the sleeve over the arm (as shown in Figure 6-12a).**

   Because this is a sweatshirt, note the space between the outside sleeve and the arm.

2. **Draw the inside shape for the lower sleeve (as shown in Figure 6-12b).**

3. **Draw the last portion of the outside sleeve (as shown in Figure 6-12c).**

4. **Complete the sleeve by adding the cuff at the wrist of the sleeve (see Figure 6-12d).**

   Observe the S-curve rhythm (see Figure 6-12e) or flow traveling from the top to the bottom of the arm.

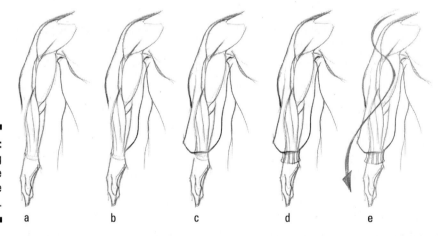

Figure 6-12:
Drawing the sleeve of the sweatshirt.

a   b   c   d   e

When the arm lifts up, note the shift of tension in the fold. Keep asking yourself which direction the shirt is being pulled toward. Look at Figure 6-12e, and observe how the small folds bunch together under the tight armpit section of the shoulder. Also, note the tension or direction of the longer folds that stretch from underneath the armpit toward the lower ribcage and across the *pectoralis* (chest) muscle group of the torso. As you explore and observe different folds, you find how closely a lot of them mimic the muscle structure of the figure that lies beneath. For example, that fold at the top of the shoulder closely resembles the structure of the pectoralis muscle. You still see how the lines of the sleeve form the rhythmic S-curve shape across the arm.

I have another trick up my sleeve (bad pun — someone stop me) that you can use when drawing the lines for the sleeves. As soon as you complete one line, draw the corresponding line on the opposite side. As the sleeve approaches the wrist, make the lines shorter. Don't forget to make sure that the lines form shapes that overlap each other. Otherwise, the arm will appear flat and two-dimensional.

The folds and wrinkles of tighter sleeves adhere closely to the form of the arm itself. Follow these steps to draw tighter-style sleeves:

1. **As shown in Figure 6-13a, draw the outside and inside sleeves close to the arm.**

   With tighter sleeves that adhere to the arm, some popular manga-ka draw the sleeves curving out away from each other in order to separate the clothing from the skin.

   Also note that you don't need as many lines to create these sleeves as you do to make looser sleeves.

2. **Add the folds emerging from under the armpits (see Figure 6-13b).**

   Draw the folds diagonally, short, and fairly straight, in contrast with the round curve forms on the loose sweatshirt.

3. **Add small folds at the joint between the biceps and forearm (see Figure 6-13c).**

   Note that the folds curve in inversely to describe forms underneath.

4. **Draw the sleeve curving outward at the end of the arm (see Figure 6-13d).**

   The V-shape and a button add nice touches to the sleeve.

The body of the shirt

The body of the shirt shares its behavior with the sleeve. The sources of tension or pull usually start under the arms, right around or slightly above the waistline, and across the chest section.

The tighter the shirt is, the closer the clothing clings to the body. In Figure 6-14a, you see multiple fold lines hugging around the hip area. Among the many fold patterns you see (especially in tight clothing), you start to recognize two common shapes: the letters "Y" and "X" (when viewed sideways). These common shapes are usually the result of multiple folds compressing together. The tighter the clothing is, the more tension is created by the clothing, and the more closely it has to mimic the figure that lies beneath. The pull in the tension that causes the folds is heightened when the body twists, turns, or bends at even the slightest degree (as shown in Figure 6-14b).

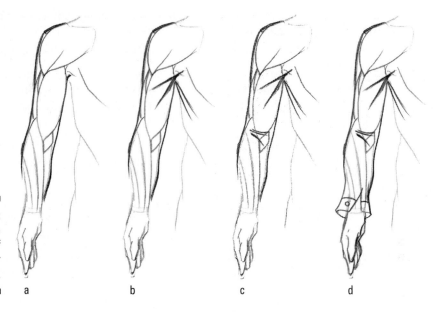

Figure 6-13:
Drawing the
sleeve of
the tighter
dress shirt.

a   b   c   d

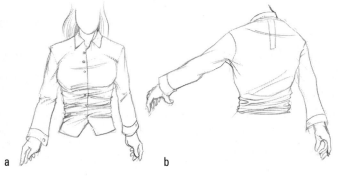

Figure 6-14:
The "X" and
"Y" fold
patterns on
a tight shirt
or blouse.

a   b

Fitted shirt

For the following directions, you need the torso that I show you in Chapter 5 with the front and side views completed. Follow these steps to draw a fitted shirt:

1. **Draw the outline of the collar and sleeve shape you want over both sides of the arms as shown in Figure 6-15a.**

   When drawing thinner and tighter clothing, quite often you don't need to worry about drawing the outside edges of the clothing after you draw the human form underneath. The fabric clings so tightly to the body that you can't see the fabric outline with the exception of subtle folds that happen where the joints bend or the body underneath creates folds (such as fat folds around the stomach when a person sits down or bends forward).

2. **Draw several bumps to show the folds hugging both sides of the lower torso (see Figure 6-15b).**

   Don't draw the bumps too big. Bigger bumps should be reserved for looser clothing.

3. **Draw folds hugging the stomach as shown in Figure 6-15c.**

   Leave the lines of the folds open and incomplete. They should be curving downward.

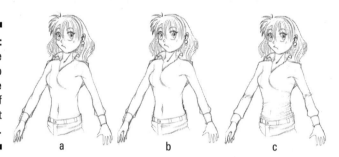

Figure 6-15:
Drawing the folds to complete the waist of a tight shirt or blouse.

a   b   c

Tight tank top

If you want to transform the fitted shirt into a tank top, all you need to do is cut off the sleeves and widen the collar opening as shown in Figure 6-16. Follow these steps:

1. **Let the neckline drop down to the middle of the torso (as shown in Figure 6-16a).**

2. **Draw a line curving from the top of the middle of one shoulder down to the middle of that side of the torso. Repeat on the other side of the body (see Figure 6-16b).**

3. **For female characters, draw the character's favorite animé character or icon, like I do in the center of the shirt in Figure 6-16c.**

   Especially in Japan, animé characters and icons are an ever-growing popular phenomenon.

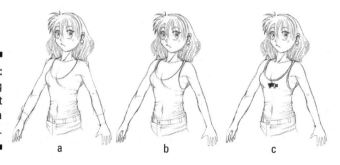

Figure 6-16:
Converting the tight shirt into a tank top.

a   b   c

Think of the tight shirt on the torso as an accordion. As I show in Figure 6-17a and 6-17b, while the torso is standing up straight from the front and side views, the folds are evenly distributed on both sides right above the waist. But watch what happens when the torso bends toward either side: Figure 6-17c shows what happens when the center line bends. The folds bunch up together in the midsection on the bent side while the tension is more dispersed on the other side. Also observe what happens in Figure 6-17d when the body bends over backward (okay, so I drew a girl who looks like a slinky). You can see the same dynamics in this fold as you do when the character bends sideways. Tension shifts to her mid-back section, and the number of folds bunching together increases on her backside. As soon as the slinky girl bends forward in Figure 6-17e, the reverse happens.

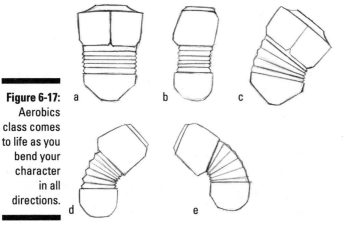

Figure 6-17:
Aerobics
class comes
to life as you
bend your
character
in all
directions.

Loose-fitting shirt

When drawing the torso of looser shirts (sweatshirts, pajamas, track suits, and kimonos), you have the freedom to draw more abstract forms. Depending on the bulkiness of the clothing, the figure may be obscured. However, a body is still buried underneath all that clothing. Starting with the central torso form keeps the clothing shapes from becoming unfocused and causing the overall figure to lose design and balance. Again, you need to bring back the torso for the following steps. In this example, I'm drawing a character who's a young Karate Champion. Follow these steps to draw a loose shirt:

1. **Draw the collar lines of the uniform as shown in Figure 6-18.**

   Observe how the collar line mimics the form of the torso.

   Drawing shirts is always easier when you start from the center collar. After you establish the center of a clothed figure, adding the smaller accessories (buttons, pockets, icons, and zippers) becomes easier and more fun. If you draw these objects without a center figure in mind, these smaller objects have no solid foundation to rest upon. You don't have a clear idea of how wide you should make the shoulder, or any way of making sure that both shoulders are the same length and distance apart. Sure, you can always guess, but think about all that time you're wasting if you get into the habit of erasing your mistakes and redrawing them in hopes that your next guess is the right one.

Figure 6-18: Starting off with the central collar lines of the uniform.

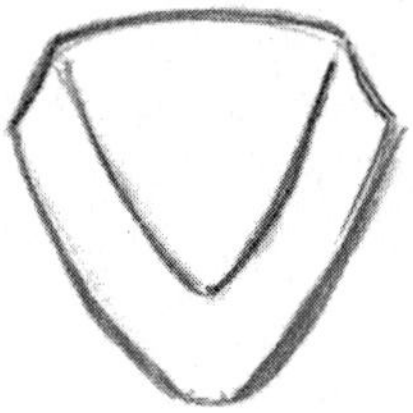

2. **Without worrying about the top of the shoulders, draw in two lines to represent both sides of the upper torso as shown in Figure 6-19a.**

   These lines shouldn't complete either side. These lines aren't skintight, but they do mimic the pectoral muscles.

3. **Complete the sides by drawing the remaining lines of the torso as shown in Figure 6-19b.**

   Observe how these lines resemble the free-falling drapery (see "Basic free-falling folds" earlier in this chapter) where the folds are dictated by gravity rather than the tension caused by pulling and twisting. These folds resemble a towel hanging off the towel rack.

Figure 6-19: Drawing the sides of the uniform.

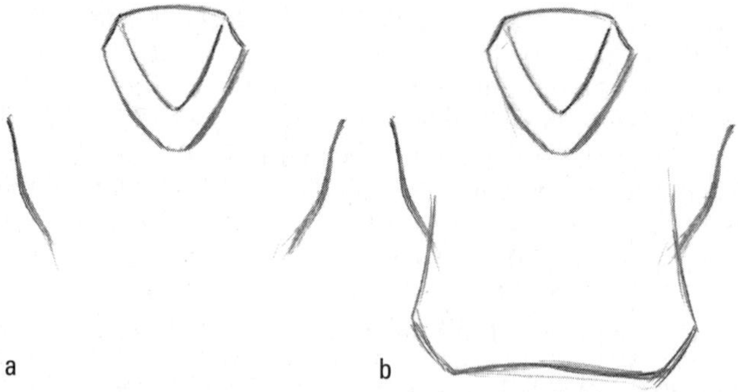
a
b

4. **Add the karate belt at the waist, the folds tucking into the belt, and the "flaps" under the belt (as shown in Figure 6-20a).**

Note that the karate belt reflects the actual width of the waist. After drawing the belt, add the folds overlapping in front of the belt to create dimension and the bagginess of the uniform.

Drawing the flaps helps show the forms coming out from underneath the karate belt. Draw the bottom end of the flap with a rounded arc.

5. **Add the sleeves to complete the top of the uniform (see Figure 6-20b).**

The final body of the uniform should resemble an hourglass.

Figure 6-20: Finishing off the karate uniform to get an hourglass shape.

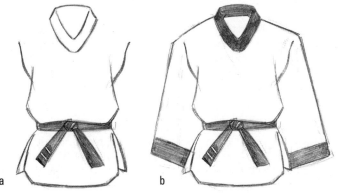

a   b

Do these jeans make my butt look big?

When you're drawing the bottom attire, your female characters once again have the advantage of being able to wear what men usually wear (with the exception of the underwear — which is why those lingerie companies are making a killing!). With the exception of the baggy pants that martial arts characters wear, most mainstream manga characters wear either long jeans or school uniforms.

Jeans are a long-standing part of manga fashion. They're so versatile that if you can't decide what your character should wear in any given situation, just draw him wearing a pair of jeans. It's a safe bet, guaranteed! Anatomically, adult women have rounder hips and rears than adult men do. Men have flatter rears that are fairly boxy or square (don't ask me why I know all this — it's a job hazard). Consistent with the trends of manga fashion and real-world fashion, which are meant to hype the human sex appeal, artists draw women wearing tighter pants and jeans than men wear. Here are two of the different shapes of jeans you should know:

 ✔ **Classic/normal fit:** These jeans are snug at the hip and upper legs and fairly loose at the bottom. These are known as the unisex jeans.

✔ **Loose/relaxed fit:** Again, you have a lot of variety within this type of fit. These jeans range from the retro bell-bottoms to the loose Goth style jeans. The extreme types have legs that are so long they cover most of the shoes.

As I mention in the previous section, folds usually form underneath the armpits, at the waist, and under the breasts for the females. With jeans, folds form at the crotch and the knees. If the jeans are the loose-fit variety, the folds at the knees typically run all the way down to the end of the jeans' legs.

I strongly recommend going over fashion magazines or looking at fashion catalogues. Although drawing rears (or, if you prefer, hind ends, bottoms, buttocks, rumps, or butts — does that about cover them all?) can be an embarrassing subject due to its sensitivity, you need to be able to draw them correctly! Believe it or not, drawing this particular part of the body can be quite tricky. The last thing you want is your readers laughing at your characters because your lead male character looks like a girl based on the way you drew his jeans.

Classic/normal jeans

Before I show you how to draw jeans, you need to bring out the hip section for males and females that I tell you about in Chapter 5. Then, proceed to read through and follow the steps on how to draw the jeans, starting from the front. I start off here with the top waist section of classic fit jeans for females:

1. **Draw the fly tab from the top of the waist to the center of the crotch.**

   Draw a center line as shown in Figure 6-21a. Don't forget to add the seams of the tab to the right of the crotch line.

2. **Add the waistband line (as shown in Figure 6-21b).**

3. **Add a button on the waistband right in the middle, above the fly tab.**

4. **Add two thin rectangle belt tabs, one on each side of the button.**

   The belt tabs should be fairly close to the buttons. Note that they extend a little further down past the waistband (as shown in Figure 6-21c).

5. **Add two more tabs, one on each side of the waist (as shown in Figure 6-21d).**

   If your character isn't going to be wearing a belt around the waist, you should draw the side belt tabs slightly curving outward away from the hips so that there's a small gap between the belt tab and the waist. If your character is wearing a belt, there's no space because the width of the belt stretches the belt tab flat.

6. **Draw two arcs, one on each side of the jeans for the pockets.**

   As with the fly tab, don't forget to add the seams at the top of the pocket.

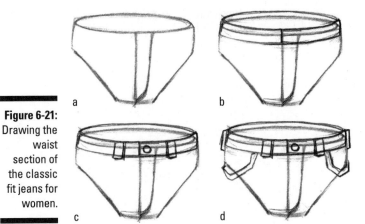

Figure 6-21:
Drawing the
waist
section of
the classic
fit jeans for
women.

a   b   c   d

Classic jeans are fairly tight (although not as tight as the tight fit jeans). Therefore, the edges of the jeans contour to the shape of the hips and legs. The only exceptions looking from the front are the places where the legs connect to the hips and at the knees. At these points, where the bearing spheres serve as a connecting joint, you may see small bumps of the folds.

7. **Draw in the upper and lower legs (including the feet), as shown in Figure 6-22a.**

8. **Add several lines from the center of the crotch toward the hips (as shown in Figure 6-22b).**

   The lines should form several "V" shapes. The tighter the jeans are, the more lines you should make. Keep in mind that these lines are showing the contours of the hips.

   The trick to making denim jeans look realistic is to place the shorter folds in tighter areas (such as the crotch, where the buttocks and legs meet, and behind the knees where the upper leg connects with the lower leg). Likewise, place broader folds in areas that have less tension of the leg movement (such as the front of the upper and lower legs).

9. **At the knees and at the hem of the jeans, add a couple of "X" folds (see Figure 6-22c).**

10. **Clean up any stray lines and shapes as shown in Figure 6-22d.**

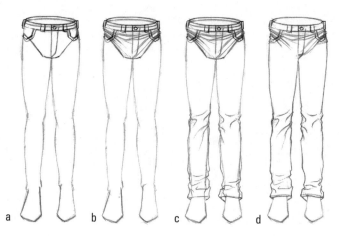

Figure 6-22:
Adding the folds to complete the classic fit jeans for women.

a   b   c   d

In Figure 6-23, I show the differences between the female classic jeans (Figure 6-23a) versus the male classic jeans (Figure 6-23b) from a ¾ view so that the difference is more clear. For the most part, these jeans are unisex, but observe how the rear and hips are toned down for the men, consistent with the differences in anatomical makeup. Also, the men's jeans are looser in the front, which means the folds are more relaxed with less tension, as compared to the female's jeans.

Drawing your male characters wearing the loose-fit jeans is perfectly acceptable, but having them wear anything tighter than the classic jeans is, for the most part, a major *faux pas*. You don't want to blatantly describe a male character's anatomy to your readers. It's just wrong (trust me).

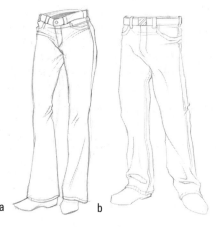

Figure 6-23:
Comparing male classic jeans to female classic jeans.

a   b

Loose/relaxed jeans

Although loose-fit jeans are for the most part unisex, female characters are more likely to be wearing slim-fit jeans to show off their figures. On the other extreme, teenage boys who fall into the rebel without a cause category tend to wear baggy, loose jeans. This character demography is known as punk or Goth. A character dressed in these jeans may be attending a punk-rock concert while chanting anti-establishment slogans.

On that note, I loosen things up by showing you how to draw the loose/relaxed jeans on your character. I compare the two types of loose jeans (regular loose versus extremely baggy loose) side by side, using a male model (you need the male torso and legs from Chapter 5). Try your hand at drawing both variations simultaneously. As you draw and compare the differences, note how much more liberal you can be with adding more décor and design to the Goth jeans. Just follow these steps:

1. **Draw the fly line from the top of the center jeans to the crotch**.

2. **On each side of the jean, draw in one belt hook at the front and one at the side.**

   The Goth jeans in Figure 6-24a have wider belt hooks than the regular loose jeans in Figure 6-24b.

3. **Draw in the belt.**

   For the belt, I draw in a dark strip that goes through the belt hooks. I draw a wider strap for the Goth belt. Note that the buckle is more decorative on the Goth jeans.

4. **Draw the sides of the jeans.**

   Because these jeans are looser than the classic/normal jeans, you need to draw both sides of the jeans. As you look at Figure 6-24, one thing that should be evident with both jeans is that the transition between the hips and the lower legs is seamless and smooth. No folds or curves are present in either example. The Goth jeans in Figure 6-24a have the longer, straighter lines that become wider toward the bottom. The normal loose jeans in Figure 6-24b have a little more curve toward the bottom.

5. **Add the folds.**

   Note the simplicity in the folds in both drawings. With the standard loose jeans in Figure 6-25b, you see a fold line stretching from the kneecap to the folds at the ankles. Compare that to the folds in the Goth jeans in Figure 6-25a. Toward the ankles, the shoes push up the hem to create a fold on the regular jeans. With the Goth jeans, the folds are closer to the ground.

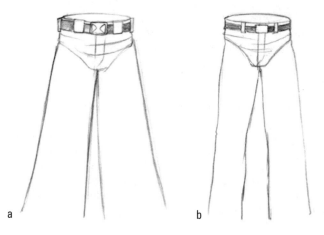

Figure 6-24:
Drawing
and
comparing
two types of
loose jeans
(Goth versus
regular).

a

b

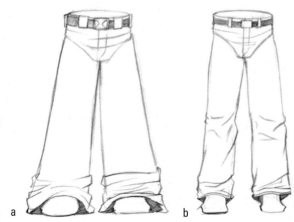

Figure 6-25:
Adding the
folds to two
types of
loose jeans.

a

b

6. Draw the décor.

Drawing the pockets is just the start. See Figure 6-26 for the interesting pocket shapes, straps, and zippers you can add to the Goth jeans (Figure 6-26a). Keep the décor on the standard loose jeans (Figure 6-26b) plain.

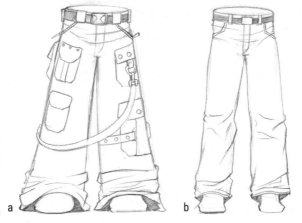

Figure 6-26: Adding décor to the Goth and regular loose jeans.

a   b

Equipped to Make a Positive Impression

After deciding on your character's basic clothing, you continue to get into style by figuring out what else he or she will wear. So many characters are walking and crawling around the pages of the popular world of manga that you want to make sure readers recognize your characters from others. I demonstrate in this section how to draw a variety of simple yet cool accessories. Drawing these accessories is easier if you start with a drawing of a young girl's head. If you haven't drawn this head yet, refer to Chapter 4.

Hair and head accessories

As you develop your own characters and stories, you may start to wonder how you're supposed to come up with something that's *truly* yours when so many manga characters look so much alike. The challenge is to equip your characters with accessories so they become recognizable to the readers. The key lies within the clothing. Like Indiana Jones who never loses his hat, you must come up with an accessory that readers immediately identify with your character. The following sections give you some suggestions.

Ribbons

Ribbons are the most popular hair items for today's manga characters. Most artists draw them for the young female characters. The age of the character or the way you want readers to perceive a character changes the size of the hair accessory. For example, you may draw a younger and more naïve female character with larger ribbons to add cuteness to her looks and personality. Try your hand at drawing a large bow-tie ribbon by following these steps:

1. **Draw the center knot of the ribbon and then lightly sketch in both sides of the bow tie (see Figure 6-27a).**

   Make sure the knot is off to the right and toward the front of the head. The sides should resemble the wings of a butterfly.

2. **Finish off with polka dots and small folds on both sides of the knot (as shown in Figure 6-27b).**

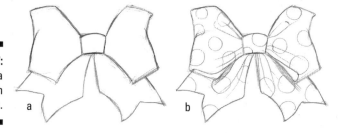

Figure 6-27:
Drawing a bow tie with polka dots.

a   b

If you're not sure whether to enlarge or shrink the size of the ribbon, follow this rule: The larger and more exaggerated you make the features on the character, the larger you need to make the accessory.

Figure 6-28 shows other sizes and shapes of bow-tie ribbons. Play around with the patterns and designs! Be open to placing the bow in different positions. Some characters may wear one behind the head while others may wear the ribbon at the bottom of a long braid.

Figure 6-28:
Other types of bow-tie ribbons that enhance cuteness.

Headbands

Headbands are another fun, easy way to manage a character's hair. As you see in the next set of steps, headbands follow the contours of the character's head. Characters who wear them typically have long hair (at least down to their shoulders) and can be older. Check out these steps:

1. **Draw a light line that follows the contours of the head (see Figure 6-29a).**

   This line helps you properly position the headband. Headbands must rest comfortably against the head or else they look awkward.

   To ensure that you draw the band properly, note the angle at which I draw the guideline in Figure 6-29a. It starts above the forehead and goes behind the ears.

2. **Draw a second line for the headband.**

   As shown in Figure 6-29b, the shape of the headband gets larger at the top and narrower at the end.

3. **Complete the band shape with rounded edges and simple decorations.**

   The edges should come all the way down to just below the top of the ear. As I show in Figure 6-29c, designs and decorations add to the visual appeal.

4. **Add the hair to finish the look (see Figure 6-29d for an example).**

Figure 6-29: Headbands are simple accessories that take care of long hair.

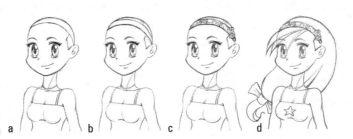

Headbands also come in handy as battle gear fashion. Although the primary function of this headband is to protect the forehead of your character, it's also a cool way to personalize your character. If he or she is a protagonist in an action/adventure manga story, consider the following demonstration:

1. **Draw a light line that follows the contour of the forehead starting from the left front of the forehead and ending toward the back of the head as shown in Figure 6-30a.**

2. **Draw a second line for the headband as shown in Figure 6-30b.**

   Be sure to draw the band wide enough for the protection plate to comfortably fit in place.

3. **Draw a personalized protection plate at the center of the forehead.**

   This plate is usually a rounded rectangle. Embellish the shield by adding a symbol that represents the character. Check out Figure 6-30c for an example.

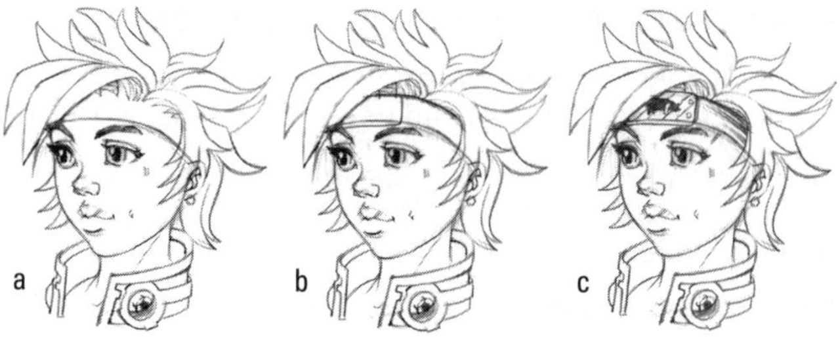
a
b
c

Figure 6-30: Headbands create a great way to personalize your character.

Fancy tiara

Headpieces, such as tiaras, bring out the class and elegance in your characters. These types of accessories are worn by princesses and other royalty. As I show you in this section, artists usually draw these items with pearls, rare gemstones, and flowers. If your character is in either the fantasy or shōjo manga genre, you should consider creating some fancy headpieces for her. Start with these steps:

1. **Draw a light line that follows the contour of the head (see Figure 6-31a).**

   This guideline helps you properly position the bottom of the tiara band. Make sure you draw the guideline across the hairline mark.

2. **Draw a jewel stone in the shape of a cross at the center, below the guideline (see Figure 6-31b).**

   REMEMBER

   Always embellish the shapes you add for the jewelry on the tiara. Observe how I add outlines or smaller shapes behind the larger ones. This detail gives the headpiece a fancier and more sophisticated appearance and more dimension.

3. **Draw a series of round pearls along the guideline.**

   As shown in Figure 6-31b, the pearls get smaller as they go away from the center.

4. **Draw more pearls above the guideline in the form of a heart on both sides and above the cross.**

5. **Finish off the headpiece by adding a rose on the end of both sides (see Figure 6-31c).**

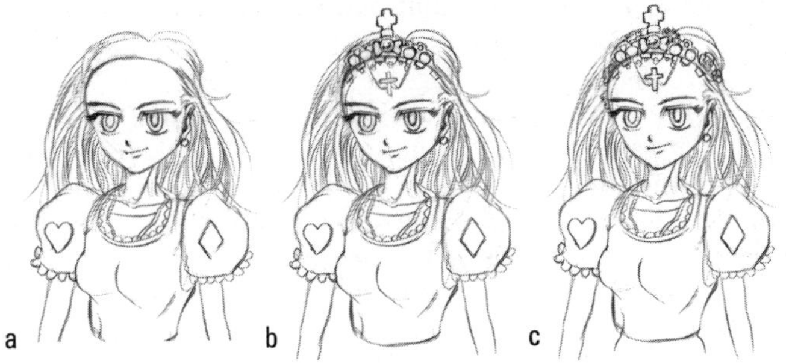
a
b
c

Figure 6-31: Fancy headpieces use pearls and roses.

Glasses

Glasses come in all shapes and sizes. They shield and protect the eyes, aid the vision, and tell about the personality of the manga characters. The shape and size of the glasses tell a lot about your character, whether she's a cunning, intelligent businesswoman or a geeky, unsocial high school kid. In Figure 6-32, I illustrate some key archetypes commonly seen in today's manga world:

- **Round glasses (Figure 6-32a):** For the innocent, naïve, young high school girl who studies very hard.
- **Box square glasses (Figure 6-32b):** For the geeky high school kid who bases his self-worth on academic performance.
- **Rectangle glasses (Figure 6-32c):** For the suave "player" who is confident that he can steal any girl's heart — anytime, anywhere.
- **Oval/pointed glasses (Figure 6-32d):** For the crafty librarian in her late 30s who can spot any overdue item a mile away.

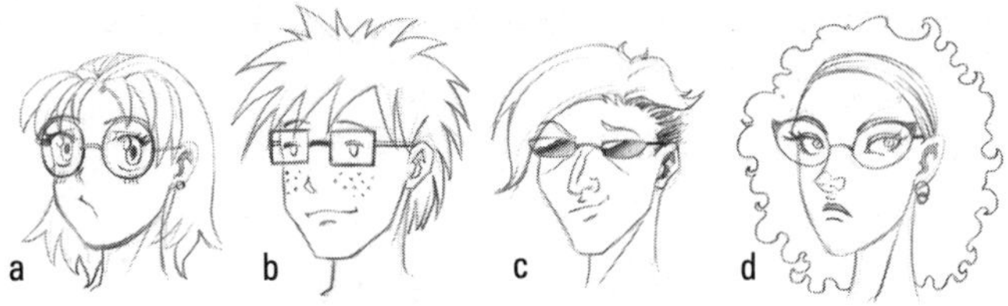
a
b
c
d

Figure 6-32: The shape and size of glasses tell a lot about your character.

The key to drawing glasses is making sure both lenses rest well in front of the eyes and are parallel to each other. Glasses are simple in nature, but beginners commonly make a couple of mistakes, which I show in Figure 6-33. One mistake beginners make is drawing the glasses too close to the head in a profile shot (see Figure 6-33a). In Figure 6-33b, I show you the correct way to draw the profile. The key to drawing glasses is making sure both lenses rest well in front of the eyes and are parallel to each other. Glasses are simple in nature, but beginners commonly make a couple of mistakes, which I show in Figure 6-33. One mistake beginners make is drawing the glasses too close to the head in a profile shot (see Figure 6-33a). In Figure 6-33b, I show you the correct way to draw the profile. Another common mistake is drawing both circles of the eyeglasses the same size when drawing the head from a ¾ view (as shown in Figure 6-33c). In Figure 6-33d, I show you what the glasses should look like. The circle for the lens that's closer to the readers should be slightly larger than the circle that's farther away.

Figure 6-33:
Common front- and side-view mistakes that beginners make with glasses.

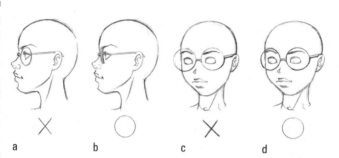

I show you what the front and side views should look like; now try your hand at drawing the glasses at a ¾ view:

1. **Draw a light line (that you can later erase) that runs right in front of the center of the eyes (see Figure 6-34a).**

2. **Draw two oval shapes for the lenses.**

   The lens that is closer to you should be slightly larger and wider than the one farther from you (as shown in Figure 6-34b).

3. **Draw the bridge of the glasses over the nose and draw the ear flap (as shown in Figure 6-34c).**

   At this stage, erase the guidelines from Step 1.

Figure 6-34:
Round glasses create an innocent character appearance.

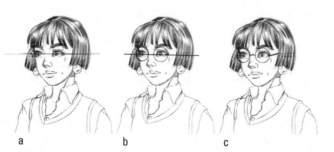

Goggles

Goggles are bulkier than glasses, so characters who wear them tend to wear them up rather than over their eyes. Manga eyes are key to communicating the emotions of your character, so drawing lead characters with their eyes completely shielded all the time isn't recommended.

Goggles create that cool "adventure" appeal, but are a bit more complicated because you have more shapes to draw and more steps to follow. They're worn above the eyes, so getting used to drawing them at an angle is a challenge. Start with these steps:

1. **As I show in Figure 6-35a, draw a light line that runs right above the eyebrows.**

   This guideline indicates the bottom edge of the goggles.

2. **Mark the midpoint of the guideline with a narrow square (representing the goggle hinge).**

3. **Draw two geometric rectangles, one on each side of the guideline (see Figure 6-35b).**

   Because the goggles point upward, you see the underside of the rectangle.

4. **Draw the sides of the goggles, which are tilting down at an angle as shown in Figure 6-35c.**

   Observe carefully and note that the side panes aren't completely square. The top line of the surface area facing the sky is angled downward more than the bottom. Without these angles, the goggles look flat and unbalanced.

   An easier way of getting this side shape down is by first drawing the angled surface area facing the sky. After that, the top of the bottom plane that is visible becomes easier to fit in.

Figure 6-35: Goggles take some time to get used to, but they look great on your character!

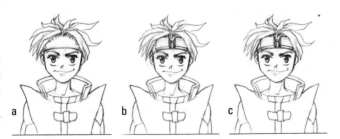

a   b   c

5. **Draw the glass window shape of the goggles as shown in Figure 6-36a.**

6. **Finish it off by adding a shadow and reflection to the goggles as shown in Figure 6-36b.**

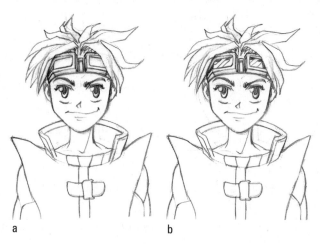

Figure 6-36: Adding the shadows and highlights to get a finished, dimensional look.

a   b

What else can we add or carry?

In this section, I show you several cool accessories that you may want to consider for your character. For more information on hi-tech tools, guns, and gadgets, check out Chapter 14.

Utility belts

Utility belts are gaining wide-spread popularity among sci-fi, fantasy, and action characters. Most of the pockets and mini-compartments on a utility belt consist of cylinders and cubes. For the following set of steps, you need the waist section from Chapter 5:

1. **Draw a wide belt around the waist as shown in Figure 6-37a.**

   The belt should be wide enough to support the extra weight of all the utility pouches and bags that are strapped around the belt.

2. **Draw the center buckle.**

   I draw a standard buckle that is rectangular with rounded edges. If, however, your character wears the utility belt as part of his or her trademark style, you should consider creating a more elaborate design. For example, the buckle can be in a shape of the character's initials, his or her team logo or mascot, and so on. Many of these fancy designs take up more space and hide the pin and notch hole.

3. **Sketch in lightly where you want the other compartment shapes to be, as shown in Figure 6-37b.**

Keeping the lines light allows you to move shapes around in case you want or need more space.

4. **Tighten up the lines and add in the details as shown in Figure 6-37c.**

   At this stage, I decide whether to use buttons, zippers, or straps with the compartments.

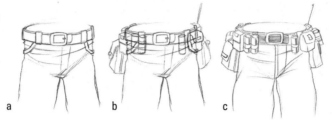

Figure 6-37: Adding many compartments to the belt.

a   b   c

Rucksacks

A rucksack is another must-have item for characters ready to embark on a long day. The larger shapes and straps imply heavy duty, whereas the smaller ones are likely to be used by grade-school children. Mid-size rucksacks are filled with all the bells and whistles a computer geek could wish for.

I show you how to draw mid-size rucksacks in the following steps. They make great props for sidekick characters (see Chapter 8) who are into hi-tech computers and number crunching:

1. **Draw a tombstone shape as shown in Figure 6-38a.**

2. **Add a smaller rectangle with rounded corners to the front as shown in Figure 6-38b.**

3. **In addition to sketching in the standard zippers, handles, and shoulder straps, I "geekify" this rucksack by adding a radio and antenna for satellite communication, a hidden camera lens, capsules, and a shoulder video recorder.**

   As I show in Figure 6-38c, you can take liberty and add lots of fun things to the rucksack. Heavy-duty sacks have more pockets and wider straps.

Figure 6-38: Designing a rucksack with a tough attitude.

a   b   c

Briefcases

Briefcases are basically geometric rectangles with handles at the top. The fun part comes when you put the finishing touches on the style. Is the case made out of metal or leather? Is it a heavy-duty case? Follow these directions to get started:

1. **Draw a thin geometric square as shown in Figure 6-39a.**

2. **Add a handle at the top (see Figure 6-39b).**

   In most cases, you see grooves for the grip underneath the handle.

3. **Finish it off by adding your personal touch, as I do in Figure 6-39c.**

   In this case, I add a heavy-duty security lock and metal corner protectors on all four corners. I also add the pig that I use for my studio logo at Piggy Back Studios.

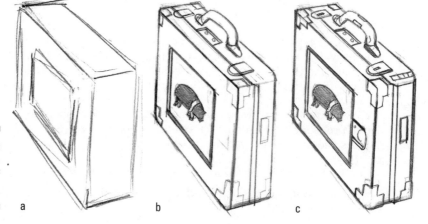

Figure 6-39: Traveling in bullet-proof style.

a   b   c

Part III
Calling All Cast Members!

The 5th Wave By Rich Tennant

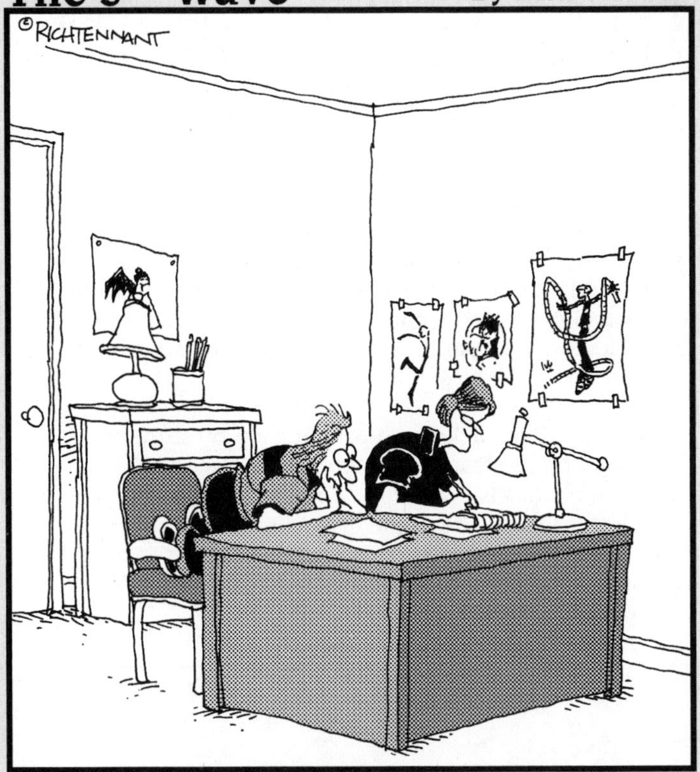
©RICHTENNANT

"Oh, Taylor, I love the way you draw close ups of people yelling. You draw the cutest esophagus."

In this part . . .

When you know how to draw a manga figure, you're ready to turn your attention toward creating your own characters. To start things off, I present you with a package of popular archetypes most commonly found in current and classic manga titles. In this case, *archetypes* are basically a set of personalities and attributes assigned to a character. An archetype may include, for example, the color of the individual's hair and eyes and the type of body build the character has. Is he or she tall, short, lean, or built like a tank?

The decision of what your character looks like is ultimately yours, but first explore and see what kind of established archetypes are out there. For those of you who already have your favorite titles, certain archetypes that you see help make a series successful for a reason. Try your hand at drawing the characters in this section. Don't be intimidated by the finished look of the final drawings. You shouldn't expect your first attempts to have a finished look. The experience of drawing an existing character is what you're after.

As a part of this package, I take you step by step through drawing popular lead characters, sidekicks, villains, wise ones, and damsels in distress. You start off posing the wire frame figure, attach the basic geometric shapes, and then add the muscle structure and the face. At the end I give some suggestions on adding the tweaks and details to finish off the character.

Chapter 7

The Main Protagonists

In This Chapter

- Drawing different types of protagonists in today's manga world
- Setting up poses that suggest strength or confidence
- Exploring various lead-character costumes

Every manga story must have a main leading character, either male or female. Readers lose interest in manga very quickly without a lead character to identify with. Even if everything else about your script is terrific, captivating the audience with memorable lead characters is crucial. In this chapter, I show you popular types of male and female lead characters in today's manga world. Think of this chapter as a casting call where you get to choose your lead cast members as the head director of a major manga motion picture!

WARNING!

If you're drawing manga characters for the first time and you've never had any drawing experience, read through Chapters 4, 5, and 6 before attempting to draw these characters on your own.

Drawing Male Lead Characters

In this section, I show you how to draw popular male lead characters. These archetypes are always expanding and changing, just like every form of popular entertainment, but you should at least recognize the common trend that has flooded the popular manga market for the past several decades.

The androgynous student

The androgynous student is usually absent-minded and quiet at first. However, deep inside, he's packing a secret: He has some kind of mystical power that he can't divulge for some reason. An androgynous quality is likely to physically appeal to both male and female readers, regardless of age. This quality paints an image that most readers can relate to — this guy is the innocent, naïve underdog who's ready to conquer the great obstacles that lay before him. Readers anticipate the radical transformation he's about to experience that will change the flow of the entire story.

Here are some traits or patterns that the androgynous student often possesses:

- ✔ **Shyness:** At least from the outside.

- ✔ **An androgynous face:** His face isn't too cute; maybe his eyes have some flare.

- ✔ **Hidden powers:** He's just figuring things out as the story progresses.

- ✔ **A lean (but not wimpy) build:** When he goes through transformation, his body changes into something more athletic, but nothing too drastic.

- ✔ **Long, jagged hair:** You're going for that disheveled *yaoi* (androgynous) look.

- ✔ **The high school uniform:** He should always be wearing it, and the top buttons should come down when his darker side awakens.

Keeping these traits in mind, follow these steps to create the androgynous student:

1. **Draw the wire figure with narrow shoulders and teenage proportions (refer to Chapter 5 for more on proportions) — approximately 6 heads tall (as shown in Figure 7-1).**

   Keep the pose simple and strong. For example, position him with one hand on his hips and the other open as if he's sensing danger around him and preparing for battle.

2. **Define the body, so that it looks more human.**

   In Figure 7-2a, I lightly draw the geometric shapes (knowing that I will erase them in the final draft). Because my character is still a teenager, I keep the width of his shoulders and waist the same (the shoulder width grows wider as a male matures).

   In Figure 7-2b, I define the basic body muscle structure, so that the figure looks more realistic and believable. Because teenagers have yet to fully develop their muscles, I keep them toned down.

   At this stage, I'm pretty sure that his school uniform will cover up his body. I keep the body lines light and fairly rough so that I can easily erase them.

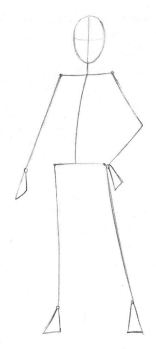

Figure 7-1: Setting up the wire figure for your lead character.

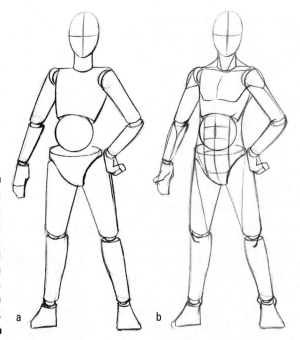

Figure 7-2: Sketching the geometric shapes and drawing the basic muscle definition.

a

b

3. **Draw the head shape and facial features, and lightly draw the under-shirt, pants, and shoes (as shown in Figure 7-3).**

I draw the yaoi hairstyle that has smoother edges in addition to the large eyes, small nose, and tiny mouth. Keep his mouth small, because this archetype is very cool and rarely displays extreme emotions by opening up to scream, laugh, or cry. To add drama to the overall feel of the pose, I keep the clothing shapes loose to give the illusion that wind and energy are blowing all around him. Keeping the lines light is still important at this stage (you want to make sure that you can make changes to the lines without too much trouble).

Figure 7-3:
Sketching in the face and clothes.

4. **Refine the head and facial features, finish the school uniform, and add some cool effects (see Figure 7-4).**

I shade in the detail of his hair and render in the eyes. To show the smooth and loose quality of his hair, I leave large portions unshaded for highlights. I also draw some loose strands of hair crossing over his forehead and eyes.

I draw the school uniform jacket with exaggerated folds. Characters who you want to portray as tough or strong should have the front of their school uniform jacket open. This trick makes the shoulders look wider and exposes the *pectoralis* (chest muscles), which are associated with masculinity.

TIP

Adding tattered bits of leaves or debris blowing around the character creates a cool effect of unseen energy flowing around him.

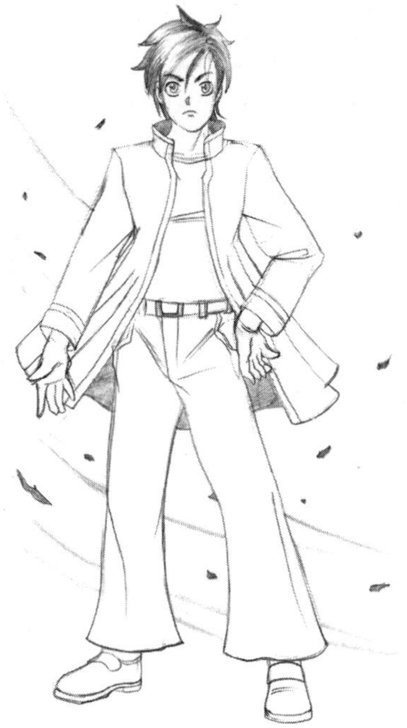

Figure 7-4: Adding the high school uniform jacket and effects.

The varsity team captain

The most popular varsity sports in manga are tennis, soccer, baseball, and martial arts. Varsity team captain characters sport the same yaoi hairstyle as the androgynous student (see the previous section), but they have fuller proportions. They're passionate about what they do and aren't afraid to bleed in order to win.

Following are some common traits of the varsity team captain character:

- **Focus:** He's all about hardcore training.
- **An underdog mentality:** Of course, he conquers all obstacles in the end.
- **Long, jagged hair:** You're going for that disheveled yaoi look.
- **A fair build that isn't too muscular.**

Keeping these traits in mind, follow these steps to draw your own team captain:

1. **Draw a wire frame that's about 6 to 6½ heads tall.**

   When I pose the wire frame figure for my character, I lightly draw a circle for the soccer ball underneath his arm and another one under his feet (see Figure 7-5). Because his posture is slightly arched and leaning forward (as opposed to standing erect), he looks shorter.

Figure 7-5:
A wire
frame figure
holding a
soccer ball.

2. **Define the body, so that it looks more human.**

   In Figure 7-6a, I lightly draw the geometric shapes over the wire frame figure (knowing that I'll erase them in the final draft). Like the androgynous student earlier in this chapter, the width of the shoulders is the same width as his waist.

   In Figure 7-6b, I define the basic body muscle structure, so that the figure looks more realistic and believable. At this teenage stage, his muscles are firm, but not developed to the point of obvious bulk.

   At this stage, I'm pretty sure that his soccer jersey will cover up his body, so I keep the body lines light and fairly rough so that I can easily erase them.

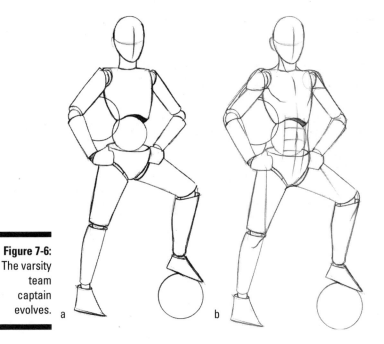

Figure 7-6:
The varsity
team
captain
evolves.

3. **Draw his basic clothing shapes, sketch his head shape and facial features, and draw his soccer gear.**

   As I fit the shorts and soccer jersey over the figure in Figure 7-7, I make sure that they're exaggerated in size to indicate that they fit loosely and aren't skintight. Most sports trunks have a "V" shape cut on the outside of both legs.

   I draw the jagged yaoi hairstyle, huge eyes, a small nose, and a thin mouth. The jagged hairstyle, which has more spikes than a porcupine's back, tells readers that he knows what it's like to train tough and he isn't afraid to take a beating in order to win a game. Draw his eyes rounder and wider than the androgynous student's.

   Soccer socks cover most of the lower leg so that the shin guards can slide underneath to protect the shins (I indicate the shin guards by drawing the outline of the shape on both legs).

   When drawing cleats, I take out my own shoes and use them for reference. You don't have to draw shoes with photorealistic detail. But many beginners overlook the different types of shoes for different types of activities. A soccer player can't play in high heels, and a combat soldier doesn't go near a battlefield if all he has are flip-flops.

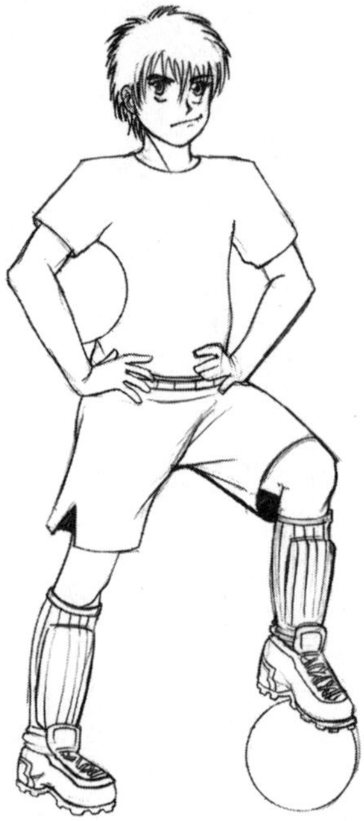

Figure 7-7: Drawing the loose soccer uniform.

4. **Complete the accessories and add the finishing touches to his features.**

   For my character, I add detail to the soccer ball, soccer jersey, and trunks, and I draw some smaller accessories, such as the wristbands (see Figure 7-8). For ideas on uniform designs, I recommend looking at soccer matches (such as the World Cup) where you see all sorts of creative wear from soccer teams all over the world. I also shade in his hair and leave some white areas for the highlights.

TIP

Adding cross-hatching marks creates the effect of dirt and scuff marks from a well-fought match. A couple of bandages show that he got some attention during a break in the match and is back on his feet for more action. Be careful not to overdo this — you want to make sure this guy's still got some fight in him and isn't ready to collapse.

Army Special Forces rookie

Another type of lead character is the young army rookie who's reckless and full of energy. He hates taking orders from the leader, yet he ends up a new man after either his bad mistakes or a fellow soldier's death.

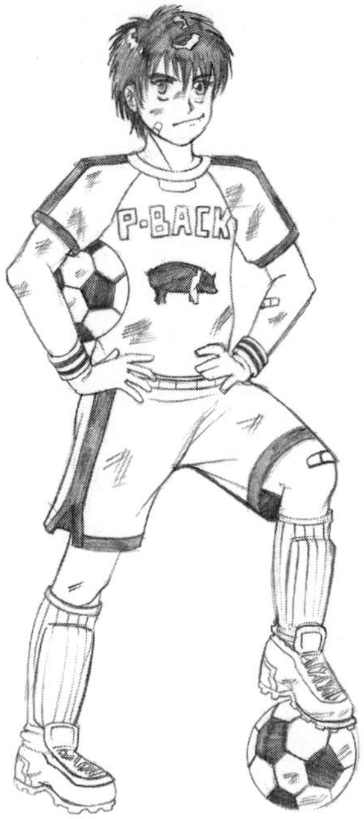
P-BACK

Figure 7-8: Finishing up the character with some accessories.

Following are some common traits of this lead character:

- **A young face:** He should be in his early 20s.
- **Heavy armor:** To protect him from artillery.
- **Guns and small gadgets:** Pay attention to the detail.
- **A smaller head:** Or at least it seems small, because he's wearing armor that makes his body appear disproportionately larger than the head.

With these traits in mind, follow these steps to create your own character:

1. **Draw the wire frame figure 8 heads tall, as shown in Figure 7-9.**

   Keep the stance wide, because later, you'll need to fit on the armor.

2. **Define the body, so that it looks more human.**

   In Figure 7-10a, I lightly draw in the geometric shapes over my wire frame figure (knowing that I'll erase them in the final draft). Since he's older than the other teenage protagonists I talk about in this chapter, I draw wider and longer geometric shapes.

   In Figure 7-10b, I draw the basic body muscle structure over the geometric shapes so that the figure looks more realistic and believable. I define the individual muscle parts so they stick out more prominently and look more developed than the varsity team captain from the previous section. Draw the neck wide to emphasize his excellent physique because armor is eventually going to conceal his entire body. Keep the body lines light and fairly rough so that you can easily erase them.

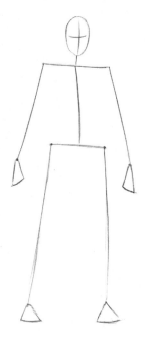

Figure 7-9:
Setting the wide stance for the wire frame figure.

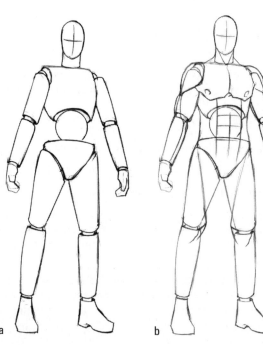

Figure 7-10:
Making the character look more realistic.

a   b

3. **Draw the head, facial features, and armor, as shown in Figure 7-11.**

   Because this type of character appears in action manga more suited to adults, I make his features smaller and more realistic. The nose is small, and I draw the thin bridge to give him a mature look (he's at least past his teen years). I also draw the contour of his hair flatter than the hair of the yaoi teenage high school protagonist I discuss earlier in this chapter.

   Many beginners make the mistake of thinking that a professional manga-ka conjures up armor design with a bat of the eye. Not so — like other creative artists, a manga-ka gathers up references for inspiration.

   TIP

   In addition to looking at what types of armor gear other manga-ka are designing, I recommend looking at riot gear, military outfits, and other forms of body armor. For inspiration, I also visit museums to see what kinds of battle armor different countries used during their history.

   Don't overload this character with overly huge armor shapes. If you go farther than I do for my character, readers may mistake him for a combat *mecha* (see Chapter 13).

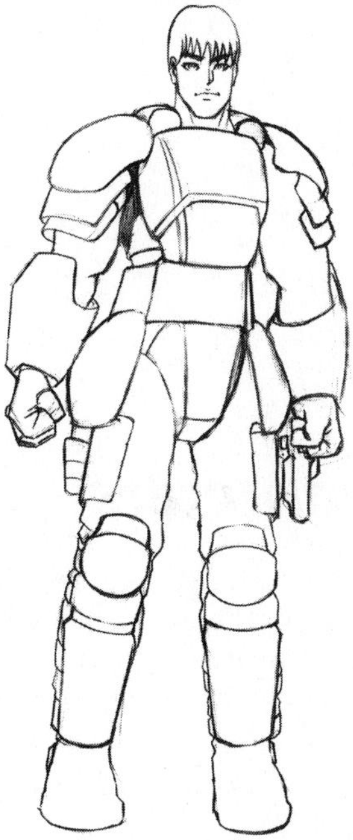

Figure 7-11: Sketching in the head and facial features, and snapping on the rookie's armor.

4. **Draw the detail of the armor and add cracks and dents to show wear and tear (see Figure 7-12), and shade in the hair.**

   I draw the straps for his side arms and add the details of the molding of his armor. An antenna next to his shoulders comes in handy for communication.

TIP

Draw overlapping shapes to give the overall image dimension. No matter how much detail you add, you character looks flat without overlapping shapes.

This wear and tear gives the sense that this rookie isn't afraid to learn things the hard way.

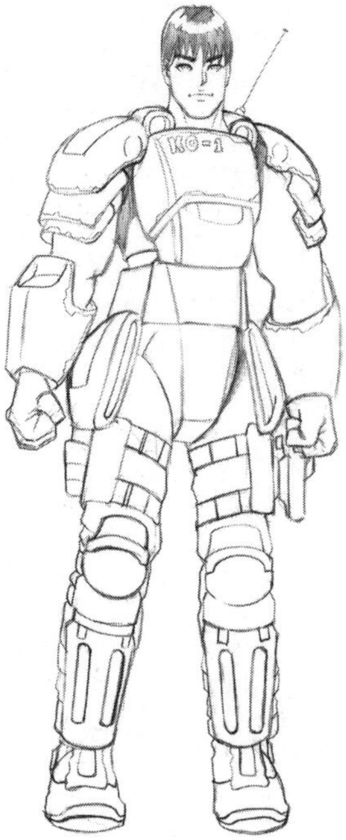
KO-1

Figure 7-12: Cleaning up the pencil marks and adding the battle scratches for realism.

Drawing Female Lead Characters

Lead female characters have dramatically evolved over the decades. While they used to play traditional maternal or supporting roles, mainstream manga titles today have aggressive females who aren't afraid to bare some skin at times. The manga world has more than just man-hating amazons, as you see in the following sections.

The daydreamer

The daydreamer is the new innocent girl on the block. She typically appears in shōjo manga (see Chapter 12), where her main adversaries are her female classmates who harass her and make it their mission to embarrass her in hopes that she will drop out and change schools. Yet, she's strong enough to weather the storm and claim the heart of the handsome androgynous male classmate.

Following are some traits of the daydreamer female:

- ✔ **Enormous eyes:** To symbolize her innocence.
- ✔ **A body that's close to being androgynous:** She has a small chest and no bulging muscles.
- ✔ **Blonde hair in fancy curls, or shoulder length brunette hair.**

With these traits in mind, follow these steps to create your daydreaming girl:

1. **Draw her wire frame to be considerably more narrow than her male counterpart's, keeping her 6 to 6½ heads tall (see Figure 7-13).**

   You also want to make sure that her stance is narrow to represent her conservative mannerisms.

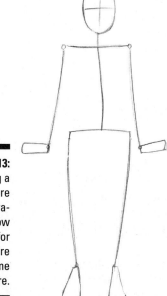

Figure 7-13: Drawing a more conservative, narrow stance for the wire frame figure.

2. **Define the body, so that it looks more human.**

   In Figure 7-14a, I lightly draw the geometric shapes over the wire frame figure (knowing that I'll erase them in the final draft). The shapes of her arms and legs are slightly thinner than her male teenage counterpart's.

   In Figure 7-14b, I draw the basic body muscle structure, so that the figure looks more realistic and believable. The muscles, breasts, and hips are minimal. The head is slightly larger and rounder (implying that she still has that "baby fat" look).

At this stage, I'm pretty sure that my character's body will be covered by her school uniform, so I draw all lines lightly so that I can easily erase them.

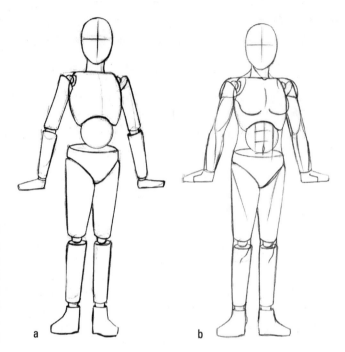

Figure 7-14:
Keeping the
overall
definition
down to a
minimum.

a   b

3. Draw her school uniform, and define her head and facial features.

These archetypes usually attend a very good high school in a very rich community. Her school uniform must reflect the conservative atmosphere as well as the school's old-fashioned etiquette expectations. See Figure 7-15.

While dressing my character (well, *someone's* gotta do it), I make sure that the short-sleeved shirt fits snuggly over her body without being too tight. Give her some frills around the opening of the sleeves and collar. The only loose item should be the short skirt. Keep the socks knee-high. In addition to drawing a vest overlapping the shirt, I attach a ribbon in front of her chest.

Draw the hair with bumpy edges to show the curls in her perm. In addition to drawing curly bangs, draw some of the curls cascading down both sides of her head. Big eyes are a must. Keep 'em wide open with ovals inside for highlights. Draw the nose and mouth small and narrow.

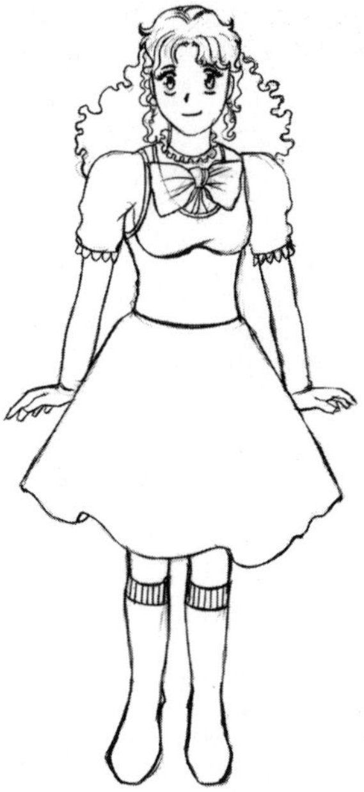

Figure 7-15: Dressing the character to match the conservative style.

4. **Add her shoes and accessories, and draw wrinkles and details on her school uniform.**

   I draw a ribbon behind her head and fancy gloves that go beyond her wrists (see Figure 7-16). Her slip-on shoes have a small ribbon on top.

   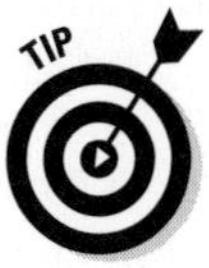

   When drawing female slip-on shoes, I add a thin band going around the ankles for the strap. The top of these shoes are open, exposing the socks.

   Draw wrinkles and folds around the bottom of the sleeves, around the waist, and down the length of the skirt. I draw a band going across the bottom of the skirt while making sure the shape adheres to the shapes of the folds. This gives the skirt shape more dimension.

Martial arts warrior

Another popular archetype is the female martial artist. She usually wears a Chinese outfit and has her hair in two buns, one on each side of the head. Unlike the teenage dreamer from the previous section, the female martial artist is outspoken and can kick some serious butt! She's strong, beautiful, and has a cocky attitude (especially toward men).

Figure 7-16:
Adding
the final
bells and
whistles.

Following are some traits of this character:

- **Full-grown proportions:** 7 to 8 heads tall.
- **Muscular arms and thighs.**
- **Hair that can dangle down:** But she must always have decorative accessories in her hair.
- **A cocky attitude.**

Follow these steps to draw your own female martial artist:

1. **Create the wire frame, setting the shoulders and hips wide, and making the pose dynamic (as shown in Figure 7-17).**

   By resting more weight upon the right hip, the shoulder tilts the other way to create an "S" shaped curve.

Figure 7-17:
Setting up a dynamic "S" shaped curve for my character's pose.

2. **Define the body, so that it looks more human.**

In Figure 7-18a, I lightly draw the geometric shapes (knowing that I'll erase them in the final draft). Draw the leg shapes, especially the thighs, wide.

In Figure 7-18b, I draw the body muscle structure over the geometric shapes, so that the figure looks more realistic and believable. The muscles need to be well defined with slightly exaggerated curves (especially the breasts and hips). The thickness of her thighs shows the power of her kick. Her neck is also thicker with more prominent muscles than that of the daydreamer from the previous section.

At this stage, the edges of her body are revealed because the outfit is very tight and clings close. Even though I still draw lightly, I know that the lines have to be accurate.

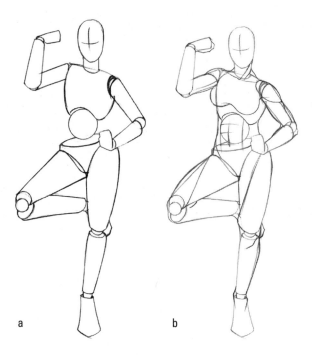

Figure 7-18:
Building a
more solid
and
muscular
definition
to the
character.

a   b

3. **Sketch in her clothing, draw her head and facial features, and refine her muscle shapes (see Figure 7-19a).**

   The popular Chinese kung-fu outfit that this archetype wears has a cylinder-shaped collar (similar to the collar of the school uniform worn by the androgynous student, earlier in this chapter). Most outfits like this one are sleeveless, and they sport a long drapery at the front and back of the hips that runs past the knees. Because this outfit is skintight, I need to draw only the wrinkles around the waist and on the clothing that flows down over the back and front of her hips. Finally, I draw in the high combat boots, which come up to the knees.

   I draw her jaw bone slightly angled and lower to show that she's in her mid-20s and no longer has any baby fat. Draw the front of her bangs and then draw her long hair going behind her back. On each side of her hair, this character wears a hair bun attached with long hair ribbons (I draw only one because her head is slightly turned away from you). Her hair doesn't overlap her eyes, but consider letting some of the bangs fall between the eyes. Draw thick eyelashes to show that she still has a feminine side underneath all that muscle.

   Although this character is strong and could probably crush a beer can against her forehead if she wanted to, her face is cute. Draw the small nose and thin lips.

I go over the basic muscle shapes from Step 2 with overlapping curves to enhance her dominant physical appearance by giving her more bulk.

4. Add details to her hair and uniform (as shown in Figure 7-19b).

For the details and accessories, I begin by drawing bracelets around the forearms and biceps. Then I draw random design patterns around the edges of her outfit and chest (also adding the outlines on the hair ribbons). I shade in the hair except for the sections for the highlights. Finally, I add the buckles to the boots and shade them in as well.

Figure 7-19:
Drawing the clothing to complete the martial artist.

a   b

Hi-tech girl

If you're familiar with manga, you've no doubt encountered this type of character a number of times. The source of every male teenage fantasy, the hi-tech girl is loaded with all kinds of hi-tech gadgets (from guns to radar-enhanced goggles) and carries out her mission in a bikini or flight suit. This archetype usually works with a team of other similarly dressed girls who are ready to take on crime or alien creatures aiming to take over the world.

The hi-tech girl is usually a teenager who exhibits some of the following traits:

- **Proportions ranging from 5 to 6½ heads tall.**
- **Fairly large eyes:** But smaller than the shōjo eyes (see Chapter 12 for details about shōjo manga).
- **Some physical definition:** But not nearly as built as the martial arts warrior.

To draw your own hi-tech girl, keep these traits in mind and follow these steps:

1. **Set up an action pose for the wire frame figure.**

   Rather than having both feet touching the ground, try posing the wire frame figure with one foot in the air. Try bending her knees or moving her arms to maintain her balance. Remember, this archetype is hyper and always on the go.

   Just to stir things up, I set the wire frame figure so that she's in running action (see Figure 7-20). I make sure that the torso is angled so that she can maintain her balance on one leg. Similar to the martial arts warrior (see the previous section), you see the "S" curvature running from the top of her head to the bottom of her supporting leg.

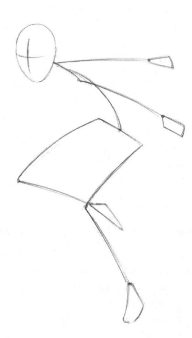

Figure 7-20: Setting up an action pose using the wire frame figure.

2. **Define the body, so that it looks more human, making sure that she looks strong and athletic with plenty of curves.**

In Figure 7-21a, I lightly draw the geometric shapes over the wire frame figure (knowing that I will erase them in the final draft). Although the character is strong and athletic, the shapes aren't bulky.

In Figure 7-21b, sketch the body muscle structure over the geometric shapes, so that the figure looks more realistic and believable. The breast size is usually exaggerated. Basically, the more curves, the better.

At this stage, I know that 80 percent of her body will be revealed, because she's wearing her hi-tech flight suit. Even though I still draw lightly, I know that the lines have to be accurate.

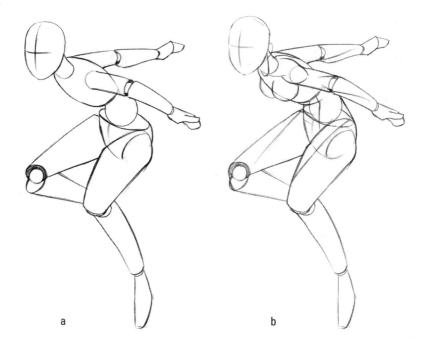

Figure 7-21: Building a more solid and muscular definition to the character.

a   b

3. **Sketch in her head, facial features, and flight suit (see Figure 7-22a).**

Characters who are hyperactive generally have bangs and long pigtails. Draw large eyes, a small nose, and a big, open-mouth smile.

The flight suit covers most of the body, leaving the neck, shoulders, and arms exposed. I draw stripes going down the thighs to her knees, and I suggest drawing bracelets and flight boots. These are fun-packed with hi-tech features, such as satellite uplinks, laser blasters, and so on.

4. Draw the hi-tech accessories to complete the figure (see Figure 7-22b).

In addition to the hi-tech forearm bracelets and flight boots, other gadgets you commonly see this archetype wearing include the following: hi-tech goggles attached to bunny radar ears, microphones, big guns, backpacks with boosters, and maybe wings so she can fly.

Figure 7-22:
Finishing
a sketch
of the
hi-tech girl.

a

b

Chapter 8

Those Loveable Sidekicks

In This Chapter

- Drawing sidekick characters in today's manga world
- Setting up poses that match each sidekick's role
- Exploring supporting-character costumes

For every lead character, you have at least one supporting cast member — otherwise known as the sidekick. These archetypes can be male, female, or neither (alien or animal). Conquering battles and winning over the hearts of loved ones gets pretty lonely without supporting sidekicks. Humans learn from interacting with each other, and that's true of manga lead characters in every story.

Readers are always curious to see how lead characters react to their surrounding characters; that's why tabloids sell so well. Lead characters look alike in so many manga stories, so the sidekicks make the difference — by either helping the lead character's mission go smoothly or by turning it into a living nightmare (usually unintentionally). Regardless of her impact, a sidekick's existence is just as crucial as the lead characters.

In this chapter, I show you popular sidekick characters in today's manga world. First I show you how to draw the male sidekicks, and then I show you how to draw the female sidekicks.

WARNING!

If you're drawing manga characters for the first time and have no drawing experience, read through Chapters 4, 5, and 6 before attempting to draw these characters on your own.

Drawing Male Sidekick Characters

In the following sections I show you how to draw popular male sidekick characters. These archetypes expand and change, just like every form of popular entertainment, but you want to at least recognize the common trend that has flooded the manga market for the past several decades.

Hustle with Mr. Muscle

This type of character is pure bulk and muscle. He's the ultimate backup for any lead character who has heavy-duty work to do. This character appears with the androgynous (classified as *yaoi*) athletic characters, such as the varsity team captain in Chapter 7.

Mr. Muscle often has the following traits:

- **Brute strength:** He's 100 percent muscle and force.
- **A rather disproportionate figure:** At 8 to 10 heads tall and 5 heads wide, his body looks a lot bigger than his head.
- **A lack of secret powers:** He just likes taking things down.
- **A love of eating.**
- **A lack of intelligence:** He's not the sharpest tool in the shed.

To create your own Mr. Muscle sidekick, keep these traits in mind and follow these steps:

1. **Set the wire frame figure at 8 to 10 heads tall and 4 to 5 heads wide to accommodate the size.**

   Because he's not the nimble, flexible type, the pose needs to be simple.

   In Figure 8-1, I have my own character with his head leaning slightly forward to make sure that the bulk of his body stands out. For this pose, I have him hunched over a bit with his stance spread apart to support his weight.

2. **Define the body with geometric shapes and basic muscle groups.**

   In Figure 8-2a, I make the geometric shapes thicker and bigger than the ones I use for the varsity team captain in Chapter 7 to give him his bulky appearance. In Figure 8-2b, I define the head, facial features, and body muscle structure. In most cases, you see these types with their fists clenched. Their pectoral muscles are larger than their head. Here, I loosely block in the placement of the eyes, nose, and mouth. I also indicate the hair shape.

   At this stage, I'm pretty sure that my character's torso and hands should be exaggerated and, therefore, the clothes I later design for him need to be tight. I draw the lines lightly knowing that I will need to refine them more accurately.

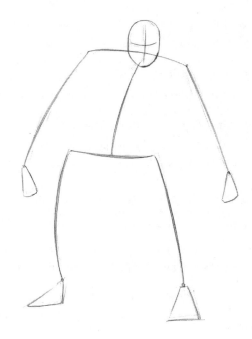

Figure 8-1:
Setting up
the wire
figure for my
sidekick
character,
Mr. Muscle.

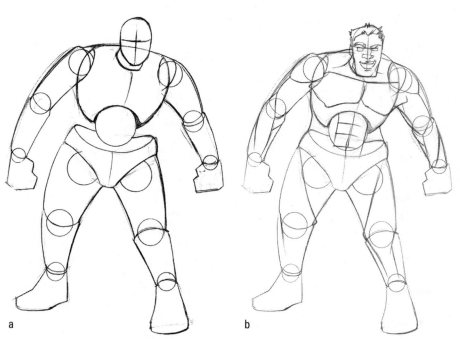

Figure 8-2:
Sketching
muscle
definition
over
geometric
shapes and
loosely
blocking in
the head.

a

b

3. **Lightly draw in the clothing and tighten up the facial features.**

   Choose clothing that doesn't hide too much of his formidable physique. Remember, you want to convince readers that this guy is packing enough muscle power to tear down a wall.

   For this particular character (see Figure 8-3), I want a heavyweight boxing outfit for his clothing. Although I draw the clothing loose, you still see the bulges of muscle around the shoulders and chest.

   Note: Because this sidekick relies on muscles to get the work done, you rarely see him carrying weaponry (he just likes to smash things with his bare hands).

   This type of character isn't afraid to show his animal-like emotions (when he has a bad temper, he lets the world know). I give my character an expression as if he's saying "Oh yeah!"

   TIP

   If the character means serious business, I like to leave the eyes as small white dots, which represent highlights from a light source and give the eyes a more realistic look.

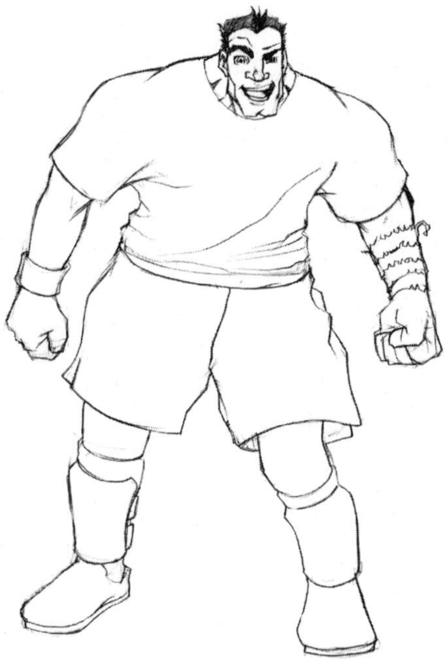

Figure 8-3: Sketching in the top, shorts, and shoes.

4. **Clean up the line work and add the details and design to his outfit, as shown in Figure 8-4.**

   Use this step to add in the details, such as the clothing design and decoration, and other smaller props, such as sunglasses.

   With my character, I add in the T-shirt design as well as the details to his boxing trunks and training shoes.

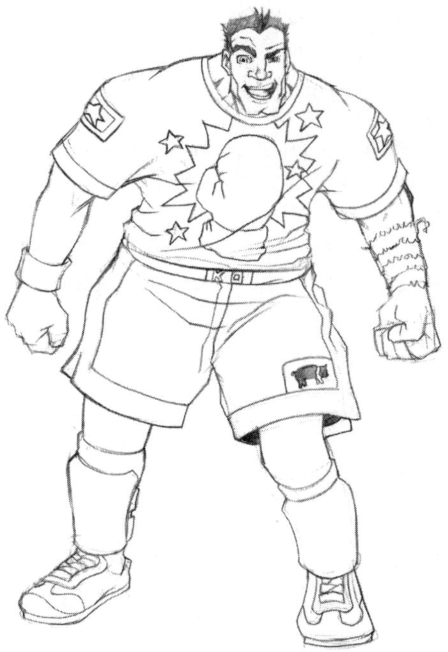

Figure 8-4: Adding the finishing touches to Mr. Muscle.

The loyal little brother

This sidekick character represents the lead character's little brother. Like the parrot to the pirate, this character makes a great companion, despite his smaller size and power. What he lacks in size, he makes up for with his loyalty to aid the lead character — even to the death. This type of flexible sidekick blends well with the following protagonist characters from Chapter 7: the androgynous student, varsity school captain, daydreamer, and hi-tech girl.

REMEMBER

Following are some traits of the loyal little brother sidekick:

- **A nerdy or geeky appearance.**
- **Always traveling with the lead character:** You never see a cover without them together.

- **Short, jagged hair:** You're going for that disheveled yaoi look.
- **Minimal muscle definition.**

Follow these steps to draw the goofy little guy:

1. **Draw your wire frame figure, deciding what kind of pose he's going to strike.**

   This character is usually 3½ to 5 heads tall. His pose should reflect a conservative youthfulness; he's a straight shooter who's eager to get the job done to help his big brother succeed.

   When posing the wire frame figure in Figure 8-5, I draw his frame much smaller than Mr. Muscle in the previous section. For his pose, I have him standing tall with his hand up against his head in a semi-salute position as if he's reporting to duty (later you see he's actually adjusting his thick glasses).

   REMEMBER

   He's the type of kid all the bullies once made fun of in class, but now he's the best friend any person can have (at least in the eyes of the lead character).

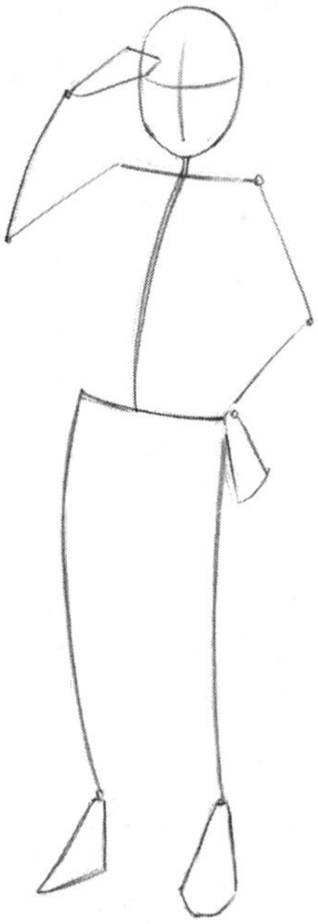

Figure 8-5: The wire frame figure that will eventually become the loyal little brother.

2. Define the body with geometric shapes and basic muscle groups.

In contrast to the bulkier Mr. Muscle, this character has a narrower body shape. Don't go overboard by drawing him too skinny — you don't want him to look like he's starving. For my character, in Figure 8-6a, I lightly draw the geometric shapes (knowing that I'll erase them in the final draft because the clothing will cover most of the body).

Keep the muscles toned down. What this character lacks in muscle, he makes up for with intelligence. In Figure 8-6b, I leave the muscle definition to a bare minimum. The pectoral muscles are almost nonexistent. I'm pretty sure that I want a "classic" appearance (I'm saying that the story in which this character appears takes place during the industrial revolution in New York City). I keep the body lines light and fairly rough so that I can easily erase them. I loosely block in the placement of the eyes, nose, and mouth. I also indicate the hair shape.

Figure 8-6:
Beginning to develop muscles and facial features.

a   b

3. Draw the clothing over the body and tighten up the features.

Match the personality of this character type with button-down collar shirts to suggest that he's conservative or nerdy. Ties or glasses are always welcome. Although his features have the yaoi look, he may also have a mischievous smirk suggesting that he's a bit of a "wise guy" unlike the more pure-looking androgynous student in Chapter 7. This character commonly wears large framed glasses.

As I draw the shirt, suspenders, gloves, boots, and pants over the figure in Figure 8-7a, I make sure that they're slightly baggy rather than skintight. This bagginess enhances the cuteness of this particular archetype. The shoes should look rugged and clunky. To enhance the nerdy look, I give him glasses so thick that you can't see his eyes. The lopsided smile adds to his smart-alec attitude.

4. **Add any accessories and details to the clothing and features.**

   For my character, I add in a messenger bag and accessories, such as the swirls that cloud inside the round glasses and the loose cap (refer to Figure 8-7b).

   If you want to, you can also add some effects with cross hatching and shading on the clothes and face to show his strong personality that allows him to stand up against injustice and abuse in the tough city.

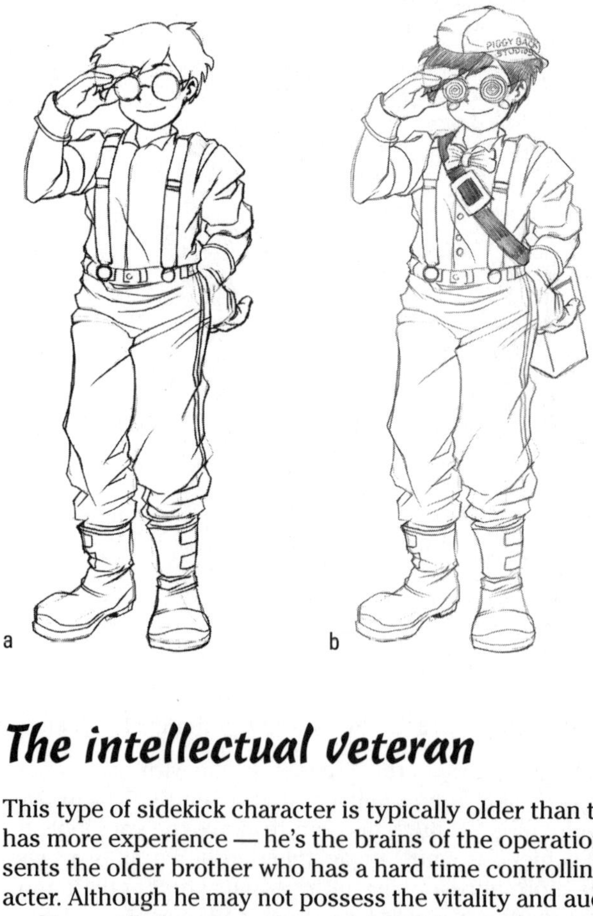
a
b
PIGGY BACK STUDIOS

Figure 8-7: Drawing the loose classic clothing and tightening up the features.

The intellectual veteran

This type of sidekick character is typically older than the lead character and has more experience — he's the brains of the operation, so to speak. He represents the older brother who has a hard time controlling the younger lead character. Although he may not possess the vitality and audacity the younger rookie usually has, he makes good decisions to help guide the team to success.

Following are some common traits of the intellectual veteran:

- ✔ **Signs of physical maturity:** His face can maintain the yaoi look, but perhaps he has slightly longer hair that has more curves. The face could also be longer with narrower eyes.

- ✔ **Greater height:** He's taller than the younger lead character; I draw him approximately 6½ to 7½ heads tall.

- ✔ **A more subdued personality:** His mind-set must be very cool in contrast to the hotheaded rookie.

Follow these steps to draw your own intellectual veteran:

1. **Draw the wire frame, making sure that the stance is wide-set to show that he's confident about his abilities based on his past experiences.**

   In addition to having a wide-set stance, you can also show his cocky attitude by either having his arms folded or resting at his hips.

   For my own character, I decided that he's the leader of the school karate team, so I have him folding his arms above his belt in front of his chest as a sign of seniority (see Figure 8-8).

Figure 8-8:
Setting the wide stance for the wire frame figure.

2. Define the body with geometric shapes and basic muscle groups.

This character shares the same body shape and muscle definition as the varsity team captain from Chapter 7.

In Figure 8-9a, I lightly draw the geometric shapes (knowing that I'll erase them in the final draft).

In Figure 8-9b, I define the body muscle structure so that the figure looks more realistic and believable. His overall muscle structure needs to be more defined, but not as exaggerated as Mr. Muscle (see "Hustle with Mr. Muscle," earlier in this chapter for more details). I loosely block in the placement of the eyes, nose, and mouth, and I indicate the hair shape.

At this stage, I'm sure the karate uniform will cover up his body, so I keep the body lines light and fairly rough so that I can easily erase them.

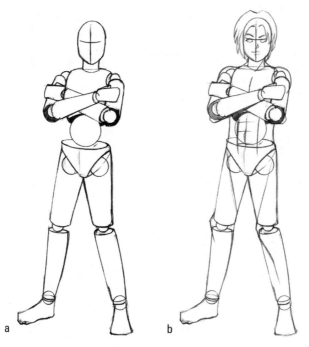

Figure 8-9:
Sketching in
the muscle
definition
over the
geometric
shapes.

a   b

3. Draw the clothing over the body and tighten up the features.

Sidekicks like this one usually appear in either a school uniform or a karate outfit; he dresses similarly to the rest of his peers.

In Figure 8-10a, I draw the uniform bottom, followed by the uniform top in Figure 8-10b.

TIP

In addition to reviewing Chapter 6 on drawing folds, I recommend looking at reference photos of karate athletes posing or sparring in their uniforms (the Internet is an excellent source).

As you tighten up the features, remember that this type's eyes aren't as big as his protagonist counterpart's eyes. The larger the eyes get, the more innocent and naïve your characters appear. Because you want your veteran to appear wiser, consider varying the eye shapes, so they aren't as round (check out Chapter 4 for more on the eyes).

With my veteran sidekick, I angle the upper eyelid to convey that cocky expression. I imagine him saying to the young rookie on their first encounter, "What's an amateur like *you* doing here?"

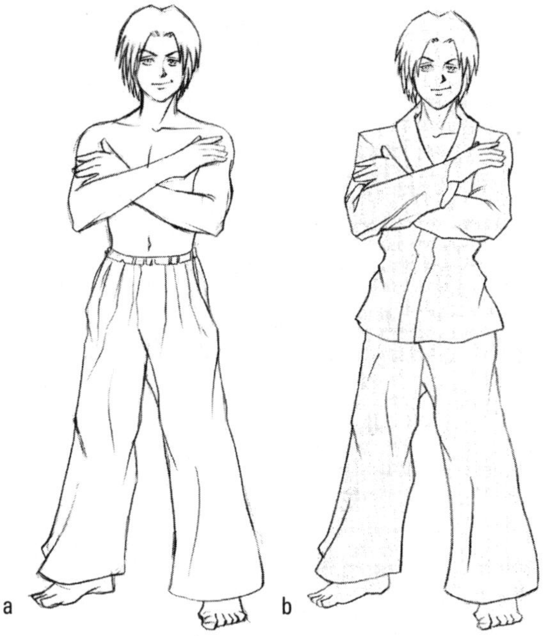
a
b

Figure 8-10: Fitting the karate uniform over the figure and tightening up the facial features.

4. **Clean up the line work and make any finishing touches (see Figure 8-11).**

   For my character, I make sure that the color of the belt is black with several stripes (indicating he's at least a third-degree black belt). Most belts have the name of the character sewn into them.

Figure 8-11:
Cleaning up
the pencil
marks and
adding the
details to
the uniform.

Drawing Female Sidekick Characters

Female sidekicks used to be virtually unheard of. Now, you see them frequently in mainstream manga (especially in those stories with lead female characters). In this section, I show you how to draw these up-and-coming characters.

The spoiled brat

Looking at her physical appearance, you see that this character is basically the female counterpart to the little brother I introduce in "The loyal little brother," earlier in this chapter. The difference is that she usually thinks of herself before others and may temporarily abandon the lead character to fend for herself in times of crisis. But this little brat usually ends up stumbling upon the key (whether she knows it or not) to solving the major obstacle of the entire manga story. This character matches well with the androgynous student and the varsity sports captain (both in Chapter 7), and she's also handy as a supporting sidekick. For example, she may be the sister of the intellectual veteran (see the previous section), and she may have a crush on the lead protagonist despite the age difference.

Following are some common traits of the spoiled brat:

- **Enormous eyes:** To symbolize just how clueless she can be.
- **An androgynous body:** Flat chest with no bulging muscles.
- **Hair that's either short or in pigtails.**
- **Tears:** Sometimes she cries when she doesn't get her way or when she's confronted after doing something wrong.

To draw your own spoiled brat sidekick, follow these steps:

1. **Draw a wire frame, making the character petite and narrow.**

   Her pose should be slightly wide to reflect her attitude that says, "I can do anything I want and there's nothing you can do to stop me." Make her head slightly larger than the rest of her body to reflect her youth.

   For my character, shown in Figure 8-12, I make the shoulders and hips of the wire frame figure slightly narrower than her male, little brother counterpart. I keep the proportion between 3 and 4½ heads tall. I'm posing the figure so that she's holding a giant teddy bear in one hand.

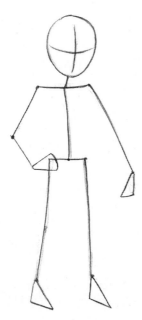

Figure 8-12:
Drawing the
short wire
frame figure
for the
spoiled brat.

2. **Define the body with geometric shapes and basic muscle groups.**

Because this character is young, the shapes need to be thin and narrow. The muscle structure should also be flat and without any exaggerated curves found in mature females.

In Figure 8-13a, I lightly draw the geometric shapes (knowing that I'll erase them in the final draft). In Figure 8-13b, I define the head, facial features, and body muscle structure so that the figure looks more realistic and believable. On each cheek, I draw an oval to show that this character is full of energy. I keep the definition minimal (no breasts or hips). Make the head slightly larger and round to imply that she has that "baby fat" look.

At this stage, draw all lines lightly so that you can draw her dress over her body and erase the old lines easily.

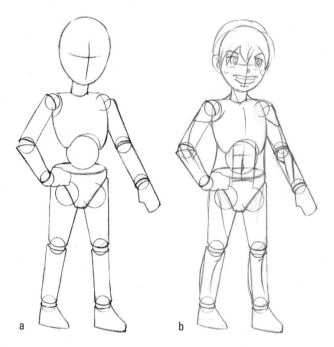

Figure 8-13:
Keeping the overall definition down to a minimum.

a   b

3. **Draw her clothing and tighten the facial features.**

I'm dressing my character as if she's the sister who gets taken to festivals and events and needs constant attention (shown in Figure 8-14).

I keep in mind that the sleeves end at the elbows without being too tight. The only loose item is the miniskirt. I keep the socks knee-high (similar to the shōjo style; see Chapter 1 for more on this and other manga styles). I also darken the lines to refine her facial features. For giggles, I render in the giant pig that she drags around as her pet.

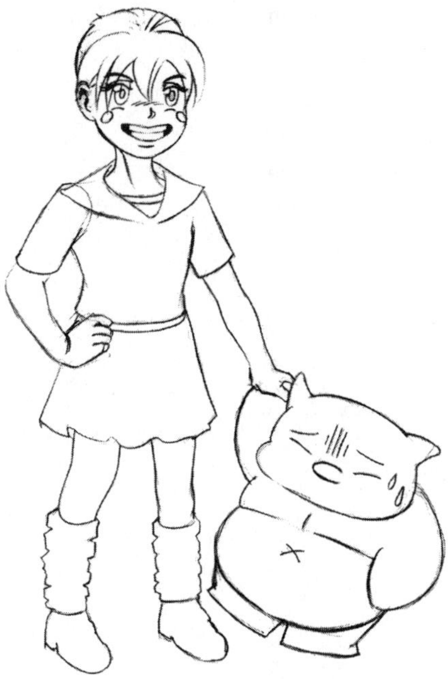

Figure 8-14: Dressing the character to match the conservative style.

4. **Add her accessories, which should reflect the shōjo way with more curls and frills (see Figure 8-15).**

   I draw the hair and a bow-tie ribbon at the front of her shirt. For her accessories, I draw a watch and bracelet. I add stripes at the end of her sleeves and on the edges of her uniform collar. I also add the wrinkles of her dress and draw in the buckle on the top of the shoe.

The nurturing and caring soul

This classic sidekick archetype represents the maternal figure who makes sure that she's there to give sage advice to the lead character in dire situations. Sometimes, in science fiction, she appears as a spirit to lead characters who can't receive physical aid when they're hurt. These characters are usually old enough to be the lead character's mother or big sister.

REMEMBER

Following are some traits of the nurturing and caring soul sidekick:

- **Full grown proportions:** 6½ to 7 heads tall.
- **Slender and elegant physical appearance.**
- **Longer hair.**
- **Down to earth:** Just like your own mother.

Figure 8-15:
Adding the
final bells
and
whistles.

Follow these steps to draw the nurturing and caring soul:

1. **Draw your wire frame, making the shoulders and hips narrow and the overall proportions fairly elongated (as shown in Figure 8-16a).**

   Because I'm drawing my character as a nun, I have more liberty with exaggerating the proportions.

2. **Define the body with geometric shapes.**

   In Figure 8-16b, I lightly draw narrow geometric shapes (knowing that I'll erase them in the final draft).

3. **Give the body and face definition, keeping in mind the breasts should be subtle and the eyes should be big to show how caring this character is.**

   In Figure 8-17a, I define the head, facial features, and body muscle structure so that the figure looks more realistic and believable. Because she's a nun, I block in the basic head piece shape. I also indicate where I want to place glasses.

4. **Draw her clothing and accessories.**

   In Figure 8-17b, I tighten up her head and facial features. When you draw the dress, make sure you leave plenty of space around the arms and legs. The clothing around the hips, however, clings closely to the figure to show how slim she is. I draw lower ends of rope coming down from her belt.

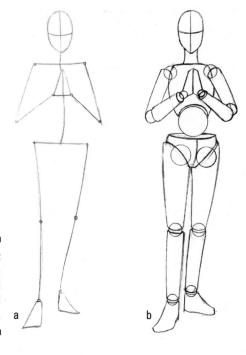

Figure 8-16:
Drawing a
narrow and
elongated
frame.

a

b

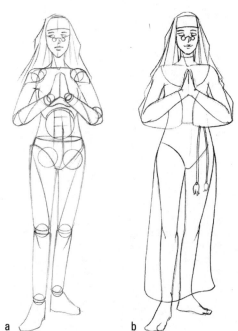

Figure 8-17:
Fleshing out
the
nurturing
character.

a

b

5. Add final details and clean up the line work.

When fitting on my character's outfit, I focus on drawing wrinkles and other ornamental shapes, such as her collar, which flows from her neck down to her shoulders (see Figure 8-18). I also make sure the folds show how tight the clothing is around the waist, and I draw her lace-less shoes. Finally, I erase the body lines under the robe and draw her necklace with a cross at the center.

Figure 8-18:
Adding the smaller clothing wrinkles, shoes, and necklace.

Chapter 9

The Dreaded Villains

In This Chapter

- Drawing popular manga villains
- Setting up poses to match the villains' personalities
- Examining the costumes that the bad guys wear

No action manga saga is complete without an opposing bad force — for every protagonist, there must be an antagonist. Otherwise, you don't have a strong plot (I talk about building a strong plot in Chapter 19).

Contrary to most American comics, where villains are portrayed as teeth-gnashing, angry, and grotesque, modern manga stories rely on good-looking, intelligent, and cunning lead villains to make the plot more interesting. In this chapter, I show you how to draw popular villain characters. These archetypes expand and change, just like every form of popular entertainment does, but you want to at least recognize the common trend that has flooded the popular manga market for the past several decades.

WARNING!

If this is your first time drawing manga characters and you have no drawing experience, read Chapters 4, 5, and 6 before attempting to draw these characters on your own.

The Handsome yet Icy-Cold Villain

This character has suspicion written all over his face. The handsome villain isn't armed to the teeth; he likely carries a sword at most. His attire is just as simple. He wears a dark cape, but the rest of his costume is one plain color.

REMEMBER

Some common traits of the handsome villain include the following:

- **Long flowing hair:** This one is a must.
- **Towering height:** He's rather disproportionately tall, ranging from 8 to 10 heads tall.

✔ **Long and beautiful features:** The overall face (particularly the nose and chin) are slightly elongated.

✔ **Mysterious power and deceit:** He plays mind games against his enemies and finds ways of increasing his physical power.

Now follow these steps to create this super villain:

1. **Draw your wire frame, making the character 8 to 10 heads tall and setting the frame very wide.**

   In Figure 9-1, the posture for my own villain is upright and proper.

Figure 9-1: Setting up the wide shoulders in the wire frame figure.

2. **Define the body with elongated, muscular geometric shapes over the wire frame figure, add curves and muscle structure, and block in the facial features.**

   In Figure 9-2a, I lightly draw the geometric shapes. At this stage, I want the waist to be narrow in relation to the shoulders. Don't draw the arm and leg shapes too narrow — he's still physically fit.

   In Figure 9-2b, I sketch in the hair, facial features, and body muscle structure. This character isn't physically bulked up, but the muscles are more defined and prominent than the androgynous student's (see Chapter 7). I give the villain narrowly set eyes, a long nose, and a small mouth. I sketch in the basic shape of the bangs and the long hair.

Draw the hands and the rest of the limbs elongated to show his graceful-ness. I draw the lines lightly knowing that I'll later refine them more accurately.

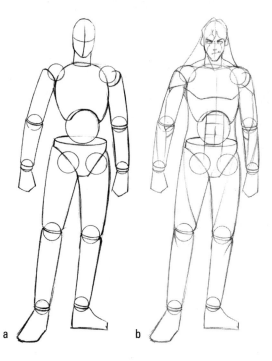

Figure 9-2:
Defining the
head and
sketching in
the muscle
definition
over the
geometric
shapes.

a   b

3. **Lightly draw the clothes, and tighten up the hair and facial features, as shown in Figure 9-3.**

   I draw the high-collared uniform top over the body first. No saggy clothes or wide folds, except maybe around the boots — other than that, everything must be tight and neat. Darken the lines of the head to solidify the hair and face. I draw the details of the eyes and draw straight hair lines behind the head to show the smooth hair texture.

4. **Clean up and refine the lines and facial features and add accessories, as shown in Figure 9-4.**

   I add a belt and a cape (which extends over the shoulders and crosses over the front of his chest), and I show the cape flowing in the wind to add to the drama of the character. I also draw the cuffs with decorations around the edges. For the shoes, I sketch a buckle that wraps around the middle section of the boots. Draw the handle grip of the sword — the rest of the weapon is hidden behind his back. Finally, shade in the hair but leave enough room for highlights.

Figure 9-3:
Sketching in
the top,
pants, and
boots for the
icy-cold
villain.

Figure 9-4:
Adding the
long cape,
belt, sword,
and other
finishing
touches.

The Awesome Warrior

This giant relies on his strength to get the job done. The awesome warrior is handsome (like the previous character), but he's more muscular, and at times during battle, he lets his emotions out — but never to a point where he's out of control. In addition to a cape, he never leaves home without his elaborate armor.

This list includes some common traits of the awesome warrior:

- ✔ **Fierce eyes**
- ✔ **Muscles**
- ✔ **Testosterone**

Follow these steps to draw the awesome warrior:

1. **Create a wire frame that's 7½ to 10 heads tall, making sure the width of the shoulders is wider than the handsome villain's to accommodate more muscle mass (see Figure 9-5).**

2. **Define the body with geometric shapes, keeping the head and facial features square and chiseled.**

   In Figure 9-6a, I lightly draw the geometric shapes (knowing that I'll erase them in the final draft because the armor will cover most of the body). In Figure 9-6b, I draw the muscle groups over the geometric shapes.

   This character is so physically buff that you need to think about and draw the muscle groups as if you're fitting a thick fur coat over the geometric shapes. I recommend starting from the shoulder muscles behind the head and neck and working your way down toward the legs. Keep the waist thin. The trick to making each bulging muscle look chiseled is drawing each one angular as opposed to the rounder muscle shapes of the female martial arts warrior in Chapter 7.

3. **Draw the clothes that lie beneath the armor, refine the muscle shapes, and sketch in the hair and facial features (see Figure 9-7).**

   Keep the folds in the material around the torso tight. Leave the arms bare so you can see the muscles. As a finishing touch for the muscles, I darken the lines that separate each muscle division.

   Draw thick eyebrows close to the small eyes. Draw the nose tall and wide. I sketch high, chiseled cheekbones on both sides of the face. For his hair, I draw jagged edges and shapes. Keep the hair short and stiff so that it doesn't get in the way of his vision during battle.

   If you want a menacing expression, draw the eyebrows thicker, pointed, and closer to the eyes. I like to add lines for the wrinkles gathering between the eyes. Having one side of the mouth slightly raised in a smirk while the opposite side angles down toward the chin adds to his dark character.

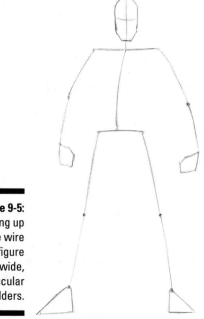

Figure 9-5:
Setting up
the wire
frame figure
with wide,
muscular
shoulders.

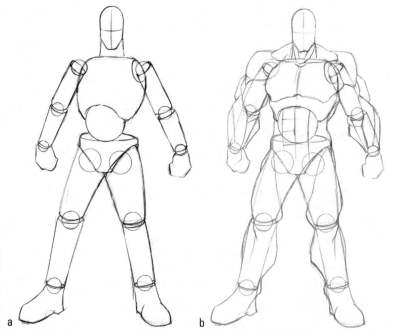

Figure 9-6:
The
awesome
warrior
bulks up.

a

b

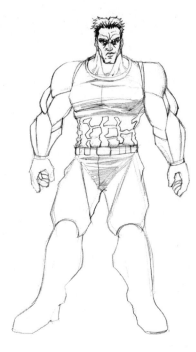

Figure 9-7:
Keeping the
basic
clothing
folds tight to
show the
muscle
structure
beneath.

4. **Sketch the armor over the figure (see Figure 9-8).**

   I lightly sketch the shoulder, breast, arm, and leg armor shapes. Hold off
   on the detail until the next step. You want to get the general shapes first.
   Keeping the direction of the body in mind is important while you fit on
   all the armor. I lightly draw a guideline down the center of the chest
   armor so that the details I later add will line up properly with the body
   that's underneath.

   Don't get overwhelmed trying to draw too much detail at first. As I show
   here, my armor shapes mimic the shape of the anatomical structures
   that lie beneath. If you're stuck and need help, I strongly recommend
   either visiting a museum with a section on armor or getting photo references. Coming up with designs is difficult when you don't have any raw
   material to work from.

5. **Add in details of the armor (see Figure 9-9a), drape the cape over the
   villain, and add the rest of the accessories (see Figure 9-9b).**

   Most armor has raised, embossed edges. For décor, I also add gems
   into the shoulder pads. Adding large spikes to a character's uniform is
   always a good indicator that he's evil. With my villain, I draw a spike on
   both sides of the armor covering his knees. Finish the accessories by
   giving him a sword that he carries behind his back. I need to draw only
   the handle because the rest is hidden from this front view.

Figure 9-8:
Blocking in
the basic
armor
shapes.

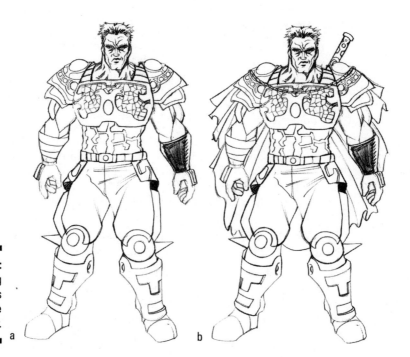

Figure 9-9:
Creating
cool designs
on the
armor.

a

b

The Military Vixen

This lady is your worst nightmare. The military vixen is the type who takes down any man or woman in charge to get power. Her personality is typically cold and ruthless. Although she's beautiful, her dark attire and evil smile are dead giveaways that you don't want to be anywhere near her.

The military vixen usually has the following traits:

✔ **A tall, thin body:** Approximately 7½ heads tall.

✔ **Dark flowing hair.**

✔ **An emotional personality highlighted by an evil, hot temper:** In quite a few manga scenarios, her brash emotions contribute to her own demise.

✔ **A dark, skintight fashion statement:** She may carry a prop to show her power (anything ranging from a whip to a scepter).

✔ **An evil laugh:** After she humiliates or defeats her opponent, she lets out an evil "Ho ho ho ho!"

To draw your own military vixen, follow these steps:

1. **Start out with a tall wire frame figure, as shown in Figure 9-10.**

   I make my vixen approximately 8 heads tall.

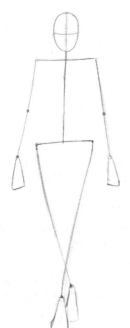

Figure 9-10: Setting the tall pose for the wire frame figure.

2. **Define the body with geometric shapes, keeping in mind that they should be more slender than those of a male villain.**

In Figure 9-11a, I lightly draw the geometric shapes (knowing that I'll erase them in the final draft). In Figure 9-11b, I block in the head, facial features, and body muscle structure so that the figure looks more realistic and believable. I also sketch the long hair shape and the front of her bangs. Although I tone down the muscle definition, I draw the chest large (this feature tends to represent a villain's power and status).

 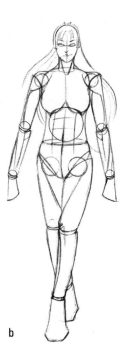

Figure 9-11: Adding geometric shapes and adding on to them.

a   b

3. **Sketch in the basic uniform shape, and define her facial and hair features, as shown in Figure 9-12.**

The collar shape is similar to the handsome yet icy-cold villain I describe earlier in this chapter. In addition to the collar, sketch in the bottom of the loose uniform jacket, and make it slightly wider than her hips. For military décor, I draw the shoulder pads, sleeve cuffs, and high boots.

In addition to reviewing Chapter 6 on drawing folds, I recommend looking at reference photos of different military uniforms (the Internet is an excellent source).

When drawing clothing over large chests, let the fold from one side of the chest overlap the fold from other side to give more dimension to the overall shape.

When defining the head, make the chin narrow and pointed. Make the eyes narrow-set with long, thin eyelashes. Give the character a tall nose and thin lips. To show that her hair is long and flowing, draw the overall rounded shape with a wider bottom like a pear.

TIP

Another trick I use to show flowing hair is to leave wavy gaps between the strands of hair. This trick gives the appearance that the hair is bouncing in the air as she's walking toward the readers.

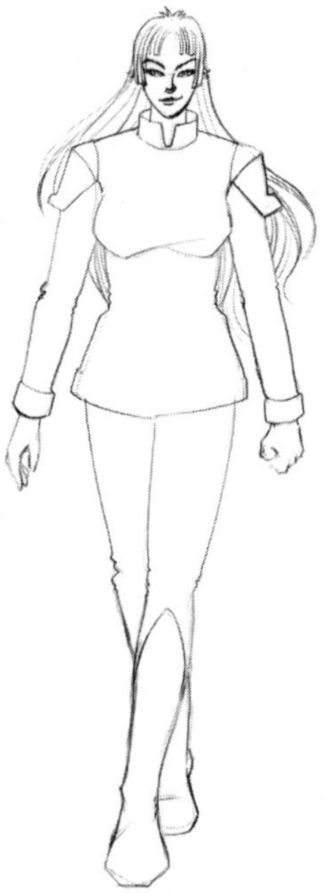

Figure 9-12: Drawing the military uniform over the figure and defining the features.

4. **Clean up the line work, as shown in Figure 9-13, and add details to the uniform and facial expression.**

   I have my own character carry a whip to symbolize her power. Because she's a high-ranking character, I draw a cape that crosses over her shoulders and pins in front, above the center of her chest. I also draw the design shapes of her uniform (in this case, the designs are partially hidden underneath her cape and continue on to her collar). Don't forget to add some of the design shapes on her shoulder pads. Draw the lines for the clothing wrinkles where the biceps meet with the forearms. I sketch a wide belt and buckle around her waist and draw two large pockets below. I complete the top uniform jacket by drawing the design strip that runs down the front of the chest and sketching the bottom hem right underneath the two pockets. For the high boots, sketch a simple symmetrical design at the top and finish it off by drawing two straps right above the ankles.

To give your vixen that evil smirk, raise one side of the smiling lips slightly higher than the other. Finally, draw a short wrinkle right next to each end of the corner of the smile.

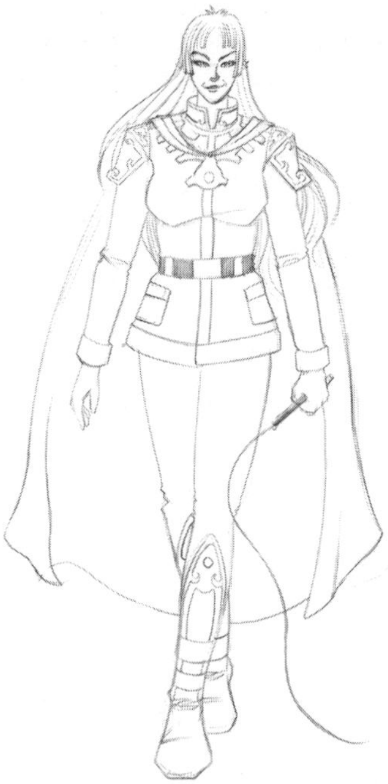

Figure 9-13: Cleaning up the pencil marks and adding the details to the character.

The Evil Sorceress

The physical appearance of the evil sorceress brings to mind the Wicked Witch of the West on steroids (younger, stronger, and more daring). With her evil magic, no one knows what demonic plan the evil sorceress has in mind. Despite her wickedness, her beauty is enough to seduce any lonely male teenager into submission.

REMEMBER

Following are some traits that evil sorceresses share:

- **Ornamental jewelry:** A huge plus.
- **A curvy body that reflects youthfulness.**
- **Wildly shaped, intensely colored hair.**
- **An evil laugh:** Like the military vixen (see the previous section), when the evil sorceress humiliates or defeats her opponent, she lets out an evil "Ho ho ho ho!"

Follow these steps to draw your own evil sorceress:

1. **Draw the wire frame so that the structure of this character looks younger and shorter than the military vixen (she should be about 5 to 7 heads tall).**

   As you can see in Figure 9-14, I make the shoulders and hips of the wire frame figure slightly smaller in relation to her head to reflect the younger age. My sorceress is 6½ heads tall.

Figure 9-14:
Drawing younger-looking proportions for the evil sorceress.

2. **Define the body using geometric shapes that are rounded and curved.**

   In Figure 9-15a, I lightly draw the geometric shapes (knowing that I'll erase them in the final draft). In Figure 9-15b, I loosely block in the placement of the head, facial features, and basic muscle structure so that the figure looks more realistic and believable. Although you never exaggerate the muscle structure on manga female characters, showing slight indications of muscle tone is okay, as I show when this character flexes to hold her magic wand. In addition to sketching her eyes and mouth, I block in the shape of her web-shaped hair that's blowing in the air, surrounded by magic.

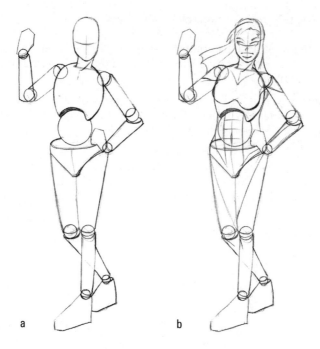

Figure 9-15:
Sketching in the basic shapes and muscle structure for my sorceress.

a   b

3. **Define her hair and facial features, and sketch in her basic costume shapes, using Figure 9-16 as an example.**

Draw the face shape round, with small eyes. Despite her youth, I don't want to draw the larger *shōjo manga* (comics geared toward teenage girls; see Chapter 1) eyes because I don't want readers to think she's innocent or sweet. I prefer to think of her as having vampire-like characteristics. I draw thick, pointed eyebrows and a wide smile exposing her teeth with fangs. I draw a simple shadow nose (refer to Chapter 4) so that the readers' attention goes straight to the eyes and mouth. To top off her facial features, draw pointed bat ears. I refine the overall shape of her hair so that it resembles that of the wings of a bat. Draw her bangs with sharp pointed tips at the end.

The overall shape of her costume is like a cross between a Halloween costume and a swimsuit. I start with the V-shaped collar around the neck (which later connects with the cape as a single shape). For the dress, I drop the V-shape to her navel. I draw long gloves that extend up to her biceps. For her footwear, I sketch in a pair of high-heel boots. To top off her costume, I draw her holding a magic wand. Because this costume is skintight, I don't draw any folds or wrinkles except around her wrists and where her arm bends. Add the finishing touches to her costume by making her nails long and sharp.

Figure 9-16: Dressing the character to match her daring fashion sense.

4. **Add her accessories to complement her costume.**

   As you can see in Figure 9-17, I add a ton of ornaments and jewelry. I draw a gem necklace, bracelets around her wrists, and a thick belt with mystic symbols. To complete her magic wand accessory, I draw some flame and smoke effects coming out of the end. I sketch in the arm and leg tattoos.

5. **Complete her costume by drawing a long cape behind her back and refining the smaller details (as shown in Figure 9-17).**

   I draw a long cascading cape, which extends over her shoulders to join part of the V-shaped collar around her neck. Draw diagonal lines from the outsides of her wrists to her middle finger's knuckle to expose her palms and fingers. Finally, draw laces along the front of her boots and the strap that goes over the top of her feet.

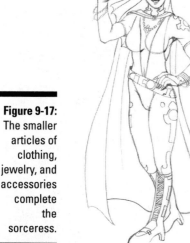

Figure 9-17:
The smaller
articles of
clothing,
jewelry, and
accessories
complete
the
sorceress.

Chapter 10

Elder Figures

In This Chapter

- Discovering grandmasters and wizards
- Using unconventional proportions
- Drawing costumes for these mystic characters

You commonly see an elder figure with whom all seek counsel in *shōnen manga* (action/adventure comics geared toward teenage boys). Genres covering fantasy and action are flooded with these archetypes. Most of these characters are old wizards or grandmasters who have immense knowledge and experience and take center stage in aiding the lead characters. Some of these characters appear at the beginning of a story as the one who has been teaching the lead character since he was born. In other instances, the lead character seeks the elder figure throughout the entire manga story and doesn't find him until the very end when the mission finally comes to an end. Traditionally, these elder archetypes are male.

The main purpose of having these characters is to build up the readers' sense of a divine figure who surpasses the abilities and powers of the lead character (no matter how strong she is portrayed).

In this chapter, I show you how to draw the popular mystic characters in today's manga world. I start with the grandmasters and follow with the wizard. If this is your first time drawing manga characters, and you have no drawing experience, read Chapters 4, 5, and 6 before attempting to draw these characters on your own.

Enter the Grandmasters

The grandmaster is an old-timer who you never see in anything other than his traditional uniform. You never really see him in full action, but readers are kept in anticipation that he can kick some serious butt when the time comes. Physically, grandmasters are either really thin or massively huge (I show you how to draw both in this section).

Following are some common traits of grandmasters:

- **Long beards.**
- **Bald heads:** A plus.
- **A no-nonsense attitude:** The large masters don't joke around.
- **A bit perverted:** The smaller, thinner masters often chase young girls or peek in the girls' locker room.
- **A staff:** The thin masters carry a staff.
- **Lack of weapons:** Both the thin and the huge grandmasters have absolutely no weapons.

The thin grandmaster

These old masters are either grumpy or comedic. As I mention in the previous list, some are perverts trying to relive their younger years.

To draw your own thin grandmaster, follow these steps:

1. **Set the wire frame figure to a short and narrow size.**

   On average, the thin grandmaster is around 4 to 6 heads tall.

   In Figure 10-1, I set my thin grandmaster to 5½ heads tall. I position my character with a wide leg stance and both forearms bent and raised to show that he's full of energy. His right arm looks like he's waving to the readers (or to a pretty young girl). In his left hand, I draw a line to represent the grandmaster's trademark staff.

2. **Define the body, so that it looks more human, and sketch in the facial features.**

   In Figure 10-2a, I draw the geometric shapes. In general, this character's upper torso and arms are thinner and shorter than the waist and legs. I make his arms short, and his lower legs slightly wider than his arms. I make his neck thin to show his advanced age. Next, I block in the fingers gripping the staff and put his other hand in the classic "V" sign hand gesture that says "all is well with life."

   In Figure 10-2b, I lightly draw the muscle structure over the basic geometric shapes and block in the facial features. Keep in mind that he's thin, but not feeble. Because he's thin from old age, his ribcage structure is more visible than the ribcage of a younger teenage character. To show thinness, I draw several diagonal curvy lines on each side of the torso, and I lightly sketch his pectoral chest muscles on the upper torso.

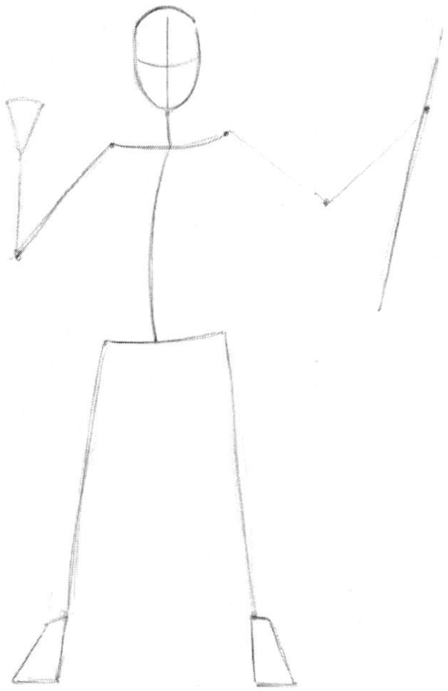

Figure 10-1: Setting up the wire figure for my thin grandmaster.

I lightly sketch the eyes and facial hair (which includes the bushy eyebrows, the hair behind his bald head, and the large mustache and beard). At this stage, I draw just two arcs for the eyes to show he's happy.

TIP

When you block in the facial hair, draw the outside ends slightly curving upward. Also, keep the eyebrows away from the eyes. I suggest drawing the eyebrow shape in the same arch shape of the eyes (as shown in Figure 10-2b).

At this stage, I know that the grandmaster's entire body will be covered by his attire, so I keep all the lines light in order to easily erase them later.

3. **Lightly draw the character's clothes, and tighten up the facial features and hands.**

   In Figure 10-3, I choose a variation of a *kimono* (the loose long-sleeved garment) with a sleeveless vest on top and traditional Japanese pants *(hakama)* for my character. These clothes are traditional for a thin grandmaster, but feel free to experiment with other options when you draw your character.

   Most grandmasters have crooked or flat noses, which make them look older and gruffer. To show that his nose is crooked from the front view of his face, I draw a long curvy line starting from my character's right eyebrow down to the center of the nose. Wrinkles underneath the eye show the age of your character.

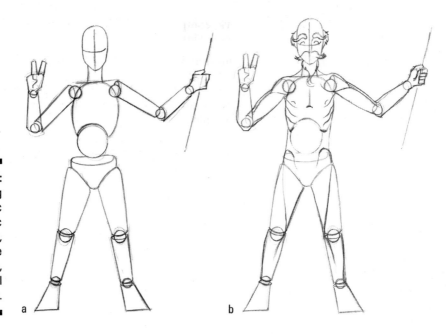

Figure 10-2:
Adding
basic
geometric
shapes,
muscle
structure,
and facial
features.

a

b

Figure 10-3:
Lightly
sketching
the grand-
master's
clothes and
tightening
up the facial
features.

4. **Clean up the line work, complete the detail on the face and clothing, and add accessories (see Figure 10-4).**

   Generally, thin grandmasters have high cheekbones and deep set eyes (as people age, features such as eyes, cheeks, and ears gradually recede back into the skull). I draw a diagonal line on each side of the cheek, upper eyelids, and just for laughs, two square-shaped highlights on his bald head to show how shiny it is.

   I finish off his kimono and vest by adding dark hemlines around the sleeves and collars. Traditionally, masters wear a unique crest mark (which is their identity) on each side of the vest. I make up my own with an "X" mark inside a circle.

   Happy-go-lucky types carry a *saké* (Japanese rice wine) flask at all times. I draw mine attached to his right hip in the traditional shape of a *Hyotan* (a Japanese gourd whose outside shell is used as a flask when dried). On his left, I draw a side bag for his miscellaneous goods. Don't forget to complete the wooden staff! Usually, the top part is blunt and deformed and the bottom is sharper. Finally, I draw in the traditional Japanese straw sandals *(wara-zōri)* for his footwear.

Figure 10-4:
Adding the finishing touches and accessories to the thin grand-master.

The huge grandmaster

The huge grandmaster is still physically active. He participates in sparring and fighting while the young fledgling looks on with awe and respect. Most of this grandmaster's emotions are less humorous and more intense than the thin grandmaster's (see previous section). Although huge grandmasters are stronger and bulkier, they aren't always tall. Some are short and rather stocky.

To draw this character, follow these steps:

1. **Set the wire frame figure to about 7 heads tall (see Figure 10-5).**

   Although proportions vary among huge grandmasters, the shoulders should be wider than the hips (which is the opposite of the thin grand-masters). The large grandmaster assumes a no-nonsense posture to reflect his inflexible intolerance toward his pupil's mistakes.

   I set the shoulders a little more than twice the width of the hips on my wire frame figure, and I draw a wide stance with his arms folded across the chest.

Figure 10-5: Setting the broad-shouldered wire frame figure for the huge grand-master.

2. **Define the body so that it looks more human.**

In Figure 10-6a, I lightly draw the geometric shapes, knowing that I'll erase them in the final draft because the character's martial arts uniform will cover most of his body.

Be sure to draw the shapes wide! With my huge grandmaster, the upper-body shapes (such as the cylinders for the arms) are as wide as, if not wider than, the shapes for the legs. A manga-ka may exaggerate the size of the arms to show how physically formidable the character is. Try it, and don't be alarmed if your grandmaster's head looks small!

In Figure 10-6b, I lightly draw the muscle structure over the basic geometric shapes and block in the facial features. To exaggerate the muscular build of the character, allow some space to fall between the basic muscle structure and the geometric shapes.

Figure 10-6:
The huge grand-master begins to come to life.

a

b

I draw the facial hair (eyebrows, beard, and moustache) straight and angled rather than arched and rounded like the thin grandmaster. I let the eyebrows angle down toward the center of the forehead to either overlap or come close to covering part of the eye. I draw his eyes narrow and smaller than androgynous eyes. The nose is identical to the thin grandmaster's, except I shorten the length a bit so that his face doesn't look as long. A simple arc for the mouth is enough for the stern character. Finally, I make the hair long, which makes him look as though he's been training without rest.

3. **Begin to sketch the character's clothes and tighten up his facial features.**

In Figure 10-7, I draw the huge grandmaster's martial arts uniform over the figure, making sure it's slightly baggy and not skintight like those superhero outfits.

Figure 10-7:
Drawing the huge grand-master's loose, classic clothing.

In this stage, I tighten up the facial features by increasing the line contrast and adding hair strands to the overall hair shape to give him a more realistic appearance. Don't forget to sketch in the wrinkle lines underneath the eyes.

4. **Add finishing detail to the character's clothes, face, and hands.**

In Figure 10-8, I draw rip and tear marks around the edges of my huge grandmaster's uniform to show that his entire life revolves around martial arts. Don't forget to draw in the black belt. To give him a scowl, draw several lines at the center of his forehead for wrinkles. You can also draw several short lines along each finger joint of his hand, so that his hands tell the story of someone who's been in a countless number of fights and tournaments. Don't forget to draw the fingernails as well.

Figure 10-8:
Adding the finishing touches to the huge grand-master's appearance.

The Wizards

Wizards and their magical powers are a huge deal in the fantasy manga world. Unlike traditional Western wizards, manga wizards have a darker, more modern appearance.

Following are some common traits of wizards:

- ✔ **Elongated body proportions and facial features.**
- ✔ **Considerably more height than the younger lead character:** Wizards are approximately 7½ to 8½ heads tall.
- ✔ **Subdued character:** Wizards don't raise their voices in anger.
- ✔ **A wooden staff with a crystal ball at the top:** All wizards must carry one.

Follow these steps to draw your own wizard:

1. **Draw the wire frame figure to reflect the tall stature of the wizard, as shown in Figure 10-9.**

   In addition to the common traits I list above, wizards tend to hunch over (as characters do as they grow older). Although I draw my wizard at 8½ heads tall, he appears shorter because his head is leaning forward toward the readers.

   If you want to show a character leaning or slouching forward, draw the head lower so that it overlaps the top portion of the torso. You don't need to draw the neck because it's hidden behind the head and out of sight.

   I draw a line to show my character holding a staff. His hands are spread out to balance his upper body, and his feet are close to each other.

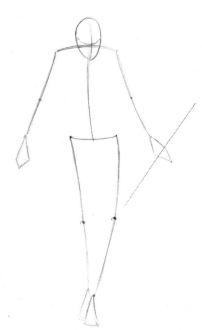

Figure 10-9: Setting the stance for the wizard.

2. **Define the body, so that it looks more human.**

   In Figure 10-10a, I lightly draw the geometric shapes, knowing that I'll erase them in the final draft. In Figure 10-10b, I lightly sketch the body muscle structure so that the figure looks more realistic, and I block in the basic facial features.

   My wizard's overall muscle structure is lanky and tall. The idea is that powerful magic has enabled him to keep his form despite more than 100 years of life. Refer to "The thin grandmaster" earlier in this chapter as you draw his muscle structure over the geometric shapes.

His features should be that of a noble intellectual elder. Make the facial hair (eyebrows and beard) longer than the thin grandmaster. Wizards are never bald. My character has long flowing hair. Don't draw any details to the eyes — leave them blank even when they're open wide. It adds to his mysterious, eerie personality.

At this stage, I'm sure I'll make dark robes to cover his body. I keep the body lines light and fairly rough so that I can easily erase them.

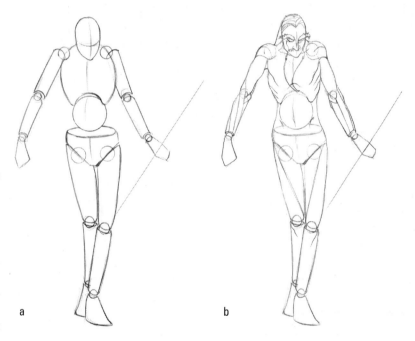

Figure 10-10: Drawing lean muscles over the geometric shapes and sketching in the face.

a   b

3. **Add basic shapes for the clothes and accessories, and further define the face and hands.**

   I draw the wizard's robes flowing from top to bottom (see Figure 10-11). Wizards live in solitude and rarely step out of their robes. I draw the tattered edges along the bottom of the robe to show the wear and tear.

   In addition to reviewing Chapter 6 on drawing folds, I recommend looking at reference photos of long robes to see examples of loose, long clothing draped over the human form. Traditionally, wizards shun technology and identify themselves with nature. In my character, I make the staff shape uneven to give a more natural appearance (as if he just picked a stick up off the ground in a forest and decided to transform it into his favorite staff). I complete the staff by drawing an abstract symmetrical base design and a crystal ball at the center. For the shoulder pads, I curl the ends out but leave the edges uneven like his staff. They should resemble the tangled branches from a tree.

Although his mouth is hidden, I lightly sketch where his mouth is with a "^" shape, and I draw his fingers long.

Figure 10-11:
Adding a
robe and
details to
make the
wizard
come alive.

4. **Finish the sketch by adding detail to clothes and accessories.**

For my character, the fun is far from over as I add an elaborate belt and ornamental design to the shoulder pads (see Figure 10-12). I embed dark crystals on each side of the pads for a mysterious touch. I draw ornamental cuffs for the robe, and the front design shape runs from behind his long beard down to the belt. I sketch the folds in the lower robe to show that he's standing in the wind while preparing to cast his next spell. Finally, I draw cloth tape wrapped around the staff for better grip and add some abstract shapes of my choice.

Figure 10-12:
Cleaning up
the pencil
marks and
adding the
details to
the uniform.

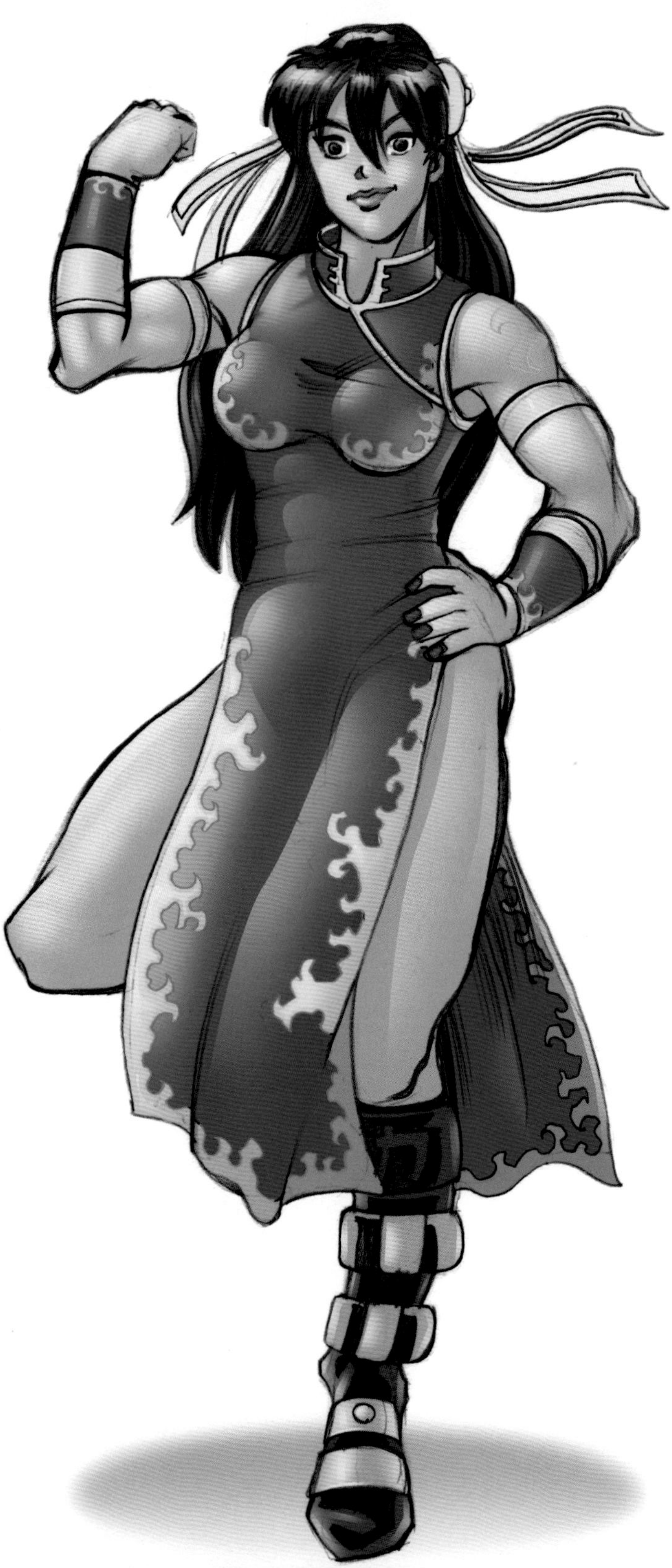

Martial Arts Warrior

This female protagonist archetype is not only physically strong but also full of confidence and pride. She's especially cocky toward her male combatant challengers and never turns down a match (or rematch). See Chapter 7 for the steps you need to draw your own Martial Arts Warrior.

Strong Grandmaster

This archetype is a lifelong teacher and mentor to his protagonist student. He's physically strong despite his age and never lets his student accept failure. You can find instructions for drawing this character in Chapter 10.

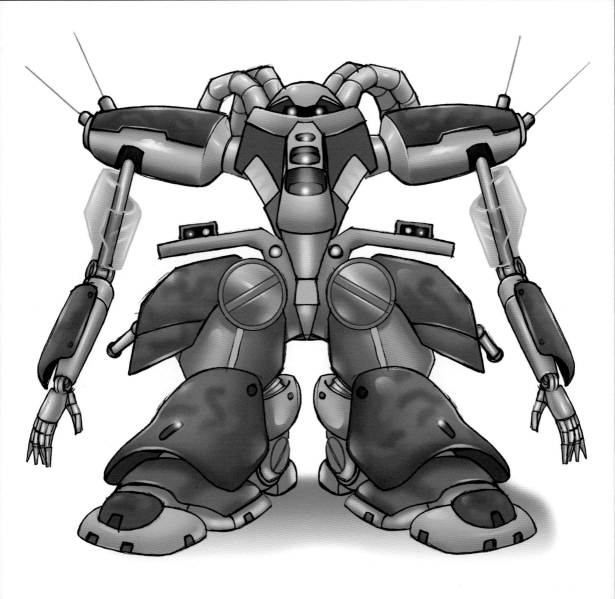

Construction Mecha

This type of mecha is built for heavy-duty construction or repair. It's large enough to be piloted by a human from the inside (the cockpit is usually located at the center chest of the mecha). Check out Chapter 13 to find out how to draw your own mecha character.

Hi-Tech Sports Car

If speed's your need, look no further. Cars like this one are constructed to be wider, flatter, and sleeker than your average civilian car for better aerodynamics. See Chapter 15 for drawing instructions.

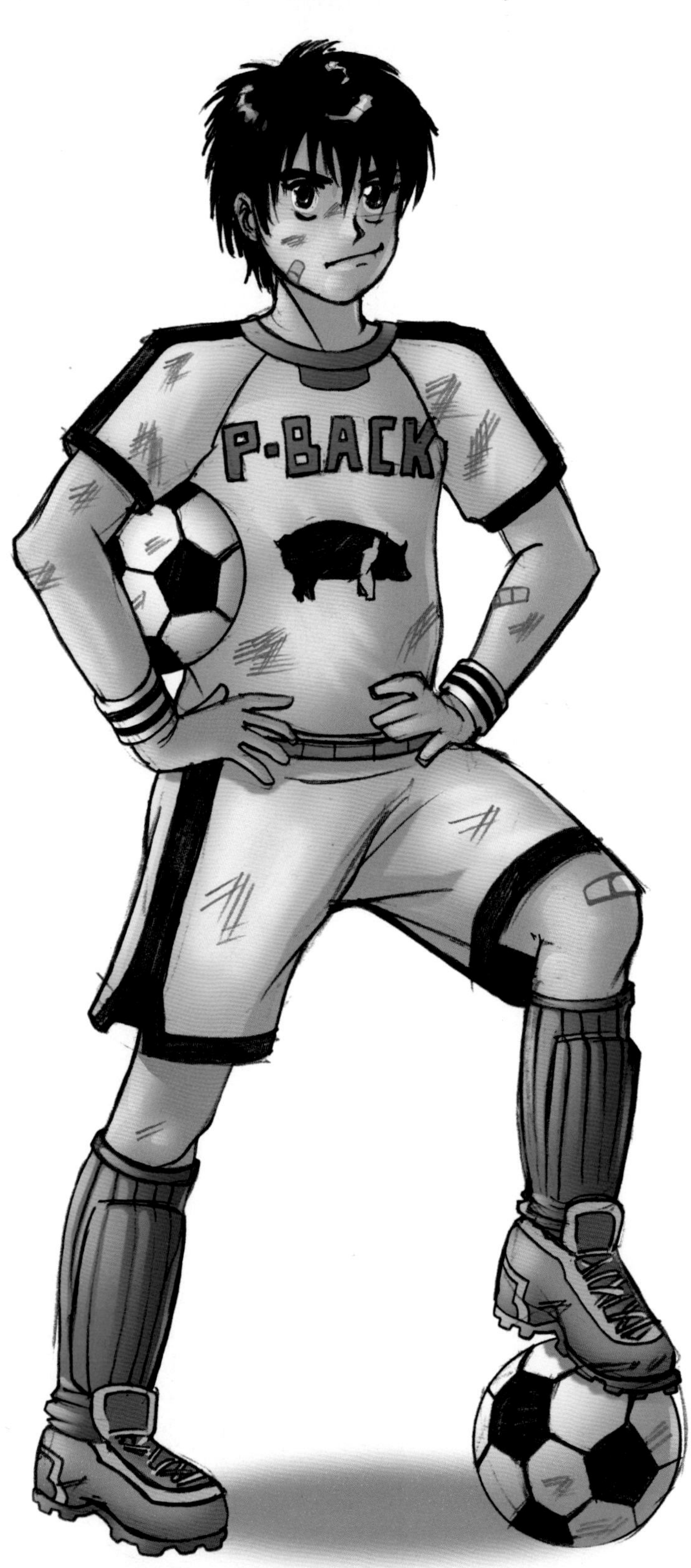
P-BACK

Varsity Sports Captain

You can't go through a manga section in your comic book store without seeing this type of lead protagonist. Sporting the ubiquitous androgynous jagged hairstyle with those large eyes, these characters never give up until the game is over. Chapter 7 tells you how to draw this male lead character.

The Spoiled Brat

Imagine your baby sister constantly getting into trouble and leaving you with no choice but to bail her out. She's cute and adorable, but this archetype is a handful, always playing the damsel in distress! Follow the steps in Chapter 11 to draw the Spoiled Brat.

Communicator

If your lead character or sidekick needs a tech-savvy device, draw one of these! From linking to a satellite to firing laser beams to washing dishes (well, maybe it doesn't go that far), this device can do it all. I show you how to draw this communicator in Chapter 14.

The Icy Cold Villain

Ladies, don't let this evil lead villain trick you with his good looks. This evil arche-type is crafty, deceitful, and cold. To draw the Icy Cold Villain, read through my steps in Chapter 9.

Chapter 11

Damsels in Distress

. . . .

In This Chapter

▶ Drawing expressions that say "Save me!"

▶ Exploring different types of hapless girls who need to be rescued

▶ Matching the face and personality with the proper costume

. . . .

*E*ver watch those silent movies featuring attractive girls in tattered clothing tied down to the railroad tracks? How about the girl who gets abducted and taken up the tall building by a giant gorilla? Well guess what — the manga world (especially shōnen manga) is flooded with these characters. Some of them are young, spoiled little princesses who have to learn their lesson the hard way by being captured and held prisoner. Others may be the brave and mature types who stand up to a greater cause even at the risk of losing their lives.

In this chapter, I show you several popular damsel-in-distress archetypes that you can use for your manga. Remember, though, these characters shouldn't steal the spotlight from your main characters; they should play a secondary role in advancing the focus of your story.

The "Little Sister" Princess

Visualize the "little sister" princess archetype by picturing a younger baby sister getting into trouble by sticking her nose into other people's business. Like it or not, the lead character has little choice but to go in to bail her out. Usually the plot to rescue these girls is based not on romance, but on emotional love.

Here are some traits or patterns to keep in mind when creating this type of character:

> ✔ **Youth:** These types are generally young (anywhere between 6 and 18 years old).
>
> ✔ **Adorable faces:** Draw them cute.

✔ **Petite body type:** This girl has no exaggerated proportions or features.

✔ **Stubborn and determined personality:** She may not always be the most pleasant person to deal with on an everyday basis.

✔ **Very high fashion taste:** She wears upscale clothing, jewelry, and hair-styles according to her culture and time setting.

✔ **A rescuer:** The lead character who eventually saves her is usually a "big brother" type lead character who loves the damsel as his "little sister."

Picture a stubborn child who's about to throw a fit after not getting her way. Or maybe a spoiled teen daughter who's irately waiting for her butler to find her pink fur coat. Then follow the steps to create the spoiled princess:

1. **Pose the wire frame figure about 6½ heads tall.**

   This character generally has her arms either folded across her chest or on both sides of her hips. Despite her attitude, she should have narrow shoulders and the narrow body frame of a normal teen or preteen youngster.

   In Figure 11-1, I pose her standing in her elegant dress while holding a parasol. Observe how the left hip is raised higher than the right when more weight is placed upon it. In her right hand, I draw a line to indicate the placement of her parasol.

Figure 11-1: Setting up the wire figure for my spoiled princess character.

2. **Lightly draw the geometric shapes over the wire frame figure, and draw the cross hairs on the face to indicate the direction of her head.**

   When drawing these shapes for this character type, keep them narrow, but not wafer thin (she's not a fashion model). Don't make them so wide that the head loses significance or balance to the rest of the body. If the character is younger, make the head larger and the body narrower. If the girl is more mature, make the body shapes narrow but longer to accommodate the change in proportion.

   In Figure 11-2, I lightly draw the geometric shapes, knowing that I'll erase them in the final draft after drawing in the clothing. I slightly arc the cross hairs on her face to show that her head is tilting up and away from the readers.

Figure 11-2:
Sketching geometrical shapes over the wire frame figure.

3. **Based upon the geometric shapes, add the curves and muscle structure and block in the facial features (see Figure 11-3).**

   Keep your character's definition to a minimum. She shouldn't look muscular or overly defined. You're not drawing a full-grown adult at this stage. Adding breasts for the older teenagers is okay, but keep them toned down.

Because her dress covers the entire body, I keep the body lines light and fairly rough so that I can easily erase them. I also angle her toes down a bit so she can fit into those high heels comfortably.

I lightly block in the facial features, which I refine in the next step. At this stage, you just want to get the placement of the eyes, nose, and mouth down. I also sketch in the shape of the hair.

Figure 11-3:
Drawing the definition and body structure over the geometric shapes.

4. **Lightly sketch her clothing shapes and refine the facial features.**

Her clothing should carry the idea of class or nobility. Keep in mind that she's the type who has been pampered all her life, and her fashion reflects that.

I lightly draw the dress and high heels (as shown in Figure 11-4). I show that her sleeves and the bottom of her skirt are baggy and loose by leaving gaps between the body surface and the clothing. In contrast, I leave no gaps between the clothing and skin when I draw the waist section. When drawing high heels, keep them elevated and pointed at the top. For her hair, I draw a large ribbon.

I refine the facial features and expression. Sarcastic and lofty expressions help sell this type of character to your readers. If your character is younger, she may be throwing tantrums or pouting in disapproval.

With my character, half-open eyelids with thick eyelashes add to her arrogant personality. Twist the smile upward to create a smirk. This expression gives readers a taste of her haughty and arrogant attitude (which hopefully changes after she's rescued from the very danger she brought upon herself).

Figure 11-4:
Refining the facial features and sketching in the dress and shoes.

5. **Finalize the clothing details and draw her props and accessories (see Figure 11-5).**

   Earrings, necklaces, and bracelets are always a welcome addition to primp up your character. Props such as hats and stuffed animals for younger characters work as well.

   In Figure 11-5, I complete the parasol for my character and add the detailed designs and frills of her dress and leg wear. Don't forget to erase the lower body beneath the dress.

   You get cool clothing effects by drawing wavy patterns along the bottom of the dress, across the chest, and around the neck.

Figure 11-5:
Finalizing
her clothing
and acces-
sories.

The Innocent Schoolgirl

The innocent schoolgirl is a classic damsel in distress who wears her school sailor uniform almost 24/7, similar to the daydreamer in Chapter 7. Likewise, she may be the subject of abuse from her female classmates. However, unlike the daydreamer appearing in popular shōjo manga, the innocent schoolgirl's adversaries are diverse, including more than just her jealous classmates. In some popular shōnen manga scenarios, rival high school students may "kidnap" this character and hold her either for ransom or as bait to get her high school's strongest student leader to fight against their own. In some science fiction or thriller genres, creatures or aliens from another radically different world may invade the real world and take her hostage.

This character endures harsh treatment and remains powerless at the hands of her captors while the main lead character devises an effective and daring way of rescuing her without getting himself killed. Don't worry, she never dies (that would *kill* the plot).

Here are some traits or patterns to keep in mind:

- **Lack of anger:** Err toward the insecure, nervous look instead of drawing her angry.
- **Big bambi manga eyes:** These eyes are always welcome.

✔ **A high school sailor uniform:** She's always wearing it.

✔ **Simple fashion:** The high school dress code in Japan generally forbids fancy jewelry, makeup, and elaborate hairstyles.

✔ **Perseverance:** Although she endures abuse from her captors, she never dies, and her knight in shining armor almost always saves her.

✔ **A savior:** The lead character who eventually saves her is usually a male classmate who is physically strong enough to stand up against the enemy high school ruffians, or who possesses the magic power to conquer the demonic forces of her captors.

Follow these steps to create your own innocent schoolgirl:

1. **Set the wire frame structure between 5 and 6½ heads tall, and make it narrow, with slightly wider shoulders.**

   You can draw a more realistic character at the standard 7½ heads tall. Use poses that are generally conservative and narrow.

   In my example in Figure 11-6, I pose the character holding her school bag while gazing toward the audience. Maybe a charming classmate who becomes her rescuer has just captivated her attention. I also draw a square shape to show the placement of her school bag.

Figure 11-6: Setting up the wire figure for my innocent schoolgirl character.

2. **Lightly draw the geometric shapes over the wire frame figure, and draw the cross hairs on the face to indicate the direction of her head.**

   Keep the shapes on this character narrow in conjunction with her wire frame figure. If you're drawing a more realistic character, make her torso wider and include more elongated shapes to match her taller proportions.

   In Figure 11-7, I lightly draw the geometric shapes (knowing I need to erase them in the final draft). I loosely draw the hairline shape on her head showing that she's facing the front.

Figure 11-7:
Loosely defining the head and sketching geometric shapes over the wire frame figure.

3. **Define her body and muscle structure and block in her facial features.**

   Regardless of her proportions, she shouldn't look muscular or too strong (she must appear to be as helpless as possible). Although her school bag hides her torso, keep in mind that her breasts and hips are similar to the daydreamer in Chapter 7.

   In Figure 11-8, I tone down her muscle definition to a minimum. Notice how straight and smooth her arms and legs are. Because the high school sailor uniform I draw in the next step covers most of her body, I keep the lines light and fairly rough, so that I can easily erase them.

   I lightly block in the facial features. At this stage, I worry only about the placement of the eyes, nose, and mouth, and I also sketch in the shape of the hair.

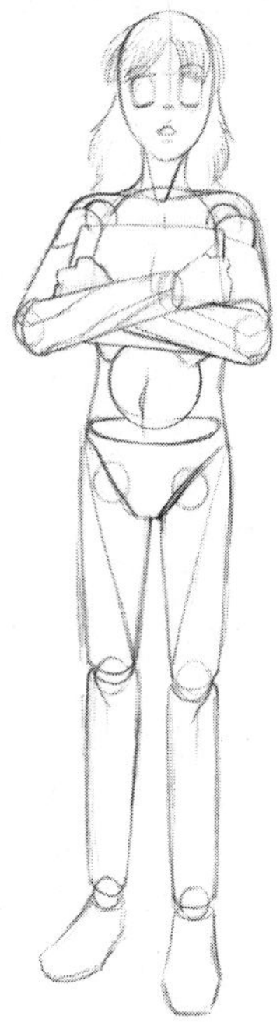

Figure 11-8: Lightly sketching the body's definition.

4. **Draw her clothes and refine her facial features.**

   Although most high school sailor uniforms are loose, draw the uniform slightly tighter. Each high school has its own uniform variation and a school emblem that's sewn or patched on either the sleeve or collar. The general rule of thumb is that the summer uniforms with shorter sleeves are white, and the winter uniforms with longer sleeves are darker (for example, a Prussian blue color).

   I lightly draw the uniform top, dress, socks, and shoes (as shown in Figure 11-9). I stick to drawing the traditional high school sailor uniform without any large ribbons. I draw the socks loose (almost like those leg warmers from the 1980s).

   WARNING!

   As I mention in the introduction of this archetype, draw her eyes large. Don't, however, draw them so big that you upset the head versus body balance. If the eyes become ridiculously enormous, the readers assume that the rest of the body should be smaller and shorter than the intended height proportions of around 6 heads tall.

   In my drawing in Figure 11-9, I draw the big eyes with larger-than-normal pupils. I also raise her eyebrows and draw her mouth slightly open to convey her innocence. I draw a very small shadow nose to enhance her cuteness. Showing several sections of her hair branching out away from the head gives the impression that she's outside the school building and enjoying the fresh spring breeze.

Figure 11-9:
Sketching in
the high
school
sailor
uniform and
refining her
facial
features.

5. Finalize the character's facial and clothing features.

Unlike the daydreamer in Chapter 7, the hairstyle should be simple. If you need to draw any jewelry such as earrings, draw them as small studs without anything shiny. Likewise, don't draw any bling into her braids or headbands. In many manga, her hair color is black (as opposed to blonde) to show her simplicity.

In my drawing in Figure 11-10, I shade in her hair and parts of her uniform. On both sides of her cheeks, I draw diagonal lines to indicate that she's blushing with love.

I add sleeve and chest stripes. For her skirt, I draw the straight folds coming out from the waistband. Although I conceal the front portion of her chest with her school bag, you may want to draw a scarf or ribbon if you have her arms dropping down. Finally, I refine her shoes by drawing in the straps.

Figure 11-10:
Finalizing
the facial
features and
adding in
her acces-
sories.

The Loyal, Selfless Damsel

The loyal, selfless damsel is generally more mature and older than the other archetypes in this chapter. She's generally in her mid-20s to mid-30s. Unlike the "little sister" princess type earlier in this chapter, the motivation behind the rescue mission for this character is romantic. This attractive female isn't kidnapped because of her nosiness or selfish, irresponsible actions; she's kidnapped against her own will, or because she chooses to submit to her captors as a sacrificial move to save her loved ones. In response, the rescuer (a courageous, daring, rookie team member, for example) goes out of his way to risk his own life in order to save her and bring her back to safety. Compared to the innocent schoolgirl (see the previous section) who lets tears from fears dictate her behavior, this damsel is able to control her emotions. Despite the torture brought upon her by her captors, she remains calm and loyal to her team members and to the ones she cares about.

Here are some traits or patterns to keep in mind:

- ✔ **Control:** She never lets her emotions get the best of her.
- ✔ **Realistic looks:** Draw her features more realistically than the other characters in this chapter.

✔ **Status:** She usually wears simple jewelry to suggest royalty or political significance.

✔ **A soft spot for children:** This usually stems from her hardships as a child and her current desire to ensure that what happened to her never happens to the children she encounters.

✔ **Very spiritual:** She's not afraid to drop down on her knees to pray to her God in the midst of a crisis.

✔ **Noble:** Although she endures abuse from her captors, she never submits to the dark side — even if it means losing her own life.

✔ **A hero:** The lead character who eventually saves her is usually a reckless male rookie or underdog who's willing to bend the rules in order to save the damsel.

Follow these steps to create your own loyal, selfless damsel:

1. **Set up the wire frame figure.**

   Make the wire frame figure taller and more elongated to show that she's an adult. The range of proportions differs according to the targeted readers' ages and the degree of mature content (equivalent to a PG-13 to R rating) in the genre of the story.

   Character types featured in stories geared toward a general audience tend to have shorter, more standard manga proportions ranging from 5 to 6½ heads tall. They also tend to be younger. The types featured in more mature stories tend to have more realistic and taller proportions ranging from 7 to 8½ heads tall.

   In my example in Figure 11-11, I go for the more challenging realistic proportions to reflect the physical and psychological maturity of my damsel.

2. **Lightly draw the geometric shapes to cover the wire figure, and draw the cross hairs on the face to indicate the direction of her head.**

   These characters have slender and elongated arms, necks, and legs. In the more serious, mature, action manga stories, these characters have longer heads and face shapes with pointed chins. The damsels of this type in the more mainstream shōnen manga (targeting early teens or younger) are an exception, and you should draw them shorter, with a rounder physique.

   With my damsel in Figure 11-12, I keep everything tall and elongated. I draw cross hairs on her face slightly arced downward to show that she's looking down and away from the readers.

3. **Based upon the geometric shapes, add the curves and muscle structure and sketch her facial features.**

Figure 11-11:
Setting up
a more
elongated
wire figure
for my loyal
damsel.

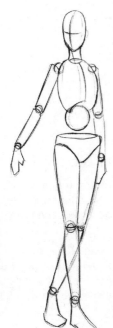

Figure 11-12:
Drawing the
slender
geometric
shape onto
the wire
frame
figure.

Never draw her muscular looking; her spirit is the source of her strength and helps her persevere over her captor's torture until she's finally rescued. You should, therefore, tone down her muscular definition. However, don't forget to add the curves to her body to show off her femininity as I do in my example in Figure 11-13. I lightly block in the facial features, placing the eyes, nose, and mouth. I also sketch in the shape of the hair.

Observe how I keep her shoulders squared and parallel to the floor. By adding the round curves to her body, the overall appearance should resemble an hourglass structure as shown in Figure 11-13.

Figure 11-13:
Adding the curves and definition over the geometric structure.

4. **Draw her clothing and refine her facial features.**

When drawing the clothing for this type of character, always think loose and flowing. The simpler the attire is, the purer she looks. The idea is that the more evil and sinister a character becomes, the more she wears heavy jewelry to match her darker costume.

I lightly draw the simple, austere robes that hang like a toga (as shown in Figure 11-14). For her footwear, I draw tattered bandages around her lower legs. Draw laces for her sandals. To preserve the image of a princess, I draw long gloves on both arms and a belt around her waist.

TIP

Draw the robes while thinking about the folds in loose drapery (see Chapter 6 for complete details on drawing folds). Think of the top and bottom of the robe as a large, soft cloth hung loosely over two bedposts as shown in Figure 11-14.

As you refine the features, draw them more realistically than the other damsels, who are much younger and potentially more emotionally unstable. I draw her eyes slightly sad by having her overall eye shape slightly triangular. I also accentuate the eyes by shading the eyelids. Be sure to keep the hair long (short hair may imply that the character is too old).

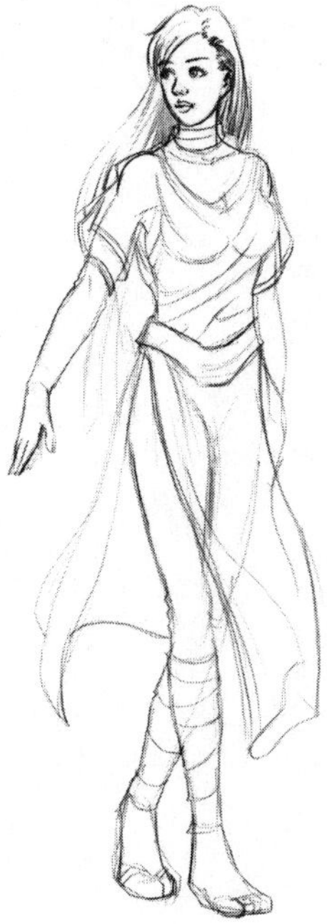

Figure 11-14: Sketching in the loose robes.

5. **Finalize the character's facial and clothing features and ornaments.**

   I finalize the features of my damsel by defining the hair shape and sharpening the contrast of her hair (you can do this by making your grays darker).

   Be sure to add simple jewelry to remind the readers that she's an important character despite the simple way she's dressed. In Figure 11-15, for example, I draw jewelry around the forehead, neck, and arms. A great place to add stones and gems is around the belt area. Simple geometric shapes work best. As you become more comfortable, you can experiment with more elaborate designs.

Figure 11-15:
Finalizing
the facial
features and
adding her
acces-
sories.

Chapter 12

Girl Power! Shōjo Manga

In This Chapter

▶ Becoming familiar with the history and evolution of shōjo manga

▶ Drawing classic shōjo manga features

▶ Discovering the simple shōjo manga style used today

Shōjo manga continues to evolve into a larger and more diverse genre since its early days of Osamu Tezuka's *Ribbon no Kishi*. Shōjo manga stories depict not only strong leading female characters, but also a range of topics from romance to the risqué topic of sexuality. As I mention in Chapter 1, women shōjo *manga-ka* (manga artists) throughout Japan and worldwide have increased as a result of this genre's rise in popularity. If you happen to browse through the manga section of your average bookstore in Japan, finding almost ¼ of the section devoted to shōjo manga is common.

In contrast to the shōnen manga, whose themes deal with humor and action adventure/fantasy, the object of a shōjo manga-ka is to relate to the psychological aspect of her readers and draw them into the character's world. For example, a classic shōjo manga story may focus on a story of romance where an orphan tries to win the heart of a prince. Another may focus on an erotic emotional tale between two men. The challenge is to find common ground with the reader's experience or emotional fantasy.

In this chapter, I illustrate some of the popular styles and effects widely used throughout shōjo manga.

Drawing Classic Shōjo Manga Faces and Hair

Classic shōjo manga-ka such as Mizuno Hideko and Nishitani Yoshinko pioneered the high school romance themed stories and incorporated the elaborate art deco/art nouveau background designs that many shōjo manga-ka still use today. Throughout the classic shōjo genre are characters who resemble the Victorian ideal. A manga-ka frequently uses ribbons, fancy curls in the hair, and big poofy dresses on young lead female characters to pump up the romance novel image. To get an idea of a classic shōjo scenario, watch the classic movie *Gone with the Wind*.

Blondes and brunettes are cool

If you're already a big manga or animé (short for Japanese animation) fan, chances are you've noticed that most of the characters, especially the female lead characters, are either blonde or brunette. The many theories behind this phenomenon include claims that the hair color varies to match the individual's personality, but I believe that you see these two hair colors because of the European influence. Specifically, I think classic Hollywood romance movies spurred this movement. In my opinion, the Japanese have a great deal of respect for Western image and culture.

Female and male shōjo faces

The eyes of a manga character are the gateway to his or her emotions. Observe the classic, big shōjo eyes in Figure 12-1a. The heavyset eyelashes and sketchy pupils with huge highlights hype up the emotional intensity of my main character. They look like they're about to burst out crying at any moment. Compare these eyes with the classic coldhearted eyes in Figure 12-1b. These eyes could belong to the cruel stepmother or stepsister who does everything possible to humiliate the main character. By thinning the eyes and eyelashes and reducing the pupils to circles without any décor, I draw out the coldhearted persona of the character.

Figure 12-1:
Comparing the shōjo manga eyes of the good versus the evil.

a   b

A shōjo manga-ka generally draws the male shōjo face more elongated to represent nobility and class. Likewise, the noses are long and tall. Although this may sound a bit odd, the eyes of the male, like the female, are heavily rendered (often with eyelashes to show their soft, gentle side).

To draw a shōjo manga head, start off with the head shape from Chapter 4. Run through these steps comparing the female and male side by side as you go:

1. **Loosely sketch the shape and placement of both eyes (as shown in Figure 12-2a and Figure 12-2b).**

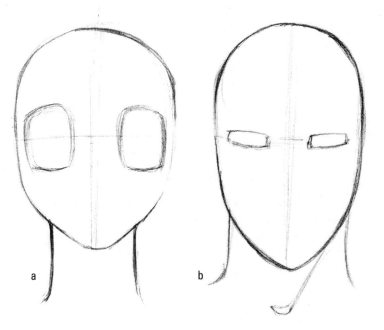

Figure 12-2: Blocking in the basic eye shapes for the female and male.

a   b

Note that I draw the eye shapes slightly larger than the normal manga eye — in fact, they're so large that you may not have enough room for the "one-eye-apart" rule that I talk about in Chapter 3. That's okay; keep all lines light for now.

2. **Draw the large circles for the eyeballs (as shown in Figure 12-3a and Figure 12-3b).**

I draw these circles very large as well. The key to getting the eyes to look aligned and cute is to cut off the top of the eyes where they meet the top eyelids and let the bottom of the eyes extend to touch the bottom lids.

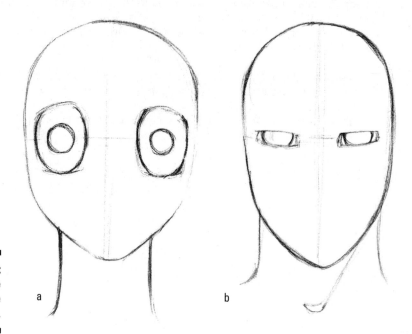

Figure 12-3:
Drawing the
super-large
eyeballs.

a   b

3. **Thicken the lines of the eyelashes on the top and bottom eyelids (as shown in Figure 12-4a and Figure 12-4b).**

4. **Darken the top of the eyeballs and finish with highlights and sparkles (as shown in Figure 12-5a and Figure 12-5b).**

   Various shōjo manga-ka use different highlight shapes, but the most common are squares and circles. I shade in the eyeballs first and then erase the shaded area to get the highlight shape I want. This technique is commonly referred to as "pulling out your highlights."

5. **Add the short, pointed nose as shown in Figure 12-6a and Figure 12-6b.**

   I draw a version of a simple nose from Chapter 4 without nostrils.

6. **To complete the face, add the thin mouth shape as shown in Figure 12-7a and Figure 12-7b.**

   I add the mouth shape slightly higher toward the nose to expose the elongated chin shape. I also darken the lips to show the character's sensuality.

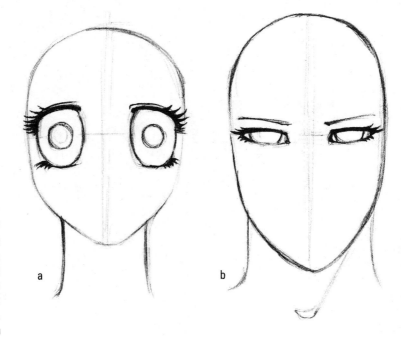

Figure 12-4:
Sketching in
the thick
bottom
and top
eyelashes.

a

b

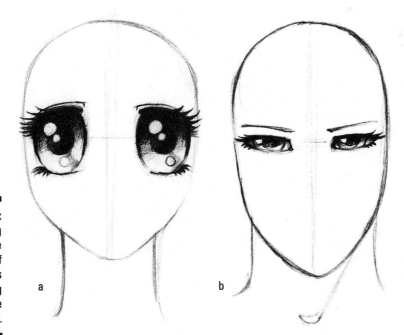

Figure 12-5:
Shading
in the
shadows of
the eyeballs
and "pulling
out" the
highlights.

a

b

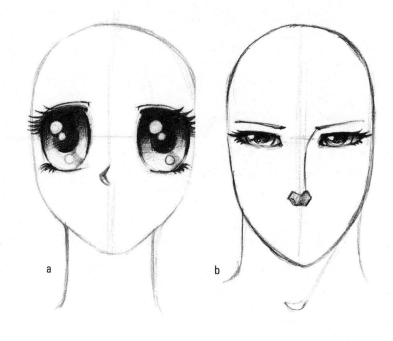

Figure 12-6:
Adding the
simplified,
elongated
nose, sans
nostrils.

a

b

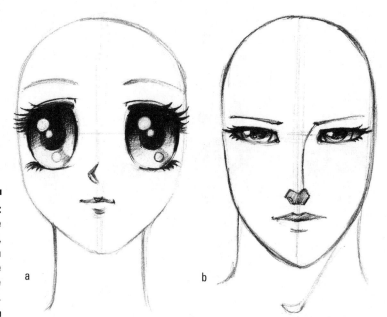

Figure 12-7:
Drawing the
darkened,
thin mouth
shape
closer to the
nose.

a

b

Traditional shōjo hair

Try your hand at drawing the shōjo manga classic female and male hairstyles. Characters (males in particular) in recent shōjo manga have adopted a more everyday, simple, *yaoi* (androgynous) hairstyle that you see in many shōnen manga stories. But the classic shōjo hairstyles are long and flowing with lots of curls. Many classic shōjo manga-ka add detailed highlights and strands to the hair to show smooth texture (just like those shampoo commercials). However, as I demonstrate in the last section of this chapter, current popular shōjo female characters wear their hair in ponytails, braids, pigtails, or sometimes just grown out and wild.

For the following steps, start off with the female and male heads from the previous section:

1. **Draw the bangs as round and as curly as possible without covering the eyes (as shown in Figure 12-8a and Figure 12-8b).**

   In my example, I draw the bangs as big shapes, as if they were large mustaches. I curl up the ends of the hair to make sure they don't obscure the character's vision. Unlike with the male yaoi hairstyle, a shōjo manga eye should be clear of any obstruction.

Figure 12-8: Drawing in the soft, round bangs on the shōjo manga head.

a

b

2. **Draw the hair behind the bangs long and flowing, as I do in Figure 12-9a and Figure 12-9b.**

   I keep both sides of the hair more or less symmetrical and curl the ends.

Figure 12-9:
Completing
the flowing
hair behind
the large
bangs.

a

b

3. **Complete the hair by shading and adding some lines to indicate highlights on the head and show specific hair strands (as shown in Figure 12-10a and Figure 12-10b).**

   In my example, I shade the areas except for the section of highlights to make the hair look shiny and glossy.

Today's shōjo hairstyles

As I mention in the previous section, current shōjo hairstyles don't necessarily follow the classic straight-and-simple shape. Although today's shōjo manga-ka still draws in the details of the hair, he breaks down the overall shape into smaller segments, which makes the hairstyle appear looser. Some current popular shōjo female characters have hairstyles that appear disheveled with strands of hair sticking out from the tangled body.

Figure 12-10:
Adding detail to the hair to complete the shōjo head.

a   b

In this section, I draw a couple of shōjo hairstyles that you're likely to see in today's popular shōjo manga. These styles are just the tip of the iceberg. If you want this style for your characters, I recommend picking up several shōjo issues at a comic book/manga convention or looking up popular titles on the Internet. As of the release of this book, www.shojobeat.com has a wide assortment of titles, and you can read previews of hot releases for free.

Shoulder-length shōjo hairstyle

The type of high school student who sports the shoulder-length hairstyle could be a bit absent-minded. Perhaps she always looks as if she just woke up 5 minutes ago. She tends to talk to herself a lot and is easily startled or disoriented.

Try your hand at drawing the shoulder-length shōjo hairstyle:

1. **Start with the basic female head shape, and lightly draw the overall "helmet" shape for the hair guideline (as shown in Figure 12-11a).**

2. **Draw in the sharp, pointed hair strands of her bangs (as shown in Figure 12-11b).**

   Starting from close to the top of her head, I draw long, pointed shapes that vary in width and length. Some of them curve to follow the contour of her forehead, while others go slightly crooked or straight (which gives her that disheveled look). The tips of the hair strands can pass over the guideline, but they shouldn't go as far as covering the character's eyes.

3. **Draw the sharp, pointed hair strands for the back of her hair (as shown in Figure 12-11c).**

   Don't draw them all going in the same direction. Like the pointed shapes for her bangs in Step 2, some of the shapes in the back of her hair should be different widths.

   The trick to making the hair look disheveled is mixing stray lines going along with the pointed hair shapes.

   For a finishing touch, I draw some stray lines outside the "helmet" guidelines. Don't forget to erase those guidelines after you're done with the hair.

Figure 12-11:
Drawing the contemporary shōjo shoulder-length hairstyle.

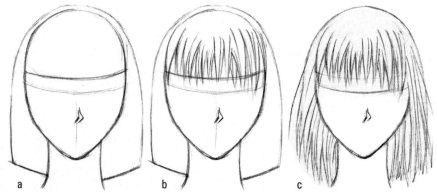

a   b   c

Long hairstyle

The archetype sporting the long hairstyle could be a type A personality who is her own worst critic. She's punctual and well organized, and she goes through emotional turmoil at the slightest failure.

Try your hand at drawing the long shōjo hairstyle:

1. **Start with the basic female head shape, and draw the diagonal parting hairline and the outside guideline down opposite sides of the head (as shown in Figure 12-12a).**

   Be careful not to draw the hairline too long (it shouldn't go past the forehead).

2. **Draw the inside hair shapes starting from the end of the parting hairline at the forehead (as shown in Figure 12-12b).**

   By completing this step, I complete the left and right hair shapes.

3. **Add a line to divide the right hair section to create the shape for the bangs that cover her forehead (as shown in Figure 12-12c).**

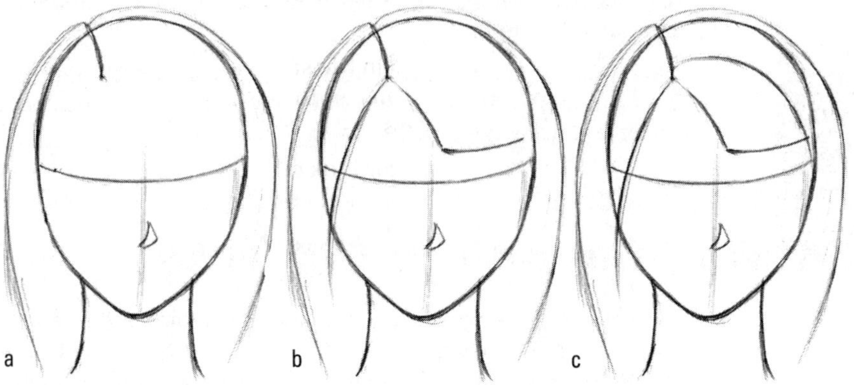

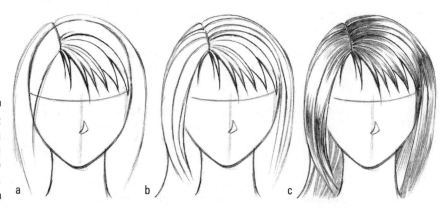

Figure 12-12:
Drawing the basic hair shapes for the long shōjo hairstyle.

a   b   c

4. **Define the bangs of the hair (as shown in Figure 12-13a).**

   Starting from the hairline, draw the pointed hair shapes. I draw the shapes in front thinner and shorter than the ones toward the top of the bangs.

5. **Define the left and right hair shapes (as shown in Figure 12-13b).**

   Starting from the front of the parting line, draw a series of lines to build up the dimension of her hair.

   The key to making the overall hair shape dimensional is decreasing the distance between the lines as they recede from the front of the face and go toward the back of the head.

6. **Shade in the value (*value* just means filling in the hair with a darker tone to create depth or contrast) to complete the long shōjo hair (as shown in Figure 12-13c).**

Figure 12-13:
Completing the long shōjo hairstyle.

a   b   c

The shading creates texture as well as contrast for the highlights in the overall hair shape.

I find it easier to start drawing my value from the opposite sides of each hair shape. Turning the page sideways sometimes is easier on the wrist when you draw the shading lines.

Drawing the Rest of the Body

In this section, I show you how to find a body to match the female and male shōjo heads. A shōjo manga-ka usually draws female characters wearing nice dresses on the covers of shōjo manga. Similarly, most male shōjo characters dress nicely too, not wearing anything that doesn't have a collar.

When drawing formalwear, I constantly use the Internet to gather references. I browse through fashion Web sites and print images that I like. Many Web sites post multiple angles of the models wearing the clothes I'm interested in drawing. You may need to spend more time searching for dresses. Try adding timeframe-specific descriptions in you search browser (such as "Victorian dresses," or "18th century gowns").

Dressing up the shōjo female

Looking through fashion catalogues is a good way to find different ideas for dresses. If your characters are younger, look at various types of sailor outfits and school uniforms. Follow these steps to draw a female shōjo character:

1. **Draw the wire frame figure.**

   Typically, a female shōjo character measures around 6 to 7 heads tall with slender proportions, and she assumes a graceful pose (almost as if she's acting onstage). Set the shoulders narrow, around 1½ heads wide.

   In my example in Figure 12-14, I pose my figure with one arm up and tilt her head up as she admires the birds flying in the sky.

2. **Fit the geometric shapes onto the wire frame figure.**

   Classic shōjo female figures should be slender (especially at the waist). Their overall structure shouldn't overshadow the head's shape or size.

   In addition to making my geometric shape narrow in Figure 12-15, I make sure that the hand doesn't get too much in the way of her face.

3. **Based upon the geometric shapes, add the curves and muscle structure and block in her facial features and hair.**

Figure 12-14:
Posing the wire frame figure for a female shōjo character.

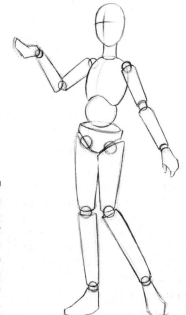

Figure 12-15:
Fitting the slender geometric shape onto the wire frame figure.

In keeping with the narrow, elongated geometric shapes, the female shōjo form should be subtle yet rounded. Don't draw any sharp angles or defined muscles. A muscular shōjo lead character is a major no-no. Although drawing the breasts and hips is fine, keep them moderate.

In Figure 12-16, I take a little liberty and exaggerate the length and slenderness of the neck, arms, and legs. Even though the joints are bent, they don't have any sharp angles.

Take this moment to loosely sketch in her hair shape and facial features.

Figure 12-16:
Adding the curves and definition over the geometric structure.

4. **Sketch her shōjo dress and refine her facial features.**

The most popular classic choices are high school uniforms, simple dresses, kimonos, and classic Victorian dresses. Recent shōjo manga characters in popular titles have been wearing more casual everyday outfits (cute overalls, T-shirts with adorable icons or phrases, tight designer jeans, and so on). The important thing is to make sure that the overall clothing shapes are simple and complement the figure of the character. Your goal is for readers to either emotionally relate to or want to be your character.

To be consistent with my classic shōjo type, I go for the Victorian dress in Figure 12-17. I sketch the basic dress shapes, which are triangular. I also lightly draw some of the ribbons and frilly designs.

I define the facial features based on my female shōjo face earlier in this chapter. Don't forget the eyelashes to accentuate the eyes!

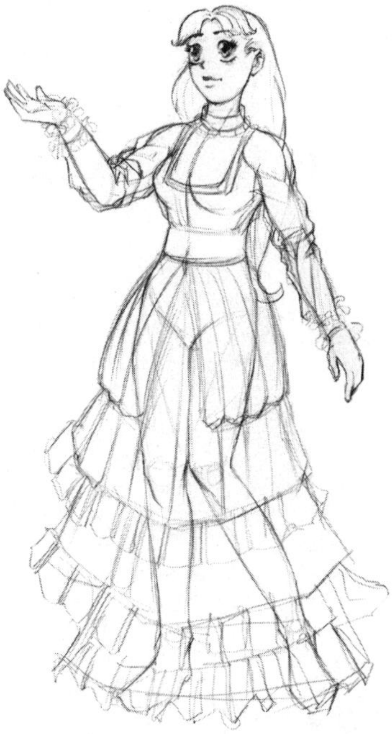

Figure 12-17: Drawing the basic dress shapes and refining the facial features.

5. **Tighten up the face and add details to your character's clothing.**

   Start nailing down what kind of jewelry and other accessories you want your character to be wearing. Ribbons have always been a shōjo favorite for the classic or younger characters. Earrings are also a must.

   TIP

   If you're a female who's out of ideas, think about what kind of cute or trendy items you want. Perhaps go through your fashion magazines to select the items that are the focus of the current buzz. If you're drawing characters for current popular shōjo manga, you want to look at what kinds of clothes your female friends wear on a casual day. If you see them wearing something you like, have them pose for a photo using your digital camera or even the camera on your cell phone.

   In Figure 12-18, I complete my classic shōjo princess's dress with all the frills and thrills. In addition to her earrings, I place a ribbon behind her head. Finally, I add in the details and highlights in her hair. I want to make sure she's the focus of all her suitors' attention when she steps onto that ballroom floor!

Figure 12-18:
Finalizing
my shōjo
lead
character.

Dressing up the shōjo male

Males in shōjo manga don't usually wear overtly fancy clothing. For the lack of a better analogy, think of the men as the parsley to the main steak of the female character. However, that doesn't mean that the male characters are expendable. They must be presented as tall, handsome, independent, caring, and as most often is the case in recent popular shōjo titles, androgynous. Check out the following steps to draw this character:

1. **Draw the wire frame figure for the classic male shōjo character.**

   Typically, classic male shōjo characters are 7 to 8 heads tall with fairly wide proportions. Make the shoulders broad, around 2½ to 3 heads wide. Although the typical age ranges from mid-20s to mid-30s, recent popular shōjo titles also include younger androgynous male characters in their late teens to mid-20s. These characters have proportions closer to their female counterparts.

   In Figure 12-19, I set my classic shōjo male character at 7½ heads tall, assuming a straight-up posture with one hand in his jacket pocket and a bouquet of roses in the other hand. I keep my pose narrow for this character.

Figure 12-19:
Setting up the wire frame figure for my shōjo male character.

2. **Fit the geometric shapes onto the wire frame figure.**

   Classic shōjo male figures should be slender. None of the shapes (especially the hips) should be wider than the shoulders.

   In Figure 12-20, I make the geometric shapes slender and slightly elongated while keeping the shoulders wide and the hips flat.

3. **Add curves and muscle structure and lightly block in the hair and facial features.**

   Like the shōjo female, keep the shapes for the male narrow and elongated. The male shōjo form should be subtle and not overly built or pumped up. A muscular shōjo male character is a major no-no, although the chest muscles *(pectorals)* are visible when he isn't wearing a shirt.

   In Figure 12-21, I make the neck, arms, and legs slim, but not as skinny as the female shōjo character's. The muscles should be slightly more defined than the female shōjo's as well.

   Take this moment to loosely block in the facial features and the shape of his hair.

Figure 12-20:
Filling in the
character's
shape with
long, narrow
geometric
shapes.

Figure 12-21:
Further
defining the
shōjo male
character
and loosely
blocking in
the facial
features.

4. **Draw the character's clothes, based on how you think he should be dressed, and add the detail to the head.**

As I mention at the opening of this section on drawing the shōjo male character, you don't have as many flamboyant fashion statements to choose from as you do with the female counterpart. The most popular classic choices are tuxedos, formal suits, and military uniforms. Artists have recently drawn shōjo male characters wearing more casual every-day outfits (sunglasses, tank tops, loose baggy jeans, and designer shirts). Unless you're dressing the male character ostentatiously for a particular purpose, tone down his attire to avoid stealing the lead female character's thunder.

I go for the classic coat and tie in Figure 12-22. Watch how I keep the shapes of his suit straight and angular (especially at his shoulders).

Draw the detail of his face using the male shōjo head from earlier in this chapter.

Just to show he has class, I draw him holding a bouquet of flowers for the lucky girl.

Figure 12-22:
Drawing in
the suit
shapes and
tightening
up the head.

5. **Add finishing touches to the head, and add the details to your character's clothing.**

   Even for the males, you should include some definition to the upper eyelids. Don't underestimate the simplicity of the attire. Make sure you get a proper reference for what a suit or tuxedo looks like.

   TIP

   Recent popular shōjo titles may have males wearing earrings to match their casual attire. If you go with the more contemporary shōjo manga style, build a photo reference of your friends wearing casual clothing. However, don't go overboard with the jewelry. If you choose to go with T-shirts and tank tops, solidify the drawing of the torso before fitting on the clothing. Remember to keep the clothing articles loose!

   In Figure 12-23, I complete my classic shōjo suit. For reference, I look at a men's fashion magazine just to make sure the collar and tie shapes are accurate. He needs to look confident enough to provide support and care to the shōjo princess!

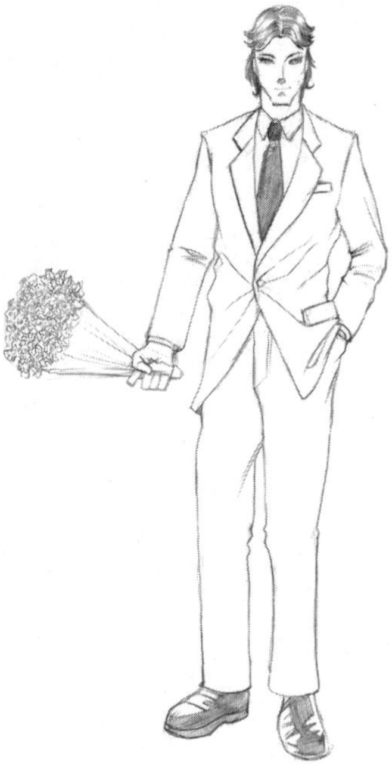

Figure 12-23: Finalizing my shōjo male character.

Art Nouveau Backgrounds in Shōjo Manga

To add to the emotional drama of a story, a shōjo manga-ka often uses a series of patterns and designs in the background, mimicking the *art nouveau* (a period that places emphasis on decorative style through ornamentation) style. The patterns a manga-ka uses range from repeating, abstract, geometric shapes (such as circles and stars) to more organic objects (such as flowers and vines). Often, a shōjo manga-ka keeps the backgrounds to a minimum — at times, the background is even blank. Instead, she adds a series of decorative patterns mimicking one another in the background or surrounding the character to help establish the mood and connect with the readers.

In this section I demonstrate several effects of shōjo backgrounds. For this exercise, you need a completed upper body of a shōjo character in a cute pose (for example, she could be holding her hands clasped in front of her chest). Then follow these steps:

1. **Beginning in the lower-right corner, draw a simple star (as shown in Figure 12-24).**

Figure 12-24: Starting the background stars.

2. **Repeat the stars at different sizes, continuing from right to left (as shown in Figure 12-25).**

   The key is to keep varying the sizes and angles of the shapes. Go back to erase or add shapes so that the overall composition is balanced.

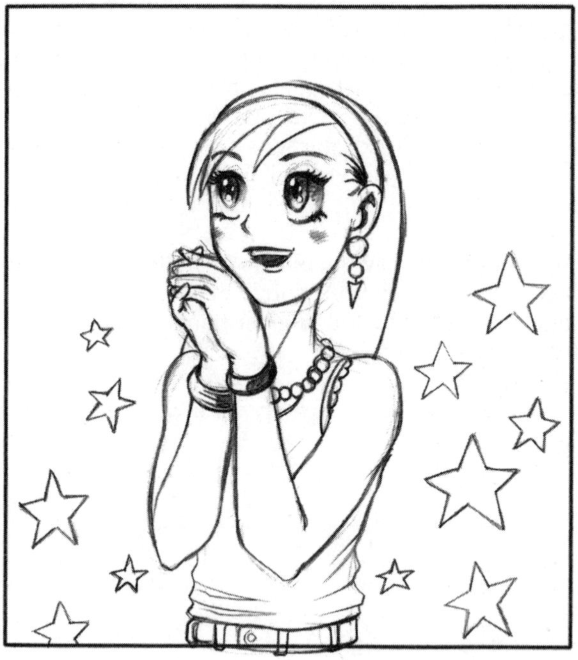

Figure 12-25: Finalizing my shōjo background.

You can replace the stars with overlapping circles. If you're up for a challenge, substitute flowers, like I do in Figure 12-26 (roses tend to be the most popular).

TIP

Ultimately, you want to select patterns and shapes that reflect the mood of either the story or the character. Be careful not to overcrowd the space around your character. She needs some empty space to breathe.

Figure 12-26:
Using other
shapes for
your shōjo
background.

Part IV
Time to Go Hi-Tech

The 5th Wave By Rich Tennant

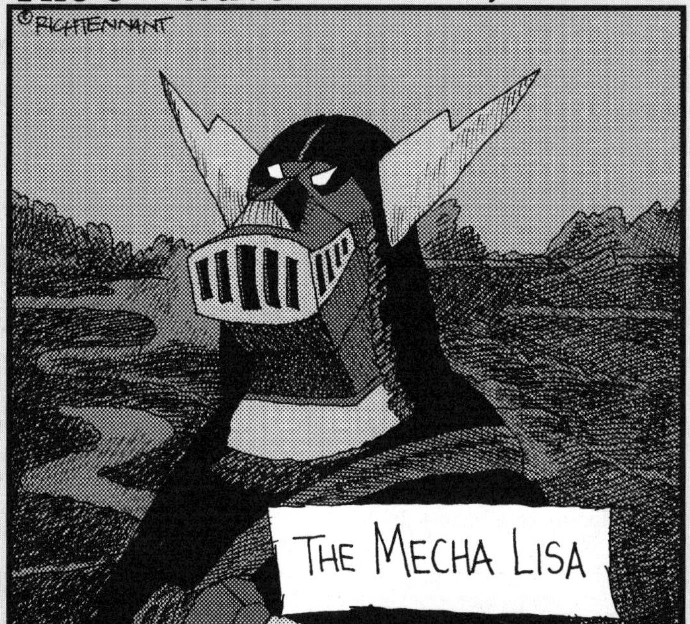
©RICHTENNANT
THE MECHA LISA

In this part . . .

Get your toolboxes out — you're going to be engaging in some awesome hi-tech projects. For those of you who are already animé and manga fans, you know what I'm talking about when I say the word *mecha*. Actually short for "mechanical," mecha is a genre name that covers everything from giant robots to sophisticated electronic devices. It also includes futuristic vehicles and types of aircraft (combat and civilian).

In this part, I demonstrate how to draw various kinds of mecha devices and weaponry ranging from the big and fearsome to the small and cute.

Overall, drawing mecha is a fun experience. However, don't be frustrated or discouraged when you don't get instant results. Like drawing the manga figure, you should take time to sit down and play around, doodling and combining different types of shapes. The tips and guides I provide are based on realism, but they're ultimately designed to build up your confidence for exploring and creating your own mecha-based devices.

Chapter 13

Designing Mechas

In This Chapter

- Becoming familiar with mechas and their distinguished roles of service
- Using basic geometric shapes to draw cute mechas
- Designing lightweight and heavyweight mechas

Mecha refers to sophisticated hi-tech robots (some of which are large enough to be piloted) or piloted vehicles that commonly appear in *shōnen manga* (comics for teenage boys) and *animé* (Japanese animation). Drawing and illustrating mecha have generated hype and opened up a huge, separate market in the manga/animé market.

Some of these mechas are as tall as or smaller than a human, but most mechas are giant humanoid machines that humans actually get in and pilot. The design and the types of roles mechas perform are more specific than they were in the early days of the original, popular *Gundam* series, more than 30 years ago. Some roles are geared toward combat while others are better suited for construction.

In addition to establishing a purpose for your mecha, think about the relationship the character has with the mecha. When readers see your mecha, they should be able to associate it with your main character.

In this chapter, I discuss several kinds of machinery and show you how to draw them.

WARNING!

If you're drawing manga or geometric shapes for the first time, please refer to Chapters 4 and 5 before tackling the illustrations in this chapter.

Creating Simple and Cute Mechas

Simple and cute mechas serve as either companions or pets. In almost all cases, these types are either created by their owners and move independently or they operate by remote control. The simpler, independent mechas don't play a role in any fighting or heavy-duty lifting — they just look cute and evoke that "awww" sentiment in your readers. The more sophisticated mechas, on the other hand, help save the day in unexpected ways that at first may appear to be trivial.

Using geometric shapes (spheres, cubes, cylinders, and cones) makes drawing simple mecha fun. Overall, even a simple mecha has some degree of human resemblance. Keep in mind, though, that you don't always need limbs and full features in order to make a mecha that has personality or that can win over the reader's affection. In this section, I select several mechas that start from a single geometric structure.

Drawing a single-shape body

In this section, I show you how to draw a mecha with a single geometric shape as its main body structure. Follow these steps to create a simple mecha based upon a single shape:

1. **Start at the center of your paper with a simple geometric shape (cube, sphere, cylinder, or cone) as shown in Figure 13-1; draw your shape large enough that you can add the smaller details or embellishments in the following steps.**

   In my example, I use my character Java's little spherical companion mecha called the Braid Maid. Her role is to make sure Java's hair (as well as the rest of her hygiene) is shipshape (because Java is kind of a big slob). This sphere is all I need to start the basic body shape.

2. **Add simple facial features as shown in Figure 13-2.**

   In keeping with the simplicity theme, you don't have to draw all the features (eyes, nose, ears, and mouth).

   As I show in my example with Java's Braid Maid, I don't even include the other eye. She's basically a Cyclopean droid. I use a small hatch to represent her mouth, which opens to reveal a Taser gun that the Braid Maid uses to wake Java up in the morning.

Figure 13-1:
Starting off
my simple
mecha with
a cylinder.

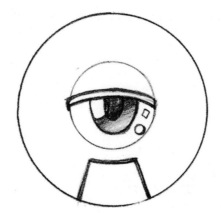

Figure 13-2:
Drawing the mecha's simplified features.

3. Draw the simplified limbs as shown in Figure 13-3.

Limbs can include a representation of an arm, leg, or even tail. Think about how these shapes move in relation to the body. Do they extend out from the body, or are they left exposed the entire time? How will they bend or twist (if they even have joints to begin with)? Again, avoid the misconception that you need to draw the limbs of these types of mechas with complicated parts or shapes.

I use popular round lids as hatch doors on both sides for the arms. The idea is that the mecha carries an assortment of hair braids in her body, and each time the arms come out, she carries a brand-new braid in her claws.

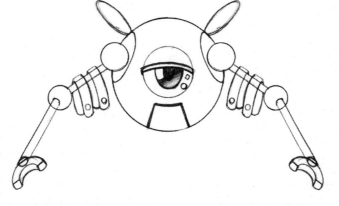

Figure 13-3:
Adding the hatch as well as the arms.

4. Finalize the small droid with your own cosmetic touches as shown in Figure 13-4.

You can add a serial or model number or design stripes that are painted onto the body. Think about what kind of accessories you can add that reflect the mecha's role or function. I shade the spherical body and darken the inside where the arm joints meet the body to give the image more realism and dimension. I paint mascara over her single eyelid as a joke fashion statement.

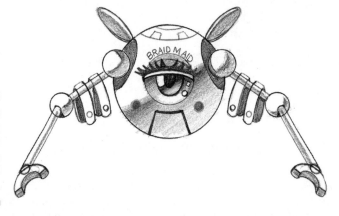

Figure 13-4:
Completing my Braid Maid with shading and makeup.

Mixing it up with a multishaped body

By adding additional simple shapes together, you give your mecha more character by increasing its humanoid functions. Follow these steps to create a simple mecha based upon multiple shapes:

1. **Draw a shape for the head as shown in Figure 13-5.**

   Because the head is usually the largest part of the body, it's a good place to start. This way, you have a better assessment of how large you should make the body. Although you can stick to the basic sphere, cylinder, cube, or cone, don't shy away from modifying the shapes by skewing or slicing off partial segments.

   In my example, I start off with a slightly squashed sphere in Figure 13-5a. Think of making this shape by imagining ground beef intended for a large meatball and squishing it to form a burger patty. In Figure 13-5b, I take my burger patty shape and slice it in half. The sliced off portion is the front of my mecha's face. For the eyes, I plunk down two large spheres on the front (like adding coals to a snowman).

2. **Draw a cylinder or cube for the neck as shown in Figure 13-6.**

   Use your own judgment to determine the width and length of the neck, but keep the overall width narrower than the width of the head.

   Because the head is rather simple and funny looking, I use a short and narrow shape for my cylindrical neck.

Figure 13-5:
Creating my
mecha's
head by
slicing a
squashed
sphere in
half.

a   b

Figure 13-6:
Giving the
head a neck
to lean on.

3. Give your mecha a torso as shown in Figure 13-7.

   If you feel confident drawing your basic geometric shapes, begin to experiment by modifying them. You can make one side of a cube smaller than the opposite side, or take half a sphere and slice the front off to make room for a control panel.

   I use my first suggestion by taking the top side of the cube and making it smaller.

4. Draw the lower portion of the mecha (see Figure 13-7).

   In this step, think about how this thing transports itself. Does it fly, walk, or roll? If it flies, consider adding a jet pack on its back. If it walks, you need to design some legs. To make it roll, make some wheels. Whatever you decide to do, keep it simple.

   In my example, I sketch in the outside shape for a caterpillar mechanism (similar to the ones found on a tank).

5. Tighten up the shapes and draw the arms, hands, and accessories.

   In Figure 13-8, I draw the wheels for the caterpillar mechanism as well as the track lines. I create the arms by using spheres for the shoulder and elbow joints and tube cylinders for the arms. I simplify the hands by drawing them as clamps. In addition, I add a jet pack on the back of the mecha so that it can fly. I draw my jet pack with a flat cube and add two small cylinders on the bottom as thrusters.

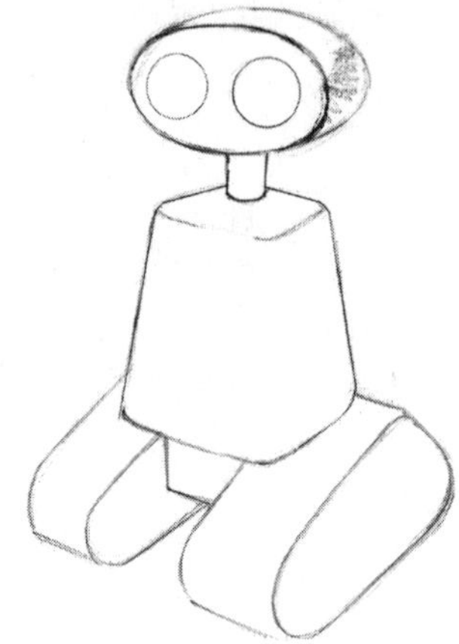

Figure 13-7: Adding your mecha's body.

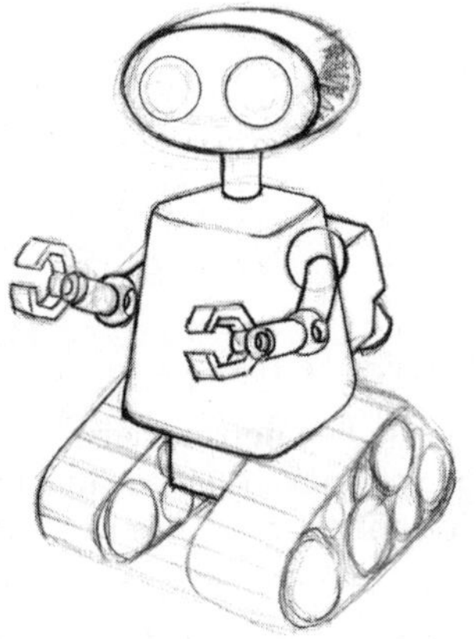

Figure 13-8: Drawing the bottom, which transports your mecha.

6. **Finalize your mecha by adding the cosmetic designs and details.**

   A lot of mecha *manga-ka* (or manga artists) add in pipes, model numbers, and decorations (either painted on or physically attached). Take a look at some of the popular *Gundam* mecha for inspiration. Although the original series is over, its impact in the mecha world continues to thrive in spin-offs where more complicated and sophisticated mechas are brought into the spotlight.

   TIP

   For a comprehensive listing of the *Gundam* mechas, visit the Web site `www.gundam.jp`. Spend time at manga/animé conventions to pick up popular manga and animé DVDs, which feature popular mechas. I also recommend looking at *Macross* (translated as *Robotech* in the United States), *Evangelion, Patlabor, L. Gaim, Appleseed,* and *Bubblegum Crisis.*

   To finish off my mecha, I add some raccoon eyes as well as a spot mark for his nose (see Figure 13-9). Just for giggles, I add a mechanical raccoon tail.

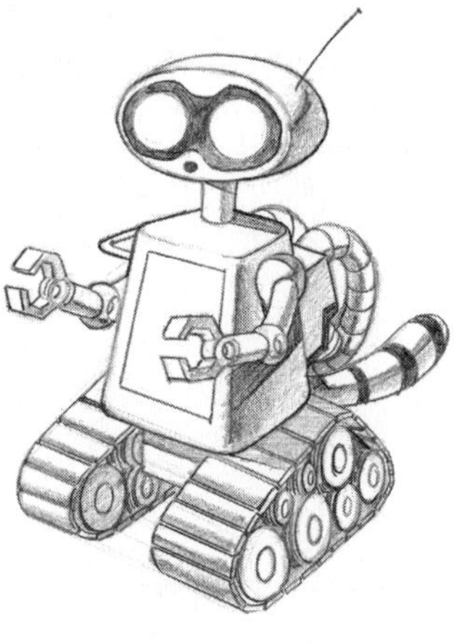

Figure 13-9: Drawing the final details and design marks on your mecha.

Drawing Pilot-Operated Mechas

In this section, I show you mechas that are large enough to be piloted by humans from the inside. Although most of them are designed for combat, some function as transportation or construction mechas. Depending on the rank or significance of the character who operates them, the mecha takes on a unique and sophisticated appearance. Usually the pilot seats him or herself at the center of the mecha's torso. Unlike the simpler mechas in the previous sections, combat mechas are more humanlike in proportion and overall look. If you haven't drawn the human figure, refer to Chapter 5. In this section, I demonstrate how to draw two types of combat mecha: the lightweights and the heavyweights.

It's all about the shapes

Before drawing the entire mecha figure, explore and get used to drawing different types of common mecha body parts and armor shapes. These parts and shapes include shoulder pads, breastplates, forearm guards, waist protectors, shinguards, and feet. In Figure 13-10, I draw some basic shapes.

WARNING!

For starters, avoid drawing the shapes from a three-dimensional angle (¾ angle). Although the ¾ angle gives a more realistic and dimensional look, it can be quite confusing and hard to grasp at first. For now, keep all the angles straight on (from the front or from the side). As you become more comfortable drawing the shapes, you can begin drawing the shapes from other dimensional angles.

Now is a good time to introduce the "X" and "A" shapes you see in mecha poses. As I show in Figure 13-11, regardless of what types of mecha you plan to draw, they should all assume a default position in the form of an "X" or an "A."

In Figure 13-11a (mecha with accessories) and Figure 13-11b (mecha without its accessories), the "X" and "A" shapes create strong, stable poses. Avoid deviating from this default pose and making the legs and arms too close to each other or the body. You need plenty of space between the body parts for the accessories to fit.

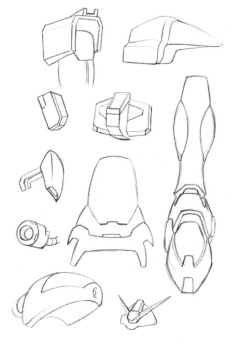

Figure 13-10:
Become familiar with drawing common mecha shapes.

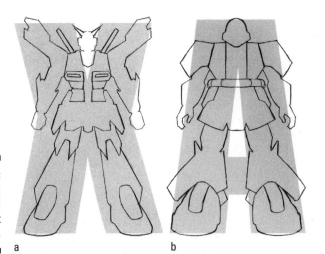

Figure 13-11:
Comparing the "X" and "A" default stances.

a   b

Enter the lightweights

The lightweight mechas excel in speed, precision, and sleek looks. In general, leaner ones are usually associated with the lead characters on the good side. While the lead character has a more slender and faster mecha that's usually white, his sidekick generally operates a darker and slightly bulkier mecha (to emphasize that he plays the backup role). In this section, I use the same wire frame figure that I use to draw my human characters to start off my mecha. I show you how to draw the mecha for the lead character, and then I show you how to draw the slightly heavier mecha for the sidekick.

Lead character mecha

Follow these steps to draw a lightweight mecha for your lead character:

1. **Pose your wire frame figure in an "X" position as shown in Figure 13-12.**

   Over the course of mecha evolution, proportions have grown. Although the average varies, the lightweight mecha is approximately between 8½ and 10 heads tall. Compared to older models, current popular models have wider shoulders — typically 3 to 4 heads wide (5 to 6 if you factor in the shoulder pads).

   I set my lightweight combat mecha at 9 heads tall.

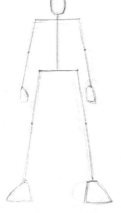

Figure 13-12: Setting my lightweight mecha's wire frame figure.

2. **Sketch the basic geometric shapes based on the wire frame figure (as shown in Figure 13-13).**

   Keep the pencil marks light and loose because you'll later go over them to refine the shapes. Start thinking about where you want to place the specific armor, air vents (where hot air is released to cool off the mecha), or other designs.

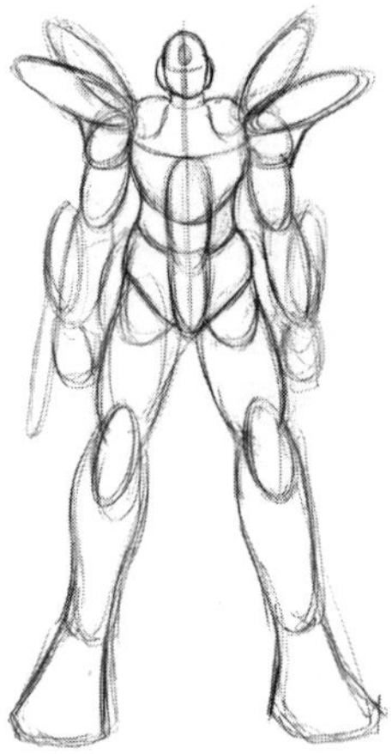

Figure 13-13: Adding loose shapes over the wire frame figure.

3. **Rough in the specific shapes for the armor over the geometric shapes (as shown in Figure 13-14).**

   Use some of the shapes that you find interesting in Figure 13-10. Don't draw the shapes too wide (remember, you're drawing a lightweight mecha). Avoid drawing the thick armor — you want to save the bulkier stuff for the heavier mecha models.

   With my mecha, I vary the shapes. I make some shapes (such as the biceps and lower legs) rounder and keep the forearm and torso shapes fairly square. I also block in the basic head shape and features.

4. **Tighten up the shapes as shown in Figure 13-15.**

   Determine which shapes you want to be rounder as well as which shapes you want to be more angular and pointed. As a general rule of thumb, rounder edges imply sleekness and elegance as opposed to angular edges, which suggest sturdiness and aggressiveness. You're not right or wrong in making either decision — leave it to your personal taste.

   In my mecha, I add a bit more angular edges. At certain sections, such as the hip protectors and sides of the legs, I let the edges come to a fine, sharp point. Note how I draw the bottom section of the legs narrow to show the slenderness.

5. **Draw the details, such as antennas, arm shields, or pipes (see Figure 13-16).**

   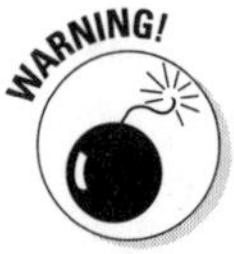
   WARNING!

   Don't overburden the mecha with too much bling. Make sure you keep the midsection between the upper torso and the hips slender. Popular places to add extra designs and small parts include the front of the torso, the back (improvise the rucksack), the forearms, and the shoulders.

Figure 13-14:
Lightly drawing the armor and other specific shapes over the geometric form.

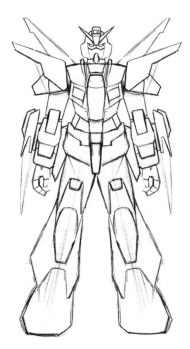

Figure 13-15:
Tightening and defining the edges of the mecha.

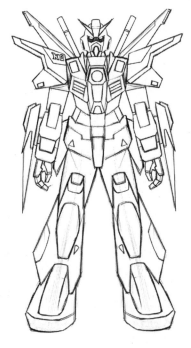

Figure 13-16:
Finishing
off the
mecha with
details and
decoration.

Be mindful of physics when drawing your mecha. If you decide to add heavier items, such as thrusters, make sure you place them where there's enough mass so that the items don't look like they're going to break off.

Based on the "X" shape I sketched in Step 1, I draw large radar equipment and two *beam sabers* (swords) protruding behind the mecha's back from the rucksack. In addition, I add some decoration marks, such as the model number on its right shoulder.

Sidekick character mecha

Follow these steps to draw the supporting backup mecha for the sidekick character:

1. Pose your wire frame figure in an "A" position as shown in Figure 13-17.

The average proportions of backup mecha have grown to approximately 8½ to 10 heads tall in recent years. Compared to older models, current popular models have wider shoulders that come in at 3 to 4 heads wide (5 to 6 if you factor in the shoulder pads). You should draw the width of the shoulders wider than the lead character's mecha because the overall shapes are thicker.

I set my sidekick combat mecha at 9 heads tall.

Figure 13-17:
Setting my
sidekick
mecha at 9
heads tall.

2. **Sketch the basic geometric shapes based on the wire frame figure (as shown in Figure 13-18).**

   Keep the pencil marks light and loose, thinking about where you want to place specific armor, air vents, or other designs.

Figure 13-18:
Beginning to
fill in the
mecha's
shape.

3. **Rough in the specific shapes for the armor over the geometric shapes (as shown in Figure 13-19).**

   Check out Figure 13-10 to get some interesting shape ideas. When creating these shapes, you want to be sure they reflect the durability, rigidity, and strength that this mecha needs to back up the lead character. Shapes can be wider and without the curves that the lighter weight mecha has.

With my mecha, I keep most of the shapes except the biceps square. I also block in the basic head shape and features. I add angular edges, unlike the straight, plain shapes I use on the mecha in the previous section. I block in a pair of large cannons (one larger for long-distance targeting). On the left side, I sketch in a radar device.

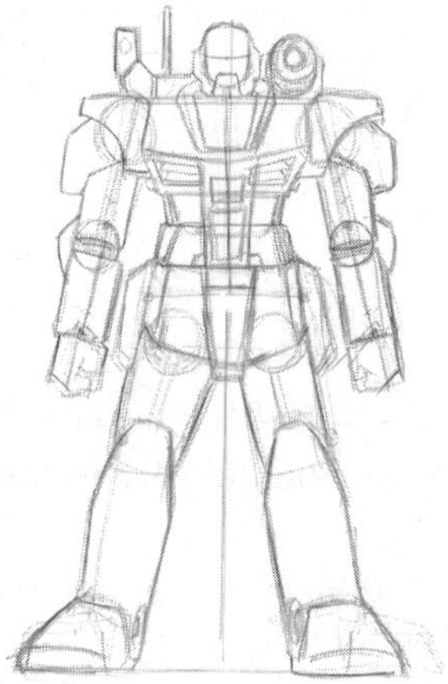

Figure 13-19: The backup mecha's strength helps the lead character.

4. **Tighten up the shapes as shown in Figure 13-20.**

   I clean up the lines. Because this mecha needs extra armor to withstand enemy fire, I also sketch thicker shoulder armor for the sides of the hips. I imagine that this mecha is fairly heavy, so I add some extra thrusters to help it move around.

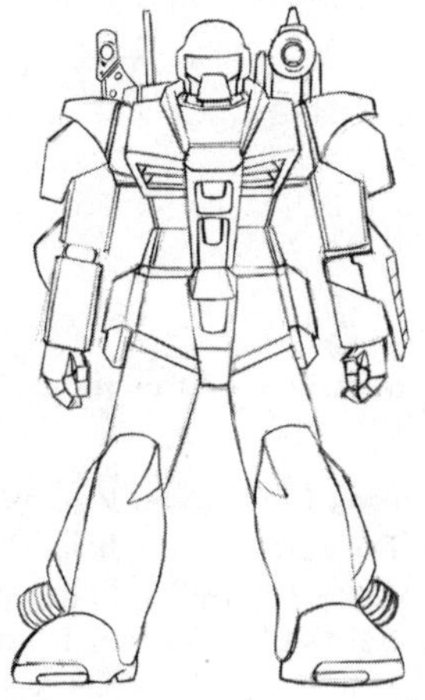

Figure 13-20: Adding extra armor and cannons to my mecha.

Here come the heavyweights

In this section, I demonstrate how to draw the heavier mecha that the antagonists or heavy-duty laborers (such as construction and transportation workers) usually use. The combat heavyweights typically have extra-thick armor and gear and usually don't fly under earth's gravity. But in space, depending upon the pilot, the combat mechas have enough boosters and power to make flying and maneuvering easy enough to take on an entire fleet. In contrast, the noncombat heavyweight mechas have wide features with solid construction, but they don't necessarily look human.

Lead villain mecha

Although the type of mecha that lead villains use isn't as graceful as the light-weight mecha, it makes up for everything with power. Most of these mechas are equipped with large bazookas or cannon weaponry that has enough kick to destroy an entire cruiser with a single blast.

Follow these steps to draw the villain's heavyweight mecha:

1. **Pose your wire frame figure in an "X" position as shown in Figure 13-21.**

   Note that because the armor adds so much bulk to this mecha's build, the approximate proportions stand between 8 and 13 heads tall. Draw the width of the shoulders wider than the lightweight mecha because the overall shapes are thicker. The shoulders also extend wider, to around 4 heads wide.

   I set my heavyweight combat mecha at 8½ heads tall.

2. **Sketch the basic geometric shapes based on the wire frame figure (as shown in Figure 13-22).**

   Keep the pencil marks light and loose, and think about where you want specific details in the overall design.

   Regardless of its bulk, don't draw the waistline, arms, and upper legs too thick. You can make the torso, hips, lower legs, and shoulders wider. Remember, this thing is still pretty darn fast in combat and must be able to twist and turn fast enough to engage its enemies.

   I exaggerate the torso of my mecha by omitting the neck shape. This technique gives the impression that this thing has armor that's at least twice as thick as the lightweight mecha's.

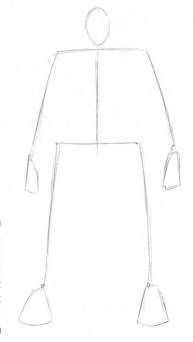

Figure 13-21:
The base
for my
heavyweight
combat
mecha.

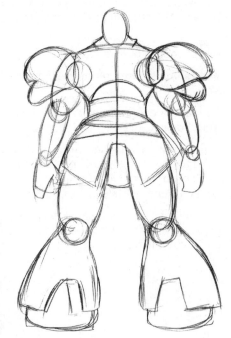

Figure 13-22:
Adding
the basic
shapes that
will become
thick armor.

3. **Rough in the specific shapes for the armor over the geometric shapes (as shown in Figure 13-23).**

   When creating these shapes, you want to be sure that they reflect the durability, rigidity, and strength of the combat mecha.

   I give my mecha plenty of armor to protect the shoulders, waist, and legs. I avoid adding the thick armor at the waist and joints where he needs to move.

4. **Tighten up the shapes as shown in Figure 13-24.**

   Determine which shapes you want to be rounder and which shapes you want to be more angular and pointed. To counterbalance the bulk of the armor, don't draw too many straight edges and lines. Otherwise, your mecha is going to look like a brick! Instead, consider adding curves to the overall structure.

   I block in a large blaster on the side of each forearm. To give this mecha a menacing appearance, I draw some spikes on both shoulders that it can use to ram into the enemy. Similar to the sidekick's mecha, this one needs extra boosters to move around quickly.

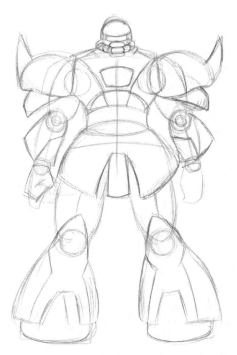

Figure 13-23: Lightly drawing the armor to protect the shoulders, waist, and legs.

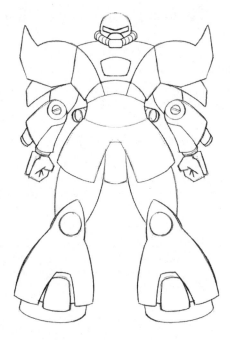

Figure 13-24:
Defining the
edges of the
mecha with
more curves
than straight
lines.

5. Draw the details, as shown in Figure 13-25.

I draw in the beam sabers behind the mecha's back. My evil mecha has simplified features for the head. Just for kicks, I give it that classic *single eye camera* (a single lens mounted at the front of the head that slides left to right for vision and target acquisition). For the final touch, I draw decorative arrow symbols around the shoulders, torso, and legs.

Construction mecha

Unlike the previous heavyweight mecha, the construction mecha is more of a giant tool. Its primary function is limited to lifting and transporting heavy objects from point A to point B.

Follow these steps to draw the villain's heavyweight mecha:

1. Pose your wire frame figure as shown in Figure 13-26.

The lower legs should be the largest part of the measurement. To keep the mecha from toppling over, the height proportions should be considerably shorter than the other mechas in this chapter; the construction mecha is approximately 5 to 7 heads tall. Draw the shoulders wide to give it strong balance and reach. Shoulders also extend around 5 to 10 heads wide.

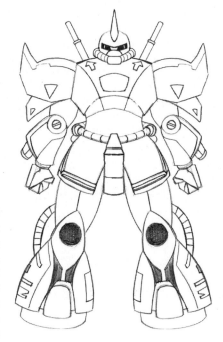

Figure 13-25:
Giving the
evil mecha
what he
deserves:
more
details.

Because this kind of mecha isn't as humanlike as the lead villain mecha,
the "X" and "A" shapes don't apply.

I set my heavyweight construction mecha to 7 heads tall.

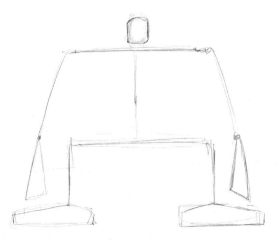

Figure 13-26:
Setting my
heavyweight
mecha to 7
heads tall
and about
10 heads
wide.

2. **Sketch the basic geometric shapes based on the wire frame figure (as shown in Figure 13-27).**

Draw the wide simple shapes to resemble smooth bubbles and lima beans. The domelike head structure is tucked into the thick torso, similar to how a turtle pulls its head into its shell. Having the head tucked in ensures that it's protected against any accidents that happen on the construction site. Having the torso way in front of the head gives the image that this mecha is meant to withstand a lot of abuse. To protect the feet from damage, I sketch large guards on each foot.

In order to support all the upper-body weight, the mecha's legs have to be large and wide so it doesn't trip and keel over from walking through debris. I draw large ball bearings at the hips to connect with the legs. Although this additional weight slows down the mecha's movement, it strengthens the leg support and balance.

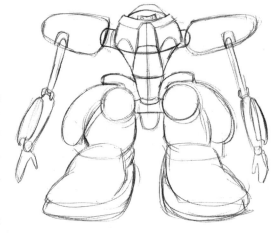

Figure 13-27:
Adding the loose shapes over the wire frame figure.

3. **Rough in the specific shapes for the armor over the geometric shapes (as shown in Figure 13-28).**

In addition to defining the armor, I add smaller design shapes, such as the squares and ovals at the center of the body, facing toward the sky. This section bulges outward so that the pilot can fit into the torso cockpit. I define the hip section by drawing metal plates on top and covering the sides of the legs. This protects the legs from any large, falling debris. I complete this step by adding the smaller shapes and detail to the feet. Toward the back of the heels, I sketch the large pin screw that secures the ankles.

When drawing the feet, which are larger and wider than the average combat mecha's feet, make sure to take the time to draw them in correct perspective. In addition to getting the perspective right, I draw the "toes" in the foreground larger and the "heel" toward the back smaller to give the mecha feet additional dimension.

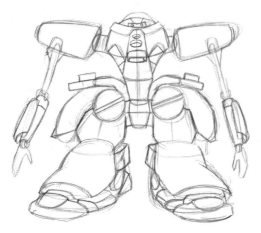

Figure 13-28:
Lightly drawing the armor and other specific shapes over the geometric form.

4. Tighten up the shapes as shown in Figure 13-29.

I clean up the image by darkening the lines and erasing any that are extraneous. I define and build up the arms by drawing metal guards around the biceps and forearms. I draw individual finger joints for the hands, and I make them elongated because the mecha needs to be able to perform intricate functions such as pressing buttons and turning dials (in addition to performing heavy-duty construction work).

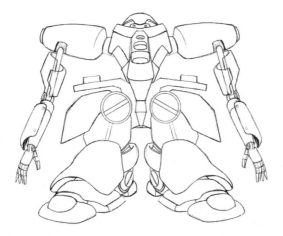

Figure 13-29:
Tightening and defining the edges of the mecha.

5. **Draw in the details, such as antennas, arm shields, and pipes (as shown in Figure 13-30).**

   With heavyweight mechas like this one, I always make sure to add four large pipes that connect from the mecha's rucksack to the back of the head. I think large pipes give mechas the appearance of a walking giant factory. I also draw two antennas on each side of the shoulders for communication, and headlights right above the hips for clear vision in dimly lit areas. Finally, I draw cosmetic details, such as seam lines between the metallic plates and small notches on the lower legs and feet.

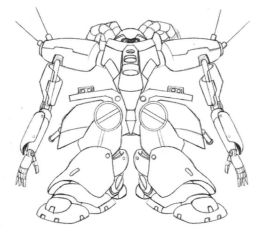

Figure 13-30: Finishing off the mecha with details.

Chapter 14

Gadgets and Weapons

. . . .

In This Chapter

▶ Drawing small, cool gadgets

▶ Improvising basic geometric shapes to create different types of weapons

▶ Discovering the tricks you need to draw metallic, sharp weapons

. . . .

*E*ver take a moment to drool over the wide range of cool gadgets and armor featured in action shōnen manga? From modern mobile phones to historic samurai swords to hi-tech battle gear and armor, characters rely on props to accomplish their missions. In this chapter, I explain step by step how to draw some of these hot items using basic geometrical shapes. Regardless of how complex the final drawings appear, they all follow the same principles. And after you get used to first laying down the overall geometric shape, you can make your own interpretations and decisions on where and how much detail you want to add.

If you have little drawing experience and you're not familiar with the geometrical shapes I talk about in Chapter 5, please take time to read through that chapter before continuing on with this chapter.

Small Gadgets

Small gadgets make great accessories because they're easy to carry and operate, yet they can perform sophisticated functions. They also serve as fashion statements to your characters as much as clothes do.

Communicators

Think of a communicator as your ultimate mobile phone that does everything except give back massages and walk your dog. It's a trendy device that can handle as many functions as you assign to it in order to meet your character's mission needs. In addition to making calls, some characters may need it for gathering classified data, and others may need to use it as a weapon or a remote control device to summon their sidekick robot.

Follow these steps to draw a communication device:

1. **Draw a thin rectangular cube for the base of the device (as shown in Figure 14-1).**

   As long as your character can hold this device comfortably, you can modify the shapes. It shouldn't be larger than the character's hand; otherwise, it loses its sleekness.

   In Figure 14-1a, I start off with a thin rectangular base and round off the edges in Figure 14-1b.

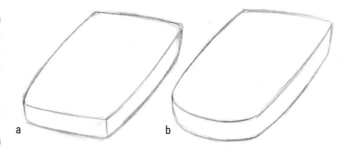

a
b

Figure 14-1: A rectangular base for a communication device.

2. **Lightly sketch a grid as your guideline, and then draw the shapes for the display interface, buttons, and microphone (as shown in Figure 14-2).**

   The display should be large enough for the character to read and is generally above the dial pad numbers.

   These features can be any shape and size you want to create them. In Figure 14-2a, I lightly sketch a grid guide so that when I draw the features, they all line up properly in relationship to one another. In Figure 14-2b, I lightly draw the smaller shapes of the buttons, displays, and so on.

a
b

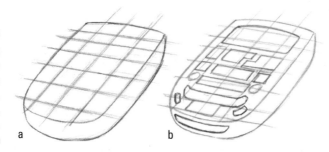

Figure 14-2: Lightly drawing the buttons, displays, and so on.

3. **At the top of the device, draw the top lid shape and its hinge (as shown in Figure 14-3).**

   This shape should be the same size as the lower shape (unless you want certain features, such as the microphone, to be exposed on the lower shape). Don't forget to draw a narrow cylindrical hinge for the lid; otherwise, the lid doesn't have anything to open or close with.

   After drawing the hinges for my device, I sketch the lid shape and an additional display and speaker set on the lid to give it that hi-tech look.

4. **Finalize the pencil lines for the communicator and add the rest of the smaller features (as shown in Figure 14-4).**

   I add the antenna and lights.

Figure 14-3: Drawing the top lid and features of the communicator.

Figure 14-4: Adding the finishing touches to the communicator.

Remote devices

Remote devices are growing more sophisticated in function and design. You can power and control not only your television, but also your DVD player, TiVo recorder, cable box, and your surround-sound speakers. The ever-increasing number of buttons are shaped and grouped according to specific functions to at least attempt to avoid confusion.

Remote devices are more challenging to draw than communicators, because they have more buttons and curves. To get started, take a look at these steps:

1. **Draw the body of the remote (as shown in Figure 14-5).**

   Instead of using a straight-edge, rectangular "candy bar" shape, experiment with skewing the edges or merging another shape into your geometric remote.

   In Figure 14-5a, I start out with a rectangular shape, but I bend the front of the head so that it curves slightly downward. In addition, I bring in another shape (a short cylinder) and merge it toward the top of the rectangular body in Figure 14-5b.

a

Figure 14-5:
Drawing the
body of the
remote
device.

b

2. **Draw a series of guidelines for your buttons, set equally far apart, as shown in Figure 14-6.**

   These lines don't all have to go straight across. Draw some of them arched or even in a ring. In Figure 14-6, I keep the straight guidelines toward the bottom and draw the arched and circular guidelines toward the top.

3. **Lightly draw the buttons around the guidelines as shown in Figure 14-7.**

   Change up the shape of the buttons — although you should keep certain button shapes grouped with other similar shapes, try drawing different shapes too.

In Figure 14-7, I group the smaller oval buttons together and add circular and arched buttons toward the top.

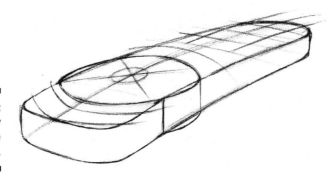

Figure 14-6:
Loosely
drawing the
guidelines.

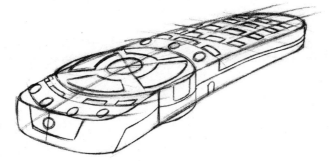

Figure 14-7:
Drawing
various
button
shapes.

4. **Gently erase the guidelines and tighten up the button shapes as shown in Figure 14-8.**

Don't be afraid of losing the button shapes while erasing the guidelines. As long as you gently go over the lines, you should still be able to see the pencil marks to trace over them again.

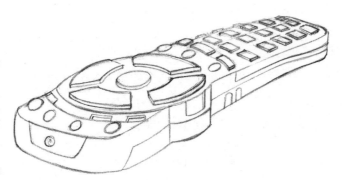

Figure 14-8:
Finalizing
the lines
and buttons
on the
remote.

Battle Arms

Combat gadgets are just as important as fashion in giving your character an identity. In this section, I demonstrate two popular battle arms by drawing a sword and guns.

Swords

A sword was considered the soul and honor of a Japanese samurai during the Edo Period in Japanese history. A samurai spent a lot of effort making sure his sword was well maintained and had a unique design.

Despite all the elaborate variations, a sword is a three-section weapon consisting of the handle, the guard, and the blade. I start off with the traditional samurai sword:

1. **Lightly draw a long guideline and a shorter line perpendicular to the long line that intersects toward the end (as shown in Figure 14-9).**

Figure 14-9:
Drawing the guidelines for the samurai sword.

2. **Block in the basic geometric shapes for the handle, protector (known as *tsuba*), and blade (as shown in Figure 14-10).**

Figure 14-10:
Adding the basic shapes for the sword.

3. **Add the decoration patterns to the handle, and sharpen the tip of the blade (as shown in Figure 14-11).**

   Pay attention to the tip of the sword where the front side suddenly curves up at the end. The back side should curve up just slightly. If your character is superstitious, you want to draw a good luck charm at the end of the handle.

Figure 14-11:
Sharpening the definition of the sword.

In Figure 14-12, I show the sword from different perspectives. In Figure 14-12a, the sword is pointed toward the readers, while in Figure 14-12b, it's pointing away. The extreme distortion you see in both images is known as *foreshortening*.

Think of the foreshortened images of the sword as thin, long cylinders coming toward and going away from you. For this exercise, you need a tube (say the cardboard center from a paper towel roll, which is about a foot long). Hold it up about 10 inches in front of you so that the side is facing you. Then gradually rotate the position so that the tube faces you until you're staring right through the hollow opening. Do you notice how the length of the tube gradually becomes shorter as it rotates to face you? It's the same foreshortening that's happening with the sword in Figures 14-12a and 14-12b.

If your character uses the sword as his main weapon, you want to design a *tsuba* for his sword. In Figure 14-12c and 14-12d, I show some *tsuba* designs. Traditionally, the engravings include the bearer's family symbol.

Guns

In this section, I demonstrate the steps you need to draw several types of guns. Smaller grip guns have smaller handles and are easier to control, while the bigger guns, such as bazookas, are heavy enough that characters need to rest them upon their shoulder for stability.

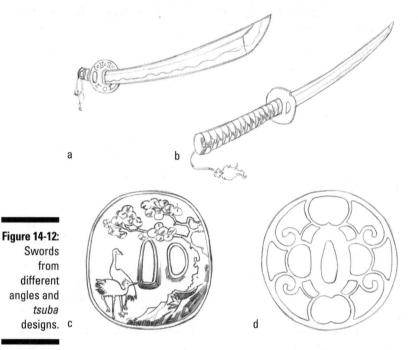

a

b

Figure 14-12: Swords from different angles and *tsuba* designs.

c

d

When drawing difficult angles of the hand gripping the gun, I take a photo, using my digital camera, of either myself or a friend posing. After I use that photo for my drawing, I save it for future reference. As you keep drawing and re-using the references, you gain the confidence and skill to draw those poses quicker and eventually from memory.

Phaser

Think of a phaser as the future of today's handgun. It has no bullets, so you don't need to reload. As a result, the chamber and barrel are often fused together into one piece, which I refer to as the main body. In place of bullets, it fires deadly laser beams and needs to be charged after each battle. Phasers are generally compact so that you need only one hand to fire them.

Follow these steps to draw your first phaser:

1. **Draw the main body (barrel and chamber) of the gun (as shown in Figure 14-13).**

   Draw the front end of the main body where the laser shoots out narrower than the back of the main body where the grip will attach beneath.

Figure 14-13:
Drawing the
main body
of the
phaser.

2. **Attach a rectangular grip (as shown in Figure 14-14).**

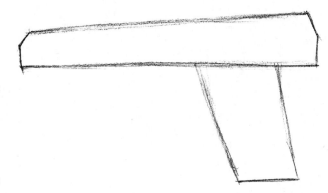

Figure 14-14:
Drawing the
grip section
of the
phaser.

3. **On both sides of the grip, draw two triangular shapes to support the main body of the phaser to the grip (see Figure 14-15).**

   The longer triangle, which is in front of the grip, has a flattened end facing the muzzle.

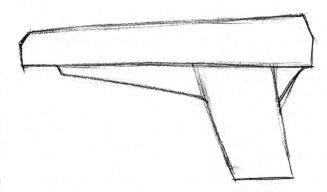

Figure 14-15:
Drawing the
support
pieces on
both sides
of the grip.

4. **Draw the trigger and add the butt underneath the grip to complete the bottom half of the phaser (as shown in Figure 14-16a).**

   The front of the butt facing the trigger should stick out and angle down so that the bottom of the character's hand rests comfortably on top.

5. **Add the smaller details to complete the main body of the phaser (as shown in Figure 14-16b).**

   Draw a square-shaped object for the back of the chamber and a digital scope above the main body. On both ends of the main body, I draw a sight on top. Finally, I add in the design lines on the body to make it look more realistic.

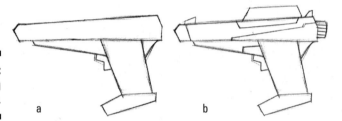

Figure 14-16:
Completing
the phaser.

a   b

Laser beam rifle

A laser beam rifle may be used by a combat *mecha* (large robots that are piloted by humans; refer to Chapter 13). This type of larger and heavier weapon requires both hands of the mecha to operate. Although it shoots laser beams like the phaser in the previous section, the rifle delivers greater accuracy, distance, and power. If your mecha is a lightweight or heavyweight combat mecha, this toy is for you!

To draw a laser beam rifle, follow these steps:

1. **Draw the main body of the rifle (as shown in Figure 14-17).**

   The main body consists of two sections — the upper and lower casing. Have fun designing the upper casing because that's what defines the overall shape of your character's or your mecha's rifle.

   First, I draw the bigger shape for the upper casing as shown in Figure 14-17a. This section represents the top portion of the main body of the rifle. The key to getting this shape right is making sure the opposite sides facing each other are parallel.

   As shown in Figure 14-17b, I draw a long rectangular shape for the lower casing coming out from under the upper casing. This represents the lower portion of the main body of the rifle, which is smaller and drawn more to the left to make room for the main grip, the trigger, and the trigger guard to the right. Make sure the bottom side is parallel to the top of the upper casing.

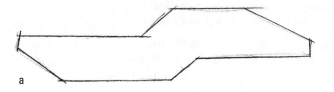

a

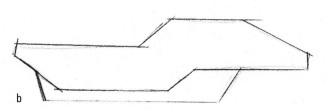

b

Figure 14-17: Drawing the upper and lower casing of the body.

2. **Draw the cylindrical muzzle protruding out from the front of the upper casing (as shown in Figure 14-18).**

   This hot dog shape attached to the front of the rifle helps the mecha shoot with more accuracy, power, and distance. Be sure to include the slits at the end of the muzzle from where the laser beam exits to meet its target. Make sure you don't make the muzzle too short — in order for the rifle to be effective on long distance targets, it needs to have a certain degree of length.

   Right beneath the muzzle, draw the red dot scope. From the side view, it resembles a square shape with the top and bottom corners cut down.

Figure 14-18: Drawing the muzzle of the rifle.

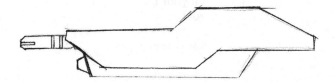

3. **Complete the back portion of the main body (as shown in Figure 14-19a).**

   You don't have to use specific shapes for the back portion of the main body. The purpose is to balance the visual weight from the front of the rifle and create a base for the main grip and trigger. The trick to getting the overall shape to look right is making sure the sides are parallel to another section of the rifle.

4. **Draw the main grip, trigger guard, trigger, and magazine grip (as shown in Figure 14-19b).**

   Unlike a normal gun, this beam rifle has a separate magazine grip located at the middle of the rifle. The magazine section should fit in slightly at an angle and look like an elongated rectangle. I draw several groove marks that prevent the hand from slipping off the grip.

I draw the main grip, which is fused together with the trigger guard. The overall shape looks like a skewed square. The trigger sits where the grip and the back portion of the main body meet.

Figure 14-19:
Fixing in the magazine grip, trigger, trigger guard, and the main grip.

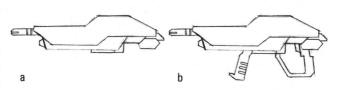

5. **Add the smaller shapes and design for the rifle (as shown in Figure 14-20).**

   As part of the shapes and design, I draw the front and rear sights (which aid targeting) as well as a long range targeting scope. Adding in the grooves and seams along the rifle adds to the realism. Other smaller shapes I add include the two trapezoidal shapes attached beneath the front of the lower main body. Some mecha weapons have numbers and letters marked on them.

Figure 14-20:
Completing the beam rifle.

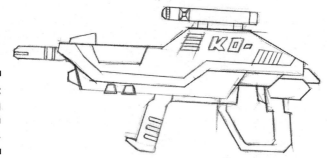

Rocket launcher/bazooka

One of the largest weapons commonly used by military and mecha, the rocket launcher/bazooka has enough power to destroy an entire space cruiser. It's heavy and clumsy looking, but here in the manga world, you can make it fun by adding cool shapes to create your own weapon of mass destruction. Mechas that use these types of weapons are heavyweight combat types (refer to Chapter 13).

To draw this powerful weapon, follow these steps:

1. **Draw an elongated rectangle for the body or barrel of the gun (as shown in Figure 14-21).**

Figure 14-21:
Drawing the
body of
the rocket
launcher/
bazooka.

This barrel is wide enough for a rocket capable of destroying a galaxy cruiser to pass through.

2. **Draw the support grip (as shown in Figure 14-22a).**

Draw the support grip approximately ⅓ from the left of the barrel. Make it at a slight angle so that the other hand can comfortably support the additional weight.

Think of the support grip as a flat rectangular cube that's tilting away from you at an angle. To emphasize that the shape is tilting away, I draw a bevel in the middle of the palm side of the grip.

3. **Draw the main grip, which is fused with the trigger guard, as well as the trigger (as shown in Figure 14-22b).**

Draw the main grip/trigger guard approximately ⅔ from the left of the barrel. The shape is similar to that of the main grip/trigger guard of the beam rifle (see the previous section) except it's larger. Copy this shape as best you can. As you continue to draw from other references, you get used to drawing the pattern of shapes.

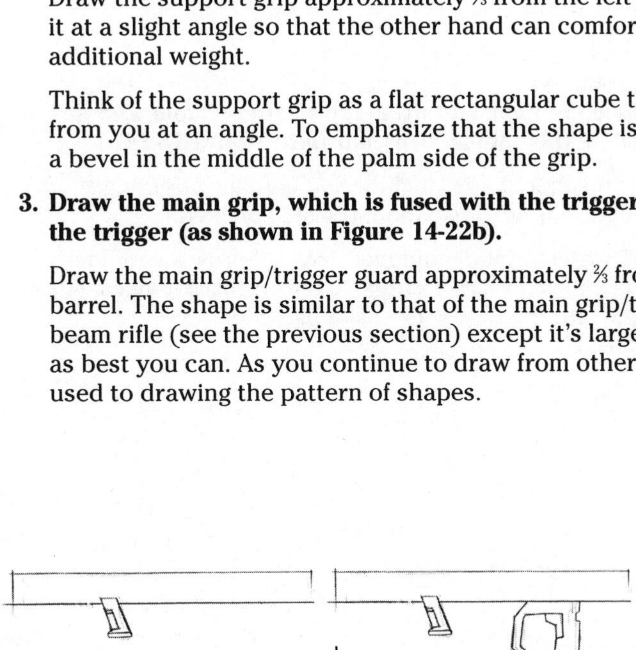

Figure 14-22:
Adding the
support grip,
main grip
(fused with
the trigger
guard), and
trigger.

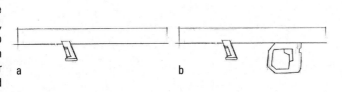

 4. **Draw the muzzle at the front of the barrel and the rocket magazine rack at the back (as shown in Figure 14-23).**

 This is where the rockets are stored and fed directly into the launcher. The muzzle is similar to the one on the rifle (see the previous section) except thicker. The magazine rack should rest comfortably behind the user's shoulder. Because of the size of the rockets, they're capable of launching only four to five rounds.

 I add some extra design elements to the muzzle, creating a "hood" effect over the opening of the barrel. I draw a slanted rectangular shape for the rocket magazine on the side rear of the barrel.

Figure 14-23:
Fixing the muzzle and rocket magazine to the launcher.

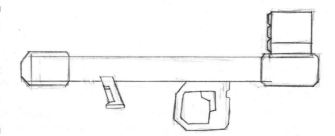

 5. **Finalize the lines and draw the smaller shapes and design to complete the launcher (as shown in Figure 14-24).**

 These smaller shapes include a long-range targeting scope, model numbers, supporting tripod, trigger, and so on.

 Along with the model number decals, I draw a shoulder rest pad as well as pipes for a more organic effect. Just for kicks, I draw the trigger sunken into the group for easier use.

Figure 14-24:
Completing the rocket launcher/ bazooka.

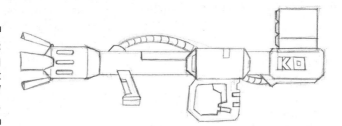

Chapter 15

Taking Off: Vehicles and Airplanes

In This Chapter

- Taking it to the road: Drawing cars
- Flying high and creating airplanes
- Understanding the differences between civilian and combat vehicles

Just about every mainstream shōnen and shōjo manga story has some type of vehicle or airplane either in the background or playing a crucial role. If you draw your character walking downtown to do some shopping, you want to make sure the streets are hustling with not just people, but also cars, which need to look convincing to your readers. Or if your main character is a race car driver whose best friend is his race car, you want to make sure that the car looks like it's the latest and greatest and not like some rusty can fished out from the bottom of the lake.

In this chapter, I provide examples and basic tips that help you become familiar with drawing different types of vehicles and airplanes. I lay out steps on how to draw the civilian versus military types. Each is designed differently to serve a different function.

Although you shouldn't feel pressured to use a ruler for every line you draw, having it handy helps, just to make sure the parts are aligned. If this is your first time drawing cars and you feel fairly comfortable using your drawing pencil by this point, I toss up the suggestion of first drawing freehand (sans ruler). You may find that you get quicker results and more fluid lines. You can always go back and use the ruler to tighten and refine the shapes if they need to be straightened.

Cars

Becoming overwhelmed by all the detail and chrome texture of a brand-new car (or any vehicle for that matter) is easy. But like drawing mecha and other hi-tech gadgets (see Chapters 13 and 14), drawing vehicles is all about using basic geometric shapes.

Throughout this chapter, you need to have a basic understanding of using one- and two-point perspectives. If you're new at drawing manga or cars, check out Chapter 16 on basic perspective.

Drawing different angles using basic shapes

Try your hand at drawing the basic car structure using elongated cubes for the body and flat cylinders for the tires. First draw the side view. After that, you can tackle the front and ¾ views.

Side view

To draw a basic car from the side view:

1. **Draw a smaller rectangle on top of a larger one (as shown in Figure 15-1).**

   Place the top shape slightly to the right to show that the left side, which now has more space, is going to be the front side. Although these shapes look like regular rectangles (because you see only one dimension when viewing objects from the side), keep in mind that you're drawing a three-dimensional object.

   You need more space at the front of most cars because that's where the engine needs to fit.

Figure 15-1:
Drawing basic rectangles for the side view of the car.

2. **Add two small circles for the tires beneath the bigger rectangle (as shown in Figure 15-2).**

   Make sure both circles overlap the shape so that you leave only half of the tires sticking out underneath. Again, even though you're drawing circles, remember that these are flat cylindrical tires.

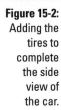
Figure 15-2:
Adding the
tires to
complete
the side
view of
the car.

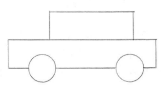

Front view

Now draw the front view of the simplified car:

1. **Draw a narrow rectangle on top of an identical rectangle (as shown in Figure 15-3).**

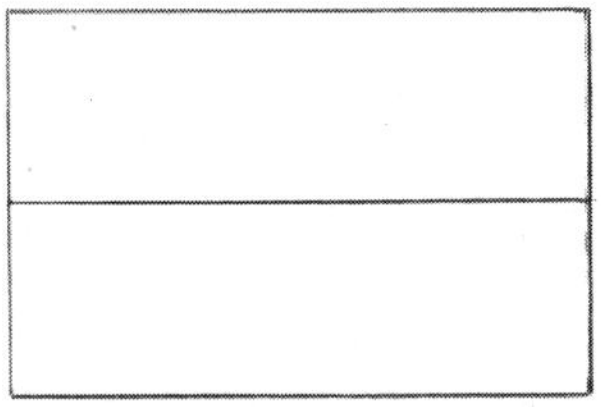

Figure 15-3:
Drawing
basic
rectangle
shapes for
the front
view of
the car.

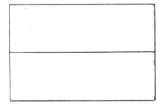

2. **Add the headlights and tires beneath the lower rectangle (as shown in Figure 15-4).**

   Use simple circles for the headlights for now. Use flat squares for the tires on each side of the bottom of the car.

Figure 15-4:
Adding the
headlights
and tires to
complete
the front
view of
the car.

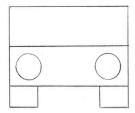

¾ view

Draw the simplified ¾ view of the same car in the previous two sections:

1. **Draw a rectangular cube above a slightly longer rectangle as shown in Figure 15-5a.**

2. **Add two dividing lines to differentiate the front view from the side view (see Figure 15-5b).**

   Insert the dividing line so that the front side on both rectangles is the same width.

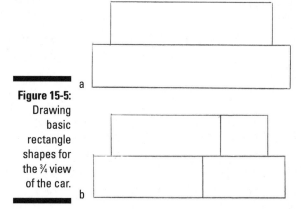

Figure 15-5: Drawing basic rectangle shapes for the ¾ view of the car.

3. **Draw all four tires under the lower rectangle and two circles for the headlights (as shown in Figure 15-6).**

   Because you see only the front-left side of the car completely, you see only two of the four complete tire cylinders. Draw only half of the cylinders for the hidden right side of the car.

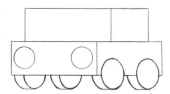

Figure 15-6: Finishing it off by adding the tires and headlights.

Right now, the car looks very mundane and flat. By applying a two-point perspective (see Chapter 16) to the ¾ view, I make the overall shape appear more dimensional (see Figure 15-7).

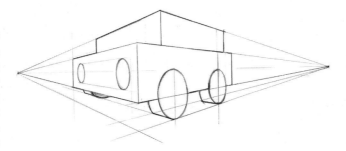

Figure 15-7:
Adding
dimension
using
two-point
perspective.

Drawing standard cars (a.k.a. "grocery getters")

For this section, I show you how to draw your standard ride using the ¾ angle model from the previous section:

1. **Taking the basic car model, draw the modified shapes.**

   As part of the adjustments, make the front and rear of the top rectangle cube and the front of the car hood slanted. You also want to raise the end of the trunk slightly for better wheel traction (see Figure 15-8a). After you finish drawing the new shapes, erase the lines from the basic model.

   In Figure 15-8b and Figure 15-8c, I illustrate the modification from the front and side views for comparison purposes.

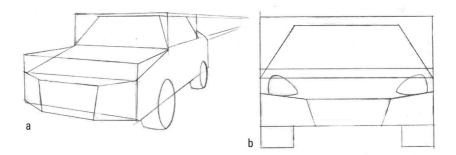

a

b

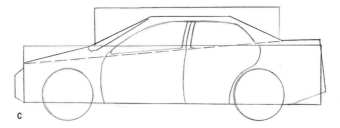

Figure 15-8:
Making the
adjustments
of the basic
car shape in
drawing the
civilian car.

c

2. **Draw the big shapes, such as the front windshield, side windows for the front and back seats, headlights, doors, front grills, and bumper (intended to decrease wind resistance).**

   See an example of these additions in Figure 15-9. Experiment with these shapes and vary them to fit your personal preferences and styles.

Figure 15-9:
Adding the big shapes.

3. **Add the mirrors and details, such as the rear windows, beveled car hood, tire treads, hubcaps, door handles, and so on (see Figure 15-10).**

   Be sure to have some car photos for references in case you need more ideas.

Figure 15-10:
Drawing the smaller details to finish off the civilian car.

Don't get overwhelmed with all the detailed shapes. My advice is to collect photos of your favorite cars and reproduce those shapes to the best of your ability. No manga-ka can possibly know how to draw everything just out of his or her head. All artists use references.

Drawing faster, sleeker cars

The main difference between fast, sleek cars and civilian cars is that these cars are wider and flatter than the standard car. Current manga gives a lot of hype and attention to street racing cars. Stories about them are one of the hottest sellers in today's shōnen manga world. The main characters usually resemble an army special forces rookie (refer to Chapter 7). Although they're reckless with their driving skills, they're calm and intelligent, and of course they sport the *yaoi* (androgynous) hairstyle from Chapter 7.

1. **Make adjustments by drawing the flatter and wider shapes based on the basic car model (as shown in 15-11).**

   In Figure 15-11a, tilt the angle of the windshield so that you see little distinction between the top section of the car and the body. In Figure 15-11b and Figure 15-11c, I show the front and side views for you to compare.

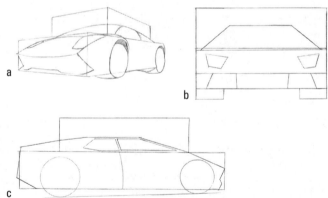

Figure 15-11:
Adjusting the basic shapes for a wider body.

2. **Draw the larger shapes, including the front windshield, side door, tires, and side wind duct (as shown in Figure 15-12).**

   Note that the car doesn't have a grill at the front or backseat passenger doors on either side. Quite commonly, faster cars don't have a backseat to reduce weight.

Figure 15-12:
Adding on
the larger
shapes
to the
sports car.

3. **Add the smaller details, such as tire treads, hubcaps, the car emblem, and headlights (as I show in Figure 15-13).**

Just like finding photos for the "grocery getters" from the last section, you should gather photos to use for references for your faster sports cars. I especially enjoy researching the new models that car companies display at auto show conventions. They're sleek, cool, and just fun to look at!

Figure 15-13:
Finishing the
sports car
with the
smaller
shapes and
designs.

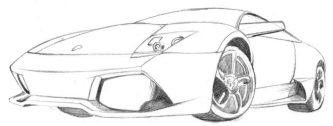

Planes

In this section, I take you through the process of drawing civilian airliners and combat jets. Although both have wings, they differ greatly in looks and serve different functions. Try your hand at building the basic body shapes for each type, starting with a civilian jumbo jet. Then go for a cool-looking F-18.

Drawing the jumbo jet

Looking at the jumbo jet, you see that the body (passenger cabin) is basically a long tube or cylinder. The engines on the wings are also cylinders. The remaining wings are what help give the overall shape character. In the following sections, I demonstrate how to draw the jumbo jet.

Top view

Start with these steps to draw the jumbo jet from the top view:

1. **At the center of your paper, lightly draw an approximately 4-by-5 inch square guide for the jumbo jet (as shown in Figure 15-14).**

   In Figure 15-14a, I divide the square guide into thirds. Next, I draw two diagonal lines from the corners of the square to mark the center (as shown in Figure 15-14b) and draw a horizontal and a vertical guideline down the middle for the cabin body.

   Use a ruler, and take your time drawing the guidelines I show you — these steps are a bit more involved and detailed. I recommend laying down the guidelines in each step before drawing the part of the plane.

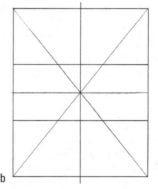

Figure 15-14:
Lightly drawing the guides for the jumbo jet.

a   b

2. **Draw the cylindrical body and the wings (as shown in Figure 15-15).**

   In Figure 15-15a, notice that the front or nose of the plane is more rounded than the sharper tail end.

3. **Place the large wings correctly within the center two guidelines (see Figure 15-15b).**

   I draw the front side of the wings straight as opposed to the rear side, which I draw angled. The front wings connect at the top of the two horizontal center guidelines.

   To place the location where the rear wing connects to the passenger cabin, divide the bottom of the two center guidelines into thirds. Next, attach the rear wing to the passenger cabin where the top third guideline meets the passenger cabin.

   I determine the location of the bend in the rear side wing by dividing the box vertically into quarters (the passenger cabin is the halfway mark). Then I draw a vertical guideline at the quarter mark on each side of the passenger cabin. The rear side of the wing bends right on the guideline of each side of the passenger cabin.

4. **Draw the horizontal and vertical guidelines for the left and right tail wings (see Figure 15-15c).**

Create the horizontal guidelines for the tail wings by dividing the bottom third of the vertical guideline in half and then taking the lower half and again dividing it into thirds.

I draw the vertical guidelines for the tail wing by taking the space between the center two vertical guidelines of the passenger cabin and dividing the space into eight sections (four sections on each side of the passenger cabin).

5. **Draw the left and right tail wings based on the guidelines from Step 4 (see Figure 15-15c).**

Copy the drawing of the left and right tail wing shapes in Figure 15-15c. Pay close attention to where the shapes of the left and right tail wings meet with the tail wing guidelines.

6. **Draw the main tail wing along the center of the passenger cabin between the left and right tail wings (as shown in Figure 15-15d).**

The center tail wing is smaller than the rest of the shapes from this particular viewpoint; you get a better look at it when I show you how to draw the plane from the side view later in this chapter. For now, copy the elongated diamond shape in Figure 15-15d. The front end of the center tail wing extends to approximately midway between the front of the side tail wings and the bottom tip of the main body wings. Pay close attention where the midsection of the center tail wing meets with the tail wing guidelines. The rear end of the center tail wing ends where the left and right tail wings attach to the passenger cabin.

7. **Add two turbo engines on each wing (as shown in Figure 15-16a).**

From the top view, draw the turbo engines as a rectangle in front of a small square that's partially hidden behind the main large wings.

Draw one of two turbo engines on each side at the front of the main wings. Use the same guideline you use to determine the placement of the rear side wing bend on each side of the passenger cabin to determine the exact placement of the engines. The second engine should fall between the first turbo engine and the ends of the main wings. I draw a vertical guideline on each side on the main wings to make sure both engine placements match the opposing side of the plane.

8. **As shown in Figure 15-16b, draw the cockpit window and nose cone (which is where the radar antenna are located).**

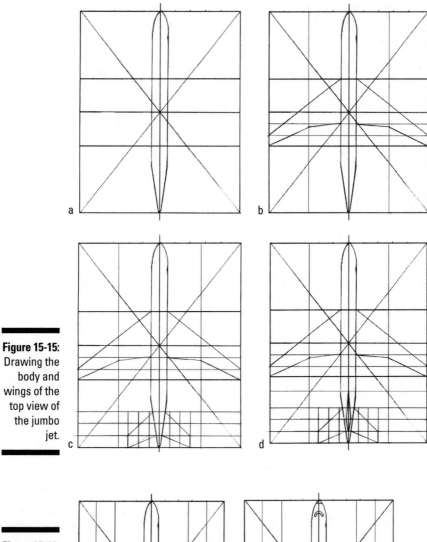

Figure 15-15:
Drawing the body and wings of the top view of the jumbo jet.

Figure 15-16:
Adding the engines, cockpit window, and nose cone to complete the top view.

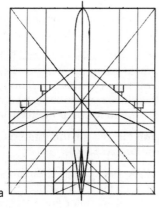
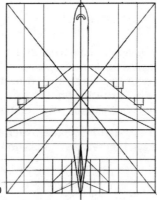

Front view

When you're ready to draw the jumbo jet from the front view, check out these steps:

1. **Draw a smaller circle within a larger circle at the center of your paper (as shown in Figure 15-17).**

   These circles are the front of the aircraft's cylindrical body (or the passenger cabin) and exist on a flat two-dimensional space.

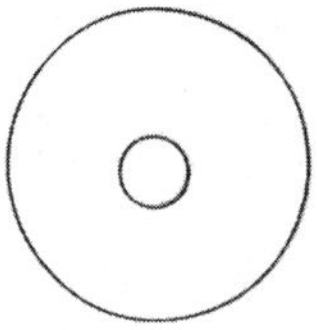

Figure 15-17:
Drawing the body for the front view of the jumbo jet.

2. **Draw a small protruding "bump" at the top of the larger circle to indicate the pilot cabin (see Figure 15-18).**

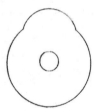

Figure 15-18:
Drawing the body for the front view of the jumbo jet.

3. **Draw the baggage compartment underneath the main cabin, as well as the wings, which angle slightly upward (as shown in Figure 15-19).**

   The baggage compartment in Figure 15-19a looks like a box with the edges cornered off. I use the width of the main cabin body as my head measurement for the wings, and I draw the wings approximately 5 body lengths wide in Figure 15-19b. The tips of the plane rest at midway level to the main cabin. The tips are pointed at the end for better aerodynamics.

4. **Add the smaller shapes, such as the circles for the engines, rear fins, and cockpit windows (as shown in Figure 15-20).**

   When drawing the smaller wings in the back, angle them up slightly — but not as much as you angle the main wings. The center fin, which helps steer the plane left and right, must be taller and thicker than the fins on either side of the cabin. Determine where to place the two engines on both sides of the wings by dividing each wing into thirds. Then place an engine below the wings at the ⅓ marking points.

Figure 15-19:
Adding on the baggage compartment and wings.

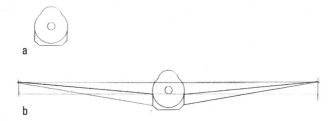

Figure 15-20:
Finishing off the front view with the windows, engines, and rear fins.

Side view

To show a jumbo jet from the side view, use the steps in this section:

1. **Draw a rectangle for the side view of the passenger cabin, and then divide it into quarters (as shown in Figure 15-21).**

   Label the guidelines from A to E.

   Keep in mind that the rectangle shape you're drawing is in fact a cylindrical tube at a side view angle.

Figure 15-21:
Adding the guidelines to the side view of the passenger cabin.

2. **Cap the front end with a rounded cone shape and add the tail piece at the back (as shown in Figure 15-22).**

These pieces should be the same width.

Make sure you draw the nose end slightly smaller to get a little space between the top of the cone and the passenger cabin (as shown in Figure 15-22a). Also, notice in my drawing that the top of the tail is straight or flat with the top of the cabin as opposed to the bottom side, which is angled.

In Figure 15-22b, I taper off the bottom of the nose cone starting from the tip of the nose cone to point B to give the airline a more realistic appearance. Also note the tapering angle cutting from point D to point E.

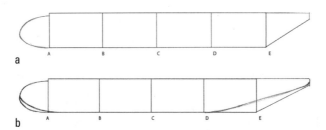

Figure 15-22:
Attaching the nose and rear tail end to the jumbo jet.

3. **Create the cockpit cabin by drawing a smooth tapered bump starting from point B and ending just slightly past point A (as shown in Figure 15-23).**

The key to getting the front part of the airliner to look realistic is to extend the front of the cockpit cabin past the passenger cabin and merge it over onto the front nose cone. Make sure the front of the pilot cabin merges at an angle with the nose cone so that the windows fit in.

Figure 15-23:
Drawing the cockpit section.

4. **Draw the side and rear tail wings along with the engines (as shown in Figure 15-24).**

Pay close attention to the shortened wing shapes in Figure 15-24a. Start from point B and draw the shape that angles up to the midsection of the passenger cabin at point D before angling back down right in front of point C. The rear side wings should start at point D and angle slightly upward as well. Because the front of the top rear wing is larger, you can let it go past the point D mark.

In Figure 15-24b, you can see that I draw the first engine midway between points B and C. The second engine falls right on point C.

TIP

The trick to drawing the engines is drawing three sets of barrel shapes that gradually get narrower (as shown in Figure 15-24c). You can add a blunt-shaped cone inside the largest tube, which secures the engine blades (not shown here).

a

b

c

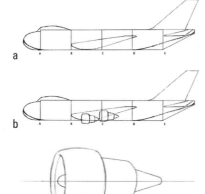

Figure 15-24: Drawing the wings and engines on the body of the plane.

5. **Add the details, such as the windows and airline logo and design (as shown in Figure 15-25).**

   A jumbo class aircraft has five doors on each side. In addition, I draw the upper deck windows behind the cockpit section. Don't forget to draw the logos on the rear tail wing as well! Finally, I add the seam marks to the wings to make them look dimensional and realistic.

PIGGY BACK STUDIOS

Figure 15-25: Adding the details to complete the side view of the jet.

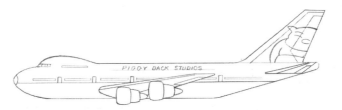

Watch what happens when I apply the ¾ angle to the side view to make things look dimensional in Figure 15-26.

Figure 15-26:
Applying the ¾ angle to the jumbo jet.

Drawing the F-18 fighter jet

In this section, I show you how to draw the front view of the F-18 Hornet combat fighter. This plane and similar planes are built for quick maneuvering and supersonic flight. They don't have large engines like the civilian jumbo jet, but they do have enough room for two pilots. Armed with an extra rear fin and twin engine thrusters, this is one fast bird!

In order to show more dimension in the drawing, the front view of the fighter jet I draw is slightly tilted to show some of the top view of the overall body. I first draw out the horizon line and vanishing point so that I can use the perspective guidelines to make sure all parts of the fighter jet are drawn from a consistent angle.

Follow these steps to draw the body of the F-18 combat fighter:

1. **Draw a horizon line at the center of your paper, and mark the center vanishing point with an "X" (as shown in Figure 15-27a).**

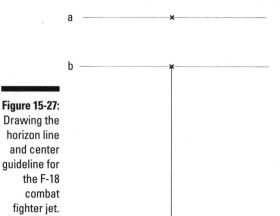

Figure 15-27:
Drawing the horizon line and center guideline for the F-18 combat fighter jet.

2. **From the "X," draw a perpendicular center guideline (as shown in Figure 15-27b).**

   You use this center guideline to draw the body of the combat fighter.

3. **Draw a teardrop shape for the body of the plane along the center guideline (as shown in Figure 15-28a).**

   Draw the teardrop shape 2 inches long and approximately ½ inch from the top of the horizon line.

4. **Starting from the vanishing point on the horizon line, draw the cockpit shape overlapping part of the body shape, and draw the nose tip.**

   The cockpit shape resembles an oval with a bite taken out of the bottom (see Figure 15-28b). The cockpit should be 1½ inches tall and should overlap the top portion of the teardrop body.

   Draw a small circle toward the bottom of the teardrop for the nose tip of the fighter plane to represent the front section of the plane from the front view.

Figure 15-28: Sketching the body and cockpit shapes of the F-18 combat fighter.

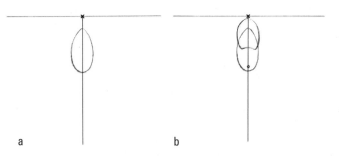

a   b

5. **Starting from the vanishing point, draw two 45-degree-angle perspective guidelines to complete the top section of the body of the fighter jet (as shown in Figure 15-29a).**

   I draw the perspective guidelines angling away from each other and the body of my combat fighter. Make sure the top-left and top-right sides of the cockpit touch the perspective guidelines on each side.

6. **Draw parallel guidelines for the main body of the fighter (as shown in Figure 15-29b).**

   Starting from the top, I draw segment A at the tip of the teardrop body shape. Next, I sketch segment B going through the points where the cockpit shape overlaps the teardrop body shape. Then I draw two diagonal lines from segment B to the bottom tip of the body to establish point C. The triangles on each side of the two diagonal lines are equilateral.

7. **Draw a tilted oval *engine inlet* (supplies air to the engines) on each side next to the body of the plane (as shown in Figure 15-29c).**

To show that the body of the plane extends further in front of the engine inlets, I draw the surface of the ovals facing the teardrop shape slightly cropped. This overlap gives more dimension to the overall body shape.

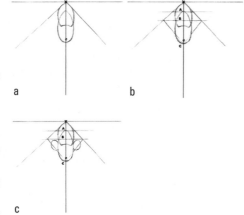

Figure 15-29:
Drawing the guideline shapes for the body of the F-18 combat fighter.

Unlike the civilian jumbo jet, the combat jet has four tail wings on the back (two on the top and one on each side). From the perspective I draw here, you see only the top two. Like most fighter jets, these two top tail wings are built at a slight angle to improve overall control and efficiency of the plane during warfare.

Continue with the body of the F-18 and follow these steps to draw the tail wings:

1. **Draw perspective guidelines above the horizon line for the tail wings (as shown in Figure 15-30a).**

From the same vanishing point I use to draw the guidelines for the body of the plane, I draw a diagonal perspective guideline at 1½ inches on each side above the horizon line.

The perspective guidelines for the tail wings form an "X" shape with the bottom perspective guidelines.

2. **Draw the thin, tall, triangular tail wings (one on each side of the combat jet); see Figure 15-30b.**

   The thin tail wings start from the points where segment A intersects with the perspective guidelines below the horizon line. The top of the wings extend up to meet the top perspective guidelines above the horizon line.

   Tilt the wings slightly away from each other (look at the two complete triangle shapes that form between the two wings as a result of the tilt).

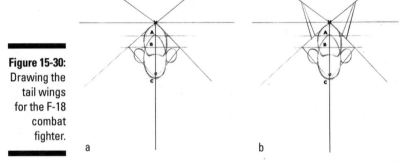

Figure 15-30:
Drawing the
tail wings
for the F-18
combat
fighter.

a   b

Designed to carry a variety of bombs and missiles, the wings of combat fighters are built parallel to the ground.

Follow these step to draw the main wingspan for the F-18:

1. **Slightly below segment B, draw a horizontal guideline for the main wingspan (as shown in Figure 15-31a).**

   Use your ruler to draw a 3-inch guideline on each side of the plane, and divide each side into even thirds (mark a notch for every inch).

2. **Draw the top surface of the wingspan (as shown in Figure 15-31b).**

   I draw the top side of the wing starting from roughly the midpoint of segments A and B. The top side extends and connects to the end of the wingspan guideline.

3. **From the vanishing point, draw another perspective guideline connecting through both ends of the wingspan (as shown in Figure 15-31c).**

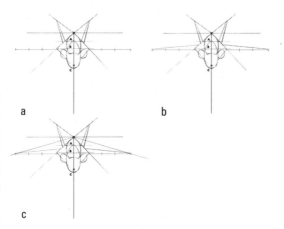

Figure 15-31:
Drawing
the main
wingspan
for the F-18
combat
fighter.

The types of *armaments* (weapons) on this combat fighter include missiles, rockets, bombs, fuel tanks, and *gatling guns* (rapid-fire machine guns).

Follow these steps to arm the fighter with bombs:

1. **Draw two hinges to secure the bombs on each side of the wings (as shown in Figure 15-32a).**

   Place the outer hinges on both sides in the middle, underneath the wings. Then draw the inner hinge (closest to the body of the jet) in the middle between the outer hinge and the body of the jet.

2. **Draw four perspective guidelines right below each hinge (see Figure 15-32a).**

   You use these perspective guidelines to make sure the bottom of the hinges and the bombs you draw in the next step are in correct perspective with the rest of the fighter jet shapes.

3. **Draw "pickle-shaped" bombs based on the perspective guidelines from Step 2 (as shown in Figure 15-32b).**

   I indicate the front tip of the bombs with a small circle to give the forms more dimension. Usually the larger, heavier armaments are attached toward the center of the jet for balance.

In the final stages, I clean up the drawing and add some shading to create a more realistic look to the combat fighter. Follow these steps to do the same:

1. **Erase the extra guidelines, horizon line, and vanishing point (as shown in Figure 15-33a).**

2. **Shade in the darkest values and use the *hito-keta* (one digit) half-tone technique (refer to Chapter 3) to define the shadows of the overall shape of the jet fighter (see Figure 15-33b).**

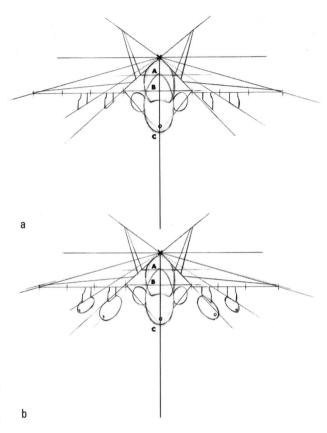

a

Figure 15-32:
Drawing the
armaments
for the F-18
combat
fighter.

b

a

Figure 15-33:
The finished
product is
ready to
take flight.

b

Part V

An Advanced Case of Manga

The 5th Wave By Rich Tennant

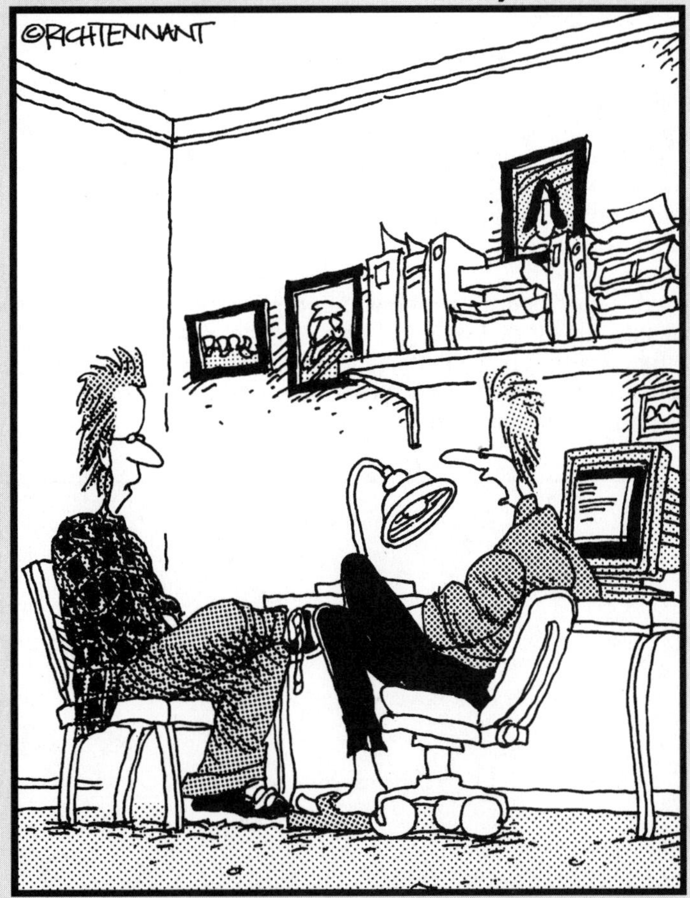
©RICHTENNANT

"If you must know, the reason you're not in any of my manga stories is that you're not a believable character."

In this part . . .

Whoa, don't be intimidated by the title! Although either reading through the first parts of this book or having some drawing experience is helpful, I still work through each exercise in a step-by-step method from start to finish.

In this part, I show you how to apply perspective to your manga drawings; I walk you through backgrounds and storyboards; I provide tips and tricks for coming up with a great story; and finally, I clue you in to the ways to get your work noticed and perhaps even published.

Chapter 16

Putting Manga into Perspective

- -

In This Chapter

▶ Using horizon lines and vanishing points

▶ Applying perspective to construct basic buildings

▶ Creating dynamic angle shots

- -

Getting the right perspective on your surroundings is crucial when drawing manga. Usually a manga story begins with an *establishing shot,* which is a panel that tells the viewers where the story takes place. The establishing shot can be anywhere from the busy streets of Metropolis to the quiet deserts in Nevada. Most importantly, these establishing shots give your characters a sense of belonging within the story. Unless your characters interact in outer space with nothing but emptiness in the background for an entire episode, readers will have a hard time seeing how your characters physically relate to their surroundings without the establishing shot. If your characters, for example, are college tourists exploring the big city for the first time, make sure you're prepared to draw some awesome scenery. No reader will be convinced that your characters are standing in front of the Statue of Liberty if all they do is point off screen or toward an empty background.

The goal of this chapter is to help you become familiar with basic perspective theories and see the benefit of applying them in your drawings, so that you can take your manga drawing up a notch.

You need a straightedge ruler and a triangle ruler for this chapter (see Chapter 2).

Creating Buildings and Backgrounds with Basic Perspective

What is perspective? *Perspective,* from an artistic standpoint, is a technique or method that enables you to turn flat two-dimensional images into three-dimensional images. It's what helps make one-sided drawings, such as squares, into more believable and realistic objects, such as cubes (see

Chapter 4). You're no longer stuck with viewing just the front side of the object — now you also know what the side, top, and even the back look like in relation to the front. Perspective is the creation of illusionary depth on a flat two-dimensional sheet of paper.

You need to know the following basic principles to understand this art:

✔ **One-point perspective:** An illusion where straight horizontal edges of simple geometric objects converge toward a single point (commonly known as a *vanishing point*) along the horizon line.

✔ **Two-point perspective:** An illusion where straight horizontal edges of simple geometric objects converge toward two separate points (commonly known as *vanishing points*) along the same horizon line.

✔ **Three-point perspective:** An illusion where straight horizontal edges of simple geometric objects converge toward two separate points (commonly known as *vanishing points*) along the same horizon line. In addition, you add a third vanishing point either above or below the horizon line where the vertical lines of the simple geometric objects converge.

In this section, I show you the basics for drawing all three perspectives.

Drawing one-point perspective

One-point perspective is the way to present a three-dimensional object in its simplest state. In manga, this perspective comes in handy when you're drawing scenes such as roads, railroad tracks, or a series of buildings where the front is directly facing the reader.

Following is an exercise in drawing one-point perspective:

1. **With your ruler, draw a horizontal line across your paper, as shown in Figure 16-1a.**

   This is the *horizon line.* By the book, it's defined as the line where the earth meets the sky. Personally, I prefer to think of the horizon line as your current eye level. If you look straight in front of you, that level of field is your horizon line.

2. **Create a dot at the center of the line, as shown in Figure 16-1b.**

   This is the *vanishing point.* It marks the point where all parallel lines you draw to create the three-dimensional shapes meet together.

3. **Draw a square to the lower left of the horizon line, as shown in Figure 16-2a.**

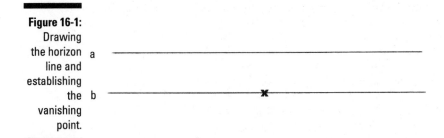

Figure 16-1:
Drawing
the horizon
line and
establishing
the
vanishing
point.

a

b

4. **Draw and connect the three corners to the vanishing point (see Figure 16-2b).**

   The technical term for these imaginary guidelines is *orthogonal lines.*

5. **Lightly draw a line between the top two guidelines, as shown in Figure 16-2c.**

   This line determines the depth of the shape.

6. **Based on where the line ends in Figure 16-2c, draw the vertical line as shown in Figure 16-2d.**

7. **Erase the extra guidelines and voila! You're done!**

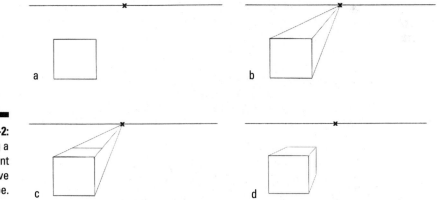

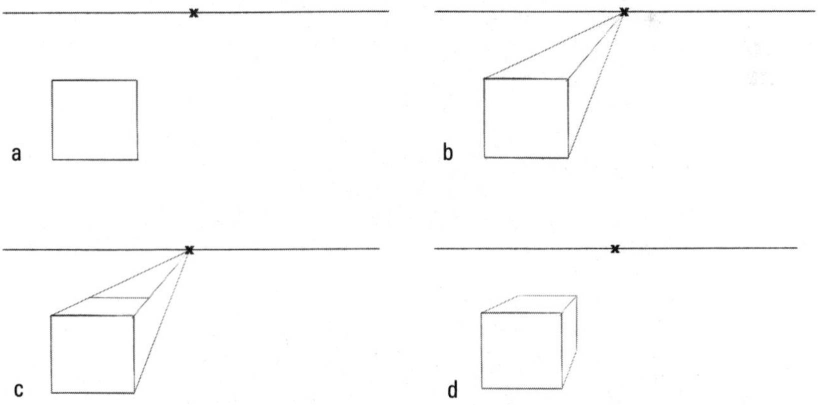

Figure 16-2:
Drawing a
one-point
perspective
cube.

In Figure 16-3, I use one-point perspective to create a city scene. With my vanishing point right in the middle, readers can tell that I'm standing right in the middle of the road, looking down at all the buildings facing me.

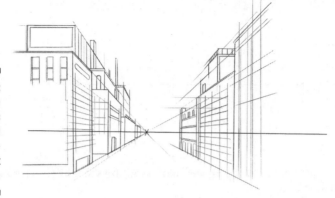

Figure 16-3:
All these buildings are created using one-point perspective.

Here's a cool trick to impress your friends. One-point perspective isn't just for drawing buildings. I can add many cubed objects into the scenario (see Figure 16-4a). You can apply these multiple simple geometric shapes to a fleet of spaceships gearing up for battle (see Figure 16-4b). When attempting complex composition where you have to draw many objects, figuring out the perspective is easier if you first use simple geometric shapes before you modify them into more complex, final objects.

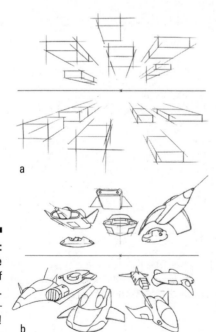

Figure 16-4:
It's a whole fleet of cubes . . . no, wait — spaceships!

Trying two-point perspective

Two-point perspective provides more viewing flexibility than one-point perspective by adding a second vanishing point on the same horizon line. You now have two separate sets of guidelines converging rather than one. This second vanishing point allows you to view the same cube you drew in one-point perspective at a rotated angle. This technique is useful when you're drawing more complex cityscapes, because not every single building you see is facing you. Instead of just one road heading toward one direction, you now have a road forking into two separate directions.

Try the following exercise in drawing two-point perspective:

1. **Set up a horizon line and place two vanishing points on both sides (see Figure 16-5a).**

2. **As shown in Figure 16-5a, draw a vertical line (segment AB).**

   This line represents the front edge and the height of the cube.

3. **From each vanishing point, draw two guidelines (see Figure 16-5b).**

   These lines set the top and bottom edges of the cube.

4. **Draw two vertical segments (CD and EF) on opposite sides of segment AB, as shown in Figure 16-5c.**

   These segments determine the depth of the cube. If you want to increase the depth of the cube, move either or both segments further away from segment AB.

   Keep in mind that by creating segments CD and EF, you are in effect creating two separate walls. One wall is formed by points ABDC, and the other wall is formed by points ABFE.

5. **Finish the cube by tightening and erasing extraneous lines (as shown in Figure 16-5d).**

If you want to draw multiple cubes in two-point perspective, you need to first establish multiple vertical lines, as shown in Figure 16-6. You can change the degree of rotation of the cube by changing the placement of the cube as well as the distance between the vertical segments in relation to the two vanishing points.

In Figure 16-7, I show a series of buildings facing a different angle. Now you get the feeling that I'm looking at the buildings from a corner of a sidewalk.

A
a
B
A
b
B
A
C
E
D
F
c
B
A
C
E
D
F
d
B

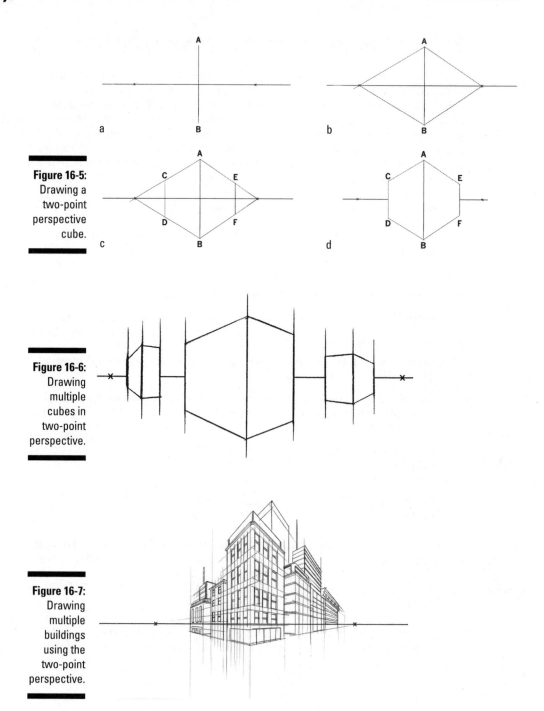

Figure 16-5: Drawing a two-point perspective cube.

Figure 16-6: Drawing multiple cubes in two-point perspective.

Figure 16-7: Drawing multiple buildings using the two-point perspective.

Shaping up for three-point perspective

Three-point perspective is achieved by adding a third vanishing point either below or above the horizon line. This perspective is useful in setting up extreme up and down shots of larger-than-life objects, such as buildings.

The three-point perspective has two categories: worm's-eye view and bird's-eye view. First, I show you how to draw a bird's-eye view. From this perspective, your character could be looking down at a building from an extreme angle in a chopper flying high above. Next, I demonstrate the worm's-eye view. From this view, your character could be looking up in awe from an extreme angle at a tall skyscraper. These extreme angles are responsible for the distortion you see in the following examples when I add the third vanishing point.

I strongly advise students to practice and become familiar with the one-point and two-point perspective theories before attempting the three-point perspective.

Drawing a bird's-eye perspective

Try the following exercise to get a bird's-eye view in three-point perspective:

1. **Set up a horizon line and place a vanishing point on each side (see Figure 16-8a).**

2. **As shown in Figure 16-8b, draw two guidelines from each vanishing point to complete the shape ABCD.**

   This shape represents the top plane of the cube.

3. **Add a third vanishing point, E, well below plane ABCD (as shown in Figure 16-8c).**

   I like to call this point a floating vanishing point because you don't need to attach it to the horizon line the way you do with the vanishing points in Step 1.

4. **From point E, draw three guideline segments to connect with points B, C, and D (see Figure 16-8d).**

5. **Draw two guidelines from the two original vanishing points meeting midway on segment CE (as shown in Figure 16-8e).**

   The further down the two guidelines meet on segment CE, the taller the cube is. Likewise, the higher and closer to point C the guidelines meet, the shorter the cube is.

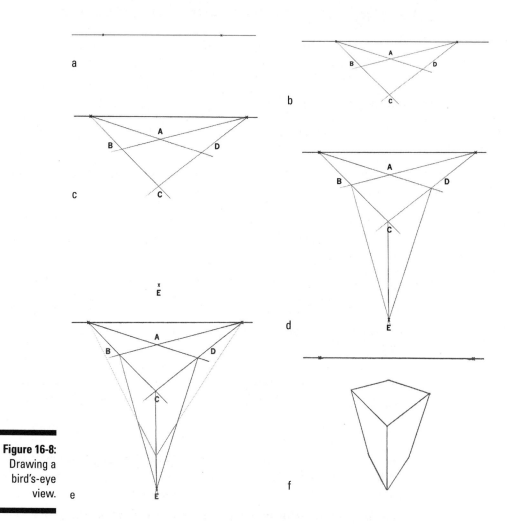

Figure 16-8:
Drawing a
bird's-eye
view.

6. **Clean up the cube by erasing the unnecessary guidelines (as shown in Figure 16-8f).**

In Figure 16-9, I apply the theory of the bird's-eye view to show an aerial view of a tall building.

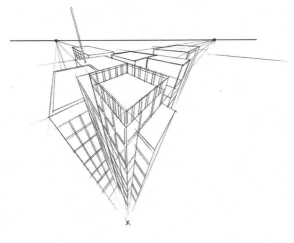

Figure 16-9:
A building
from a
bird's-eye
view.

Drawing a worm's-eye perspective

Here I show you how to draw a worm's-eye view perspective. The process is essentially the same as creating the bird's-eye view (see the previous section). The big difference is that the floating vanishing point is now above, as opposed to below, the horizon line.

To try this worm's-eye perspective, follow these steps:

1. **Create the horizon line and two vanishing points as you do in Step 1 for the bird's-eye view, and draw a vertical line for segment AB, as shown in Figure 16-10a.**

   This line represents the front edge and the height of the cube.

2. **Draw two guidelines from each vanishing point to points A and B (as shown in Figure 16-10b).**

   These segments determine the height of the shape.

3. **Add the floating vanishing point over the horizon line and above point A, as shown in Figure 16-10c.**

   I recommend that beginners place the floating vanishing point above the middle or tallest segment. As you become more comfortable, you can try moving the floating vanishing point slightly to the right or to the left.

4. **Draw two guidelines from the floating point down to the bottom guidelines that connect with point B, as shown in Figure 16-10d.**

5. **Erase the extra guidelines to tighten up the drawing, as shown in Figure 16-10e.**

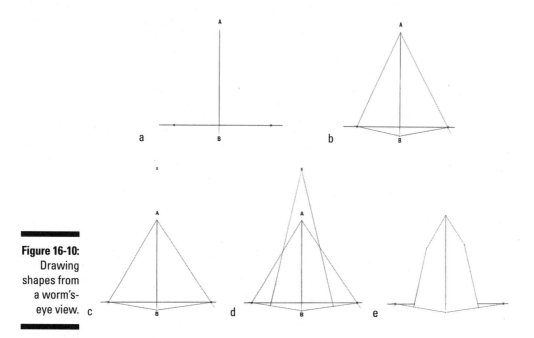

Figure 16-10:
Drawing
shapes from
a worm's-
eye view.

In Figure 16-11, I demonstrate the effect of a worm's-eye view on a tall building.

Figure 16-11:
Drawing a
tall building
from a
worm's-eye
view.

Students ask "How far up should I place the floating vanishing point?" The answer is, "As far up as you want it to be." One key trick to remember is that the farther up or away you decide to place any vanishing point, the less extreme or exaggerated the perspective becomes. For example, when you're standing close to a desk, pinpointing the location of the vanishing point isn't easy, because the edges of the desk are so close to you that they appear almost completely parallel. Even if you have the longest ruler, the guidelines don't find their target for miles.

Adding People to the Environment

In order for characters' interactions to be credible to the viewers, the characters must abide by the same perspective rules that govern their environment. In this section, I show you some techniques on applying basic perspective theory to your characters. ***Note:*** Throughout this section I assume you know how to draw the figures. If you don't, I recommend reading through Parts II and III.

When you're drawing characters interacting in a large background with a lot of perspective, solidify the background first before working in the detail of the characters. You'll find drawing believable characters easier and more efficient if you first resolve the bigger environment. You don't want to spend hours perfecting your character's appearance only to have to erase and redraw him later because he's too big in relation to the background.

No character can exist outside of her environment. Whether the character is flying in the open blue sky or fighting 10,000 soldiers in middle of New York City, an indication of where she stands in relation to the environment is always necessary. The bigger setting dictates the relationship with the character.

One-point perspective characters

Start with a simple one-point perspective building in the background, and try your hand at drawing two characters using one-point perspective:

1. **Draw a series of parallel lines for the ground, and then determine the height of the figure by drawing vertical line AB, as shown in Figure 16-12a.**

   Note that the distance between the parallel lines increases as they come closer.

   When deciding where to place line AB in relation to the background buildings, I look at my horizon line and see where it levels with the building doors, and compare it to the would-be height of my character. In this case, the bottom of the chin rests along the horizon line.

A
B
a
A
VI
B
b
A
C
VI
D
B
c
A
C
VI
point 1
point 2
point 3
D
B
d
A
C
VI
point 1
point 2
point 3
D
B
e

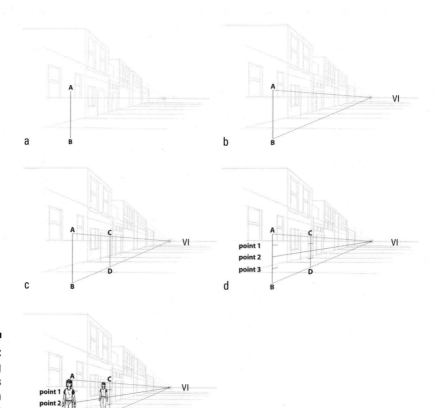

Figure 16-12: Constructing two figures based on one-point perspective.

The longer you make line AB, the larger, taller, and closer to the readers your characters must be. The shorter you draw line AB, the smaller, shorter, and farther away from the readers your characters must be. As long as the level of the neck rests along the horizon line (in this particular case), your characters exist comfortably within the environment.

Don't draw your character so short that his legs can't reach the ground. If you do, your character looks like he's either flying or levitating in space.

2. **Draw two guidelines from the vanishing point (V1) to points A and B, as shown in Figure 16-12b.**
3. **For the second person, draw another line (CD) between segment AB and the vanishing point (see Figure 16-12c).**
4. **Divide segment AB into quarters, and draw a guideline to cut the segment in half like I do in Figure 16-12d.**

The halfway mark (point 2) is the crotch point. Point 1 marks the center of the torso. Point 3 marks the knee area.

5. **Based on these division marks, complete both figures as shown in Figure 16-12e.**

Two-point perspective characters

As I mention in the section "Trying two-point perspective," earlier in this chapter, you need to have a second vanishing point linked to the same horizon line as the first vanishing point to draw in this style. For clarity, I begin Step 1 in this section from where I left off in Step 5 of the last section ("One-point perspective characters"). In the following steps, I establish my second vanishing point and go on to build a two-point perspective character. As you see by the end of this demonstration, the final picture has a lot of depth and movement as I add more people based on a separate vanishing point. Continue with these steps:

1. **Mark a second vanishing point (V2) as shown in Figure 16-13a.**

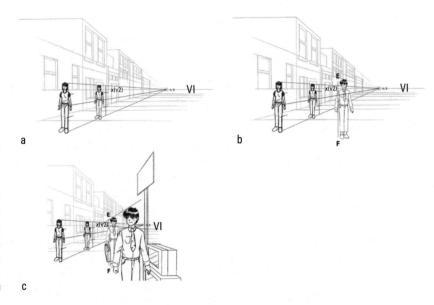

Figure 16-13: You get a lot of depth perception with these two-point perspective characters.

2. **Create two segments and divide them into fourths.**

As I show in Figure 16-13b, the depth perception is greater when your figures are based upon a second vanishing point.

3. **While finalizing the two new figures, add some simple objects (in this case, I add a suitcase, a newspaper vendor, and a bus sign).**

   The additional items aren't important, but as I show in Figure 16-13c, they help secure the new characters to the environment.

Three-point perspective characters

In this section I show you how to control the narrative tension when your characters interact in a three-point perspective environment. Because your characters and buildings exist on the same horizon line, they must abide by the same vanishing points. As I mention earlier in this chapter, the farther away you place a vanishing point from an object (building or human), the less exaggeration or distortion you get. However, readers can get queasy after looking at too many frames of characters drawn under extremely close perspective guidelines.

While exaggeration certainly helps hype up the tension in a story, using it in every frame isn't a good idea. Readers either become bored or confused as to what's going on if every frame has them looking up underneath your character's nostrils or right above her head.

Drawing characters from a bird's-eye view

Take a look at the examples where I draw a character on top of a tall building. In Figure 16-14, I have two scenes — in one, I place the floating vanishing point farther away from the objects, and in the other, I place it closer to the objects. In Figure 16-14a, the character appears to be relaxed, sitting on top of the building. You can see space between the readers and the objects in the frame. But look what happens when the floating vanishing point is closer in Figure 16-14b. I draw a different girl and a different building, but you sense the tension of height awareness of the building that she's peering over. The focus suddenly shifts from the girl to her environment.

Drawing characters from a worm's-eye view

Take a look the examples where I draw a character from a worm's-eye view. In Figure 16-15, I draw two different scenes, varying the placement of the floating vanishing point. In Figure 16-15a, the character is standing below a large skyscraper. The building is so much taller than the person that the perspective effect on the character is small. The focus is not so much on the character, but on the exaggerated environment.

a
b

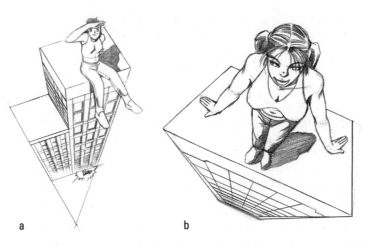

Figure 16-14: Examples of the floating vanishing point's nearness to the building and character.

As massive objects (such as Caribbean cruisers, giant skyscrapers, or galactic space stations) recede back into perspective distance, you want to either simplify the detail or make the lines lighter.

If you want to shift the focus from the environment to the character, check out Figure 16-15b. Here, the floating vanishing point is closer to both the elevator and the character inside. The drama is on the character, and he looks like he's reporting for duty for an important mission.

X(floating vanishing point)
a
b

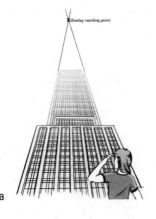

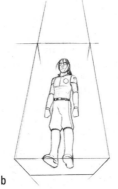

Figure 16-15: Drawing a worm's-eye view for the characters without the third vanishing point.

Ultimately, conjuring up complicated environments (such as large cities) is hard when you're establishing a vanishing point. If you're having difficulty, I recommend taking a photo and using it as reference.

Using Perspective and Camera Angle to Tell the Story

If you read the earlier parts of this chapter, you know the basics of perspective. In this section, I show you how to apply these theories and principles to help tell your story. Manga is no different than a movie — in both, being able to tell a story well and convincingly is key. You're the director and producer working with an unlimited budget — your creative resources. Think of the movie camera as your eye: It sees what you want the audiences to see. You control it and you're in charge of making sure that every framed shot develops the plot and storyline.

As I mention at the beginning of this chapter, strong perspective shots help communicate to the readers not only where the story takes place, but also how your characters relate to their environment. Now I show you how perspective angles can communicate to the readers the way objects and characters relate to each other psychologically. Specifically, I want you to ask questions like "What kind of reaction do I get from the audience by using this type of perspective shot on this character?" If you're ready to discover the answers to this and other questions, keep reading.

Creating strong establishing shots

Establishing shots are important in setting the opening scene of any story. The shots usually have specific backgrounds to show where the story takes place, and the perspective angle you decide to use also determines the tone.

In this section, I pull examples from my creator-owned series *JAVA!* to help illustrate my point. The story focuses on a satirical future city in the year 2073; in Neo Seattle, coffee takes over the whole world. Everyone must drink coffee or perish. In the midst of a society wrapped in turmoil, Java emerges as a high-powered caffeine girl who fights crime. In Figure 16-16a, you see an opening one-point perspective shot of the slums of Neo Seattle, taken from a spin-off of the original published miniseries. I use a single vanishing point to evoke the feeling of a quiet, run-down city. In Figure 16-16b, I use a worm's-eye view to create the perception of a massive coffee storage depot where everyone is rushing to get a caffeine fix.

When drawing a worm's-eye view of huge buildings where the vanishing point is off the paper, extend the paper by taping another sheet to the page and use a ruler to extend the guidelines to find your vanishing point.

Figure 16-16:
Using perspective to create establishing shots in Neo Seattle.

Armed with your ruler, take a walk downtown to an area with a lot of build-ings. You can also go to a grocery store or a library where the aisles are lined up in perfect order. Any location with large geometric structures will work. See whether you can identify where your horizon line is. (Hint: It's wherever your current eye level is.) Then, find your vanishing point(s). Extend your arm out with the ruler and see whether any of the guidelines running from the objects in the foreground meet.

Establishing the strong versus the weak

In Figure 16-17, I show two examples where you can use extreme camera angles to give the illusion that a character is larger or smaller than he is. By applying the third vanishing point that I talk about in the section "Shaping up for three-point perspective," your character can either look overpowering or overpowered. In Figure 16-17a, the fighter (skilled though he may be) is feeling outgunned by the mysterious visitor. In Figure 16-17b, I use a slight worm's-eye view to make my villain female character from *JAVA!* look more menacing even though she's shorter than the male characters in my book.

If you want your shots to look dynamic, tilt the angle of the camera so that the ground is slightly diagonal. Next time you go see an action movie, take note of all the dynamic camera angles and establishing shots with a wide range of perspective angles. If you carry a small drawing pad and pencil with you, quickly sketch a thumbnail of what you remember.

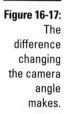

Figure 16-17:
The difference changing the camera angle makes.

a

b

Chapter 17

Using Speed Lines to Create Motion and Emotion

∙ ∙

In This Chapter

▶ Drawing speed lines

▶ Exploring different ways of making things go fast

▶ Using lines to show the emotion of the character

∙ ∙

*I*n mainstream manga, *speed lines* are key in showing motion and emotion. In a stationary, two-dimensional world, you can't make things on paper physically travel fast. Instead, you must imply movement with lines. Similar to film, sometimes your subject (person or object) does the moving, and at other times, the camera moves around or alongside your subject. Regardless, each manga frame is equivalent to a movie frame that the cameraman and director — you — are shooting. These motion and emotion lines show the relationship between the camera and the subject to create the environment.

In this chapter, I explore different ways of creating various types of speed lines to accomplish different types of movement and emotions. As you see throughout these steps, adding these lines helps establish the overall environment of the frame in which your character breathes. Sure, creating gorgeous landscapes and elaborate city backgrounds are important skills to have. But, sometimes, without the motion and emotion that speed lines convey, the focus on the characters may get lost within the complex background, or worse yet, your readers won't have a clue about how to interpret what your character is experiencing in his or her crucial moment.

For this chapter, make sure you have a ruler, French curve, and thumbtack handy. (Refer to the materials list in Chapter 2 for more info.)

Getting Your Character Moving

I start by showing you different ways of making your character go faster or slower. For this section, you need to either copy or draw your own profile of a running figure as your "control" frame. As you see in Figure 17-1, the background is simple, with no indication of movement. The drawing looks as if I took the remote control and pressed "pause." Without anything to suggest interaction between the background and the foreground, this frame is just boring. In this section, I show you how to press the "play" button.

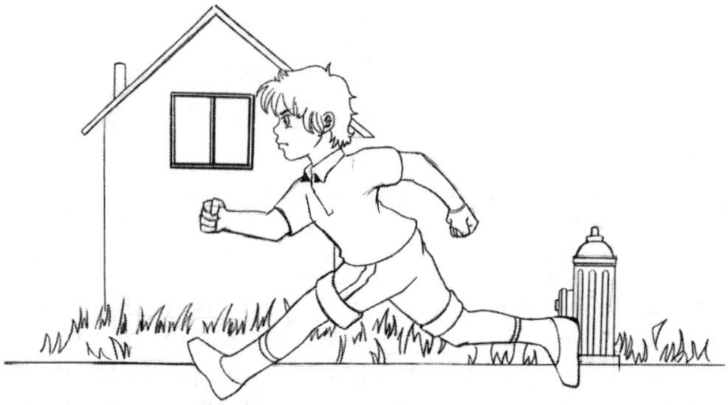

Figure 17-1: The character here looks as if he's suspended in eternal "pause."

Making your character move fast

By making the lines trail behind the boy from Figure 17-1, I create the illusion that he's zipping by the camera (as shown in Figure 17-2a). Follow these steps to get this desired effect:

1. **Starting at the top of the head, draw a series of straight speed lines using a straightedge ruler.**

   The key to getting this effect right is to vary the gap spaces between the lines. If they all bunch up together equidistantly, the space looks flat and uninteresting.

2. **Keep drawing the lines extending to the bottom as shown in Figure 17-2b.**

   TIP

   Observe how I let some of the speed lines overlap the back of the figure. The idea is that he's running so fast that some of his features are blurred or obscured. Now you have a better idea of what's happening. You see not only *that* he's running, but also *how fast* he's running in relation to the background.

a

b

Figure 17-2: The character is now zipping past the camera.

Creating the illusion of moving along with the character

But wait, there's more! What if you want the camera to follow the boy? In this case, readers need to move along with matching speed (regardless of how fast or slow the character is traveling).

Speeding along with your character

Suppose you're drawing a series of sequences where your character is delivering an important monologue as he's zipping along. The camera and readers must stay close by so they can hear everything.

You keep up with the character by extending the lines to fill the space between the boy and the background. Follow these steps:

1. **Completely erase the background.**

2. **Starting from the top of the frame, use the straightedge ruler to draw the lines as shown in Figures 17-3a and 17-3b.**

The camera is now going so fast to keep up with the boy that the entire background is a blur. Because the viewer is now traveling at the same speed as the boy, the boy no longer has speed lines.

Make sure you vary the lines. When covering larger areas, I make the gaps in the speed lines slightly wider. That way, the subject matter isn't overshadowed by too much detail in the background. Toward the bottom section, you can let some of the lines overlap the figure to give the illusion of wind rushing by. Just make sure you don't overlap the face or other parts that are the focus of attention.

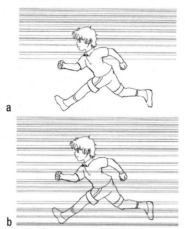

Figure 17-3:
In this
illustration,
the camera
is zipping
along at the
same speed
as the
character.

a

b

Moving with your character at a slower pace

If you want to slow down the speed of your character, keep the background image and decrease the number of lines. Follow these steps:

1. **Starting from above the head of the character, draw speed lines that extend to the bottom (as shown in Figure 17-4a).**

2. **Erase some of the background between some of the lines (see Figure 17-4b).**

   This technique takes some practice because you have to rely on your instinct when deciding how much of the background you want to erase. If you erase too much, the background becomes too obscure to recognize.

a

Figure 17-4:
Adding
speed lines
to the
background
sets the
camera in
motion.

b

Making objects and characters come toward readers

Speed lines don't have to be parallel or go straight across the manga frame. When I draw a series of speed lines stemming out from a vanishing point behind an object, as shown in Figure 17-5, I create the illusion of an object shooting right toward the audience (for example, a pitched baseball from the batter's viewpoint). This vanishing point represents the *origin of trajectory* (the location from which an object is being thrown).

Follow these steps to draw a baseball going toward the readers:

1. **Mark the origin of trajectory with an "X" for the vanishing point.**

2. **Draw the ball several inches to the right of the vanishing point.**

   As shown in Figure 17-5, the ball should be larger to reflect the extreme angle of trajectory. I draw mine approximately 2½ inches in diameter.

3. **Using a ruler, draw the perspective guidelines at the bottom and top of the ball.**

   As shown in Figure 17-5, the rest of the speed lines should fall in between. Draw some of the speed lines overlapping the ball to make the overall image look more dimensional.

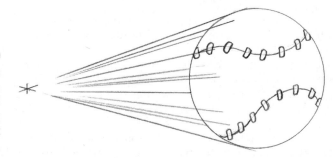

Figure 17-5:
Drawing a baseball coming straight at you.

By the same token, you can reverse the perspective so that the vanishing point heads toward the *target of trajectory* (the target an object is being thrown at). Now the speed lines I draw make the ball look as if it's hurdling toward a target in the distance (perhaps a catcher's mitt).

Just follow these steps to draw a baseball speeding away:

1. **Mark the vanishing point with an "X," and draw the baseball to the right of it.**

   The smaller the ball, the greater the distance between it and the readers. When you draw the baseball closer to the vanishing point, the angle at which the ball is being thrown becomes more exaggerated.

2. **Using the ruler, draw a series of speed lines originating from the vanishing mark (as shown in Figure 17-6).**

   If you're not sure of the perspective terms I'm using, be sure to read Chapter 16.

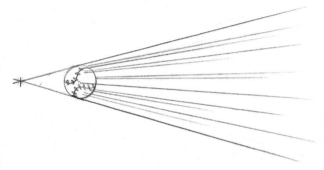

Figure 17-6: Making the speed lines recede in perspective.

You can apply the advancing ball perspective technique to your character to show him or her rushing toward the readers (as shown in Figure 17-7).

Instead of always using a straightedge ruler to draw my speed lines, I sometimes switch to the French curve to add variation to my character's advancing movement. In that case, I use a thumbtack to secure my vanishing point because the French curve can be an awkward tool to use.

For this demonstration, I start with a youth armed with a sword and posed for battle. Follow these steps to create the effect that he's rushing toward the readers (or the enemy):

1. **Display your character without any speed lines.**

   In Figure 17-7a, my character looks like he's just standing there waiting for the enemy to bring it on.

2. **Draw a vanishing point to the right of your character and mark it with a thumbtack.**

Generally, the vanishing point is located outside of the frame (I crop my frame in the last step to show you the final results). I draw my vanishing point around the character's shoulder level.

3. **Rest the long edge of the French curve ruler facing toward the bottom of the thumbtack, and draw speed lines, varying the gap or distance between the lines (as shown in Figure 17-7b).**

   Make sure they all start behind the figure and run all the way in front and off the frame.

4. **Crop your character so that all speed lines fill the frame completely (as shown in Figure 17-7c).**

   My character is now rushing to meet his enemy. Thanks to the speed lines, I don't even need to show the entire figure for my readers to understand that he's running.

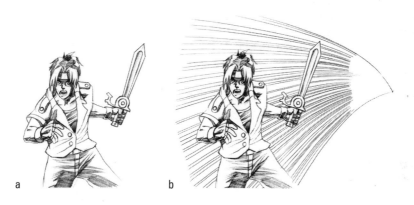

a   b

Figure 17-7: Drawing speed lines to make my character charge forward.

c

Slowing down your character

Just because they're called "speed lines" doesn't necessarily mean that the objects they accompany are traveling at the speed of light. As I show in Figure 17-8, I can make this super fast boy go super slow by changing the type of lines. When I use wavy lines, he looks like he's been running for the past 24 hours, ready to collapse with exhaustion! To achieve this effect, follow these steps:

1. **From the middle top of the head, begin sporadically placing curvy lines going from left to right as shown in Figure 17-8a.**

2. **End the lines somewhere around the hip area (see Figure 17-8b).**

3. **Add some tear-shaped sweat drops at the back of his head to emphasize just how tired this kid is (as shown in Figure 17-8c).**

   You see not only that he *is* going slow, but also *how* slow!

The key to getting this effect right is not drawing the line completely across the frame.

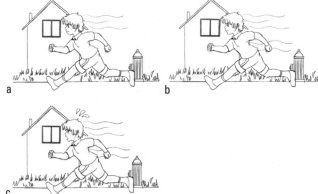

Figure 17-8:
Adding
variety to
the lines
produces
drastically
different
results.

A good way of thinking of these lines is to imagine tying up any loose gaps between the negative space (your background) and the positive space (your subject matter). The lines help guide or direct your reader's eye toward what's important in the frame.

Zooming Around for Emotion

Similar to cinematography, you can use speed lines to communicate shock or surprise. This technique is mostly used on frame shots closing up on the character (usually from the torso up). In this section, I show that by adding the speed lines, readers get the sense that the camera is zooming in on the character's expression.

Note: You can certainly get many other emotional effects using other types of speed lines. In this segment, I show you only fear and shock, because they're the most popular and widely used in mainstream manga. I strongly recommend taking time to go through manga books that you have or like to see what other variations of speed lines manga-ka use to generate other ranges of emotion.

Striking fear into your character

Figure 17-9 is my control image without any speed line effects. The character does look scared, but all that negative space surrounding her takes away from her emotions. You don't get the feeling that she's about to let out a blood-curdling scream; her emotion isn't convincing enough.

Figure 17-9:
She doesn't look frightened enough without any speed lines!

Follow these steps to change that:

1. **Off to the back side of the head, place a thumbtack for the vanishing point.**

   Mark the vanishing point at approximately the same level as her nose (as shown in Figure 17-10a). I recommend letting the vanishing point extend beyond the frame.

When you don't have enough room to place the vanishing point on the paper, attach additional paper to the original artwork.

 2. **Go on to complete the series of speed lines using the French curve (see Figure 17-10b).**

 3. **Crop in the image so that the entire frame is centered on the character and the lines fill in the background (as shown in Figure 17-10c).**

As I show in Figure 17-10d, you can draw a series of parallel lines angling up at the petrified girl to create an expression of fear. In this case, you don't need to draw the speed lines based on any vanishing point. Use a straightedge ruler, and make sure you keep a steady hand when drawing the parallel lines.

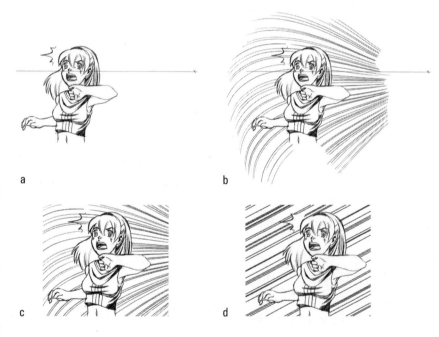

a

b

Figure 17-10:
Using the
French
curve and
straightedge
to strike fear
into your
character.

c

d

Shocking your character

Picture a scene where your character enters the room and discovers that the entire place has been turned upside down. You need to focus on the head or eyes to capture that instant reaction. The camera zooms in, up close, toward the character. In Figure 17-11, I show two control images without any speed lines. Both characters appear to be shocked, but all that open negative space in Figure 17-11a makes the character's expression less convincing. In Figure 17-11b, I draw the eyes according to what I tell you in Chapter 4. Without the speed lines, her immediate reaction to what's in front of her isn't clear. In this section, I demonstrate radial speed lines where the center of focus becomes the vanishing point.

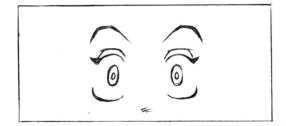

Figure 17-11:
Without speed lines, the effect of shock isn't there.

a

b

For the following steps, you need to start with two images similar to those in Figure 17-11:

1. **Mark the center of attention with a vanishing point.**

    In Figure 17-12a, the vanishing point is slightly lower than the face because you need to account for the rest of the upper body. In Figure 17-12b, however, the vanishing point is right between the eyes.

2. **Using the straightedge ruler, draw the speed lines as shown in Figure 17-12c and Figure 17-12d.**

The key to getting this technique right is to first lightly draw single long lines equidistant from each other. Then, draw shorter lines on both sides to fill in the negative gap spaces. When all is done, you end up with a series of speed lines forming a series of arrows.

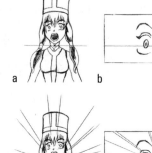

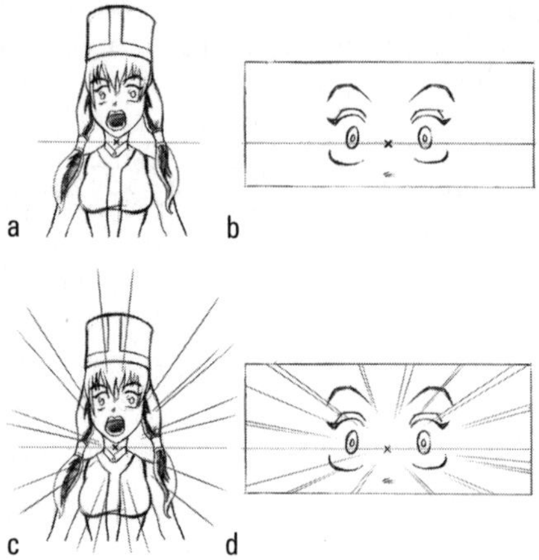

Figure 17-12:
Radial
speed lines
add the
intensity of
emotional
shock to the
character.

A close-up of a face with too many speed lines may be too obscured (see Figure 17-13).

Figure 17-13:
With too
many speed
lines, my
character
looks like a
porcupine!

Chapter 18

Thumbnails and Scenery

In This Chapter

▶ Creating your own storyboards

▶ Making thumbnails work for you

▶ Drawing basic types of scenic backgrounds

As you might guess, without an environment surrounding any characters you create, your readers won't have a world in which to identify with those characters. In this chapter, you find out how to take characters you created based on previous chapters and place them into a believable environment where they can interact with other characters. (*Note:* I put this chapter in the advanced section of the book because you need to first have an understanding of not only drawing figures but also basic geometric objects in correct perspective before you tackle anything in this chapter.)

Creating Effective Thumbnails

"What's a thumbnail?" you ask? Well, a *thumbnail* (often mistakenly confused with a storyboard) is to manga as an outline is to a novel. *Thumbnails* are basically miniature rough sketches of a manga page that a *manga-ka* (manga artist) uses to get his or her ideas onto paper before going to the final full-size page.

Why bother with a thumbnail?

Some consider thumbnails as an extra step (that the readers never see), but it saves the manga-ka hours of frustration and energy. Some of the many benefits include the following:

✔ **When working on a larger page size, you often get caught up with the details and lose sight of the overall drawing.** With an established thumbnail sketch as a guide, a manga-ka gets a better overall sense that the final image reflects the initial "feel" being described in the smaller image.

Thumbnails versus storyboards

In case you were wondering, the concept behind thumbnails and storyboards is identical. Both are used as planning stages for the development of the final product. Though often confused with each other, manga and comic book artists and illustrators use the term *thumbnails* exclusively to describe a series of brainstorming sketches that lead to the development of either a comic/manga book or an illustration. A *storyboard* is a finished product that describes an established script for a commercial, movie, or a theatrical performance. Storyboards are more neatly drawn than thumbnails (which are rougher) because high-end corporate clients or a large group of directors who see the final product need to have a clear picture of what's going on. However, the biggest visual difference is that a storyboard sequence is drawn out frame by frame rather than a bunch of frames grouped together page by page.

✓ **Thumbnails are an essential brainstorming method that helps you preview how the pictures in the frame ultimately flow throughout the entire story.** The manga-ka looks over the small sketches and may change the sequential order, or decide to make certain frames larger or smaller in order to better communicate with the readers.

✓ **Thumbnails help the manga-ka plan the pages so that each episode ends when it's supposed to without running over the allotted page count.** Ruining the ending of a well-illustrated and exciting story just because the manga-ka doesn't have enough open pages left is a nightmare.

So, the moral of the story is to always, *always* get into the habit of drawing thumbnails for your pages before heading into the final larger pages. It saves time, headaches, and money you spend on materials.

Practicing thumbnails

A professional manga-ka shows thumbnails of his pages to the publishing editor or to the writer who then gives feedback to the manga-ka during the development stage before he or she spends hours creating the final pages. As an freelance illustrator, I also draw thumbnails to show art directors what kinds of ideas I have in mind before I develop the final product. It also helps my art directors get a clearer idea of what to expect. In Figure 18-1, I show some examples of page thumbnails.

Try this thumbnail project working from a script:

1. **Select a comic book script (pages without any images — just the frame-by-frame dialogue and description of what's going on) and read through the first five pages.**

If you don't have a script, you can send a request to a publisher for a sample copy, or have a friend write a five-page script describing an existing comic book that you don't know. Make sure to have her indicate the page and panel number as well as dialogue and characters.

2. **Take several blank sheets of regular photocopy paper and fold them in half to create your own minibook.**

3. **Read through the script several times and then quickly sketch out the entire page-by-page sequence according to the script.**

Rather than drawing the panel frames around the completed rough image, first draw all the frames before drawing any of the images inside. Drawing the frames first allows you to better judge how big or small you need to draw images inside. As you sketch your manga images inside the panel frames, I recommend also sketching where you want to fit in the *word balloons* (empty space for dialogue). You don't want to face the shocking reality after you spend all those hours drawing that you have no space left for the word balloons. Unavoidably, small portions of your final manga art get covered by word balloons — you need to make sure that whatever space is covered up isn't too important.

Transferring the thumbnails to final paper

When you're done with the thumbnails, you're ready to transfer them onto larger drawing paper. The most common mistake beginners make is trying to redraw the entire storyboard at a larger size to match the larger paper. This method has many problems. First, you're wasting your time trying to duplicate the energy that you spontaneously generated in your thumbnails. The energy and flow that you have in your smaller sketches are difficult enough to reproduce as it is. Second, redrawing the entire thumbnail just isn't practical. In fact, obtaining the same overall feel is impossible when your vision and hand coordination become overwhelmed with having to compensate for such a large space to fill.

What I recommend is quite simple: Go to a copy machine and, for less than 10 cents a copy, enlarge your sketches to the size of your final drawing paper. After that, take the enlarged photocopy and place it over a *light box* (a box with a translucent lid fixture with florescent light bulbs inside). Place your final manga paper over the enlarged sketch so the position of the rough sketch frames matches roughly where you want the final frames to be. Don't worry if the placement doesn't match up 100 percent — you want to use the rough sketch underneath as a guide to draw a more accurate outline drawing from which you can further refine. After that's done, turn off the light box and you're ready to render and refine your manga drawing on your final manga paper (you no longer need the rough sketch from this point). This may seem like a lot of steps, but it's the cheapest and most efficient method.

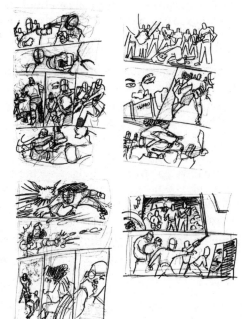

Figure 18-1:
Examples of
typical
rough
thumbnails.

Sketching Scenic Backgrounds

In this section, I share some tips and methods on creating scenery for your characters. Three elements go into creating a dimensional composition: a *foreground, middle ground,* and *background.* Try to include all three; they're especially effective when you're drawing establishing shots to show readers where your story takes place.

The key to creating the illusion of depth is creating overlapping shapes (I say illusion because you're trying to fool the eye into thinking that it's seeing a three-dimensional object on a flat, two-dimensional space.) As I show you in the following examples, foreground objects should overlap objects in the middle ground, which in turn go in front of the background images.

Cityscapes

In Chapter 16, I show you how to create basic cityscapes using one-point, two-point, and three-point perspectives. Adding more layers to the background behind the basic cityscape not only makes it more dimensional, but also tells the reader more about the character and time setting of the scene.

In this exercise, I demonstrate how adding a middle ground and background behind a foreground setting helps create depth within your establishing shot:

1. **Draw a set of buildings using one-point perspective (as shown in Figure 18-2).**

   My example is a passable establishing shot. The readers know that the story takes place in some city downtown (which is the foreground level for this particular example).

2. **Add simple, abstract building shapes behind the foreground perspective (as shown in Figure 18-3).**

   Observe that the building objects run fairly parallel to the horizon line. I vary the perspective of the buildings by having some of them face completely forward while I turn others at an angle. By completing this step, you're letting the readers know that the city is quite large.

   TIP

   To differentiate between the foreground buildings, you can leave the lines open as I do.

3. **Draw a skyline in the background of the city (as shown in Figure 18-4).**

   You don't have to draw the images in detail. In fact, the farther away the objects get, the less detail you should see. In my scene (as shown in Figure 18-4a), I draw simple abstract cloud shapes and a sun setting behind the buildings. In Figure 18-4b, I use the cross hatching and line technique from Chapter 3 to show that it's getting darker.

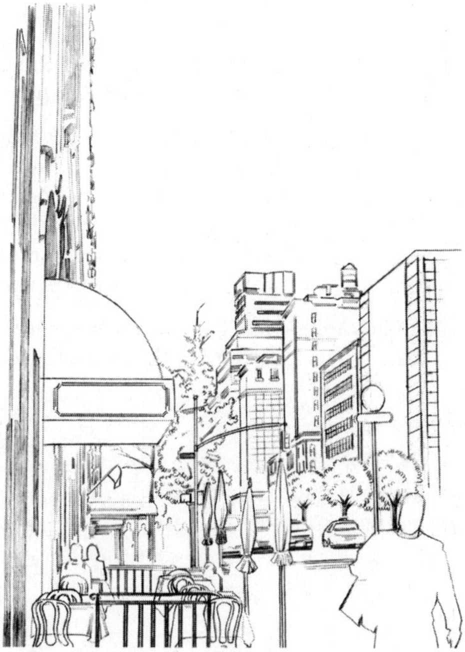

Figure 18-2: Starting with a one-point perspective downtown shot.

Heading to the country: Trees, bushes, and pastures

Don't let the complex forests on those nature shows fool you into thinking that drawing trees is impossible. In this section, I start you off with the basics of drawing simple tree variations. From there, I demonstrate more complex scenes.

Single circle-based trees

First, I show you how to draw a single tree using a simple circle and triangle as your guide. These types of trees are fun and quite addicting.

1. **Lightly draw a circle at the center of your paper (as shown in Figure 18-5a).**

   I recommend keeping the circle small at first (no larger than 1½ inches in diameter). Remember, your circle guide needs to be drawn lightly (otherwise, erasing it when you no longer need it is difficult). The circle doesn't need to be drawn perfectly. In fact, less perfect circles make more interesting trees.

2. **Draw a narrow triangle for your tree trunk intersecting at the bottom of the circle (see Figure 18-5b).**

   It's easier to work with a triangle with a blunt tip. The degree to which the triangle needs to overlap the circle depends on how long you want the trunk to be. The lower you draw the triangle, the longer your trunk becomes.

3. **Refine the tree trunk to make it more realistic and use the circle guide to add smaller bumps for the outside tree shape (see Figure 18-5c).**

   Draw the roots of the trunk as well as the top branches going into the top circle of the tree. At the end of the branches, you want to cap them off with short squiggly lines (make sure the bumps face *toward* the branches and not away). This gives a more dimensional look to branches. Lightly erase the circle line, but leave enough so you can see and use it to draw a series of uneven blunt squiggly lines around.

   To make your tree look believable, draw the length and width of the branches and roots as random as possible so they don't look artificial.

Multiple circle-based trees

Now I step it up and show you how to create larger trees using more than one circle. The concept is similar to using just one circle in the previous section, but here you get more artistic freedom and more interesting shaped trees.

Figure 18-3:
Adding the middle ground layer behind the foreground buildings.

Figure 18-4:
Adding the background to the scene.

a

b

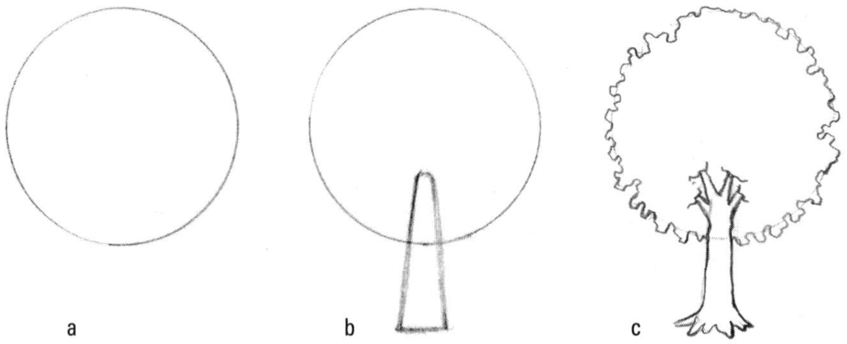

Figure 18-5:
Drawing a
single circle
tree.

a   b   c

1. **Lightly draw several different shapes of overlapping circles around the center of your paper (as shown in Figure 18-6a).**

   Make sure your circles overlap each other to create the illusion of depth. I recommend keeping the largest circle no larger than 1½ inches in diameter.

2. **Draw a narrow triangle for your tree trunk intersecting at the bottom of the circles (see Figure 18-6b).**

   The triangle is the same one you use for the single circle tree from the previous section. Instead of determining the midway point of a single tree like you do in the previous section, you want to determine the centermost point based on the length of both bottom circles combined. But don't bother measuring the length to find the mark, just make your best guess. Then go ahead and draw the triangle for the trunk.

3. **Refine the tree trunk to make it more realistic and use the circle guides to add smaller bumps for the outside tree shapes (see Figure 18-6c).**

   Draw the roots of the trunk as well as the top branches going into the top circle of the tree. Cap off the ends of the branches with short squiggly lines. Lightly erase the circle lines, leaving enough so you can see and use them when you draw a series of uneven blunt squiggly lines.

   When drawing these squiggly lines, determine which circle you want to place in the foreground, middle ground, and background. I recommend using either circle on the bottom as your foreground or middle ground (the top circle usually sits in the background). You can show one circle in front by completing the squiggly lines as opposed to leaving the remaining two shapes either incomplete or partially hidden behind the other.

Using ovals to create taller trees

In this section, I show you how to create taller more slender trees using ovals instead of circles. The process is virtually identical to the previous tree using three circles. The only difference is the shape of the body I use in Step 3.

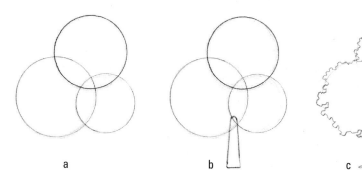

Figure 18-6:
Adding multiple circle shapes to the tree.

1. **Lightly draw several different shapes of overlapping ovals around the center of your paper (as shown in Figure 18-7a).**

   Make sure that you draw the ovals vertically and that they overlap each other to create the illusion of depth.

2. **Draw a narrow triangle for your tree trunk intersecting at the bottom oval (see Figure 18-7b).**

   Because taller and narrow trees usually have longer trunks, draw the triangle for your trunk either lower or slightly longer.

3. **Refine the tree trunk to make it more realistic and use the oval guides to add smaller bumps for the outside tree shapes (see Figure 18-7c).**

   The key to getting this tree right is to first complete the center bottom body of leaves first. With taller trees, draw the squiggles pointing toward the sun (as does happen with taller and thinner vegetation). From there, draw another pair of branches shooting into the tree oval to the left and complete that form with the same squiggly lines to complete the leaves (just make sure you indicate that a portion of it is hidden behind the first body of leaves). Keep repeating this for the remaining ovals.

Triangle-based trees

Triangle-based trees have sharper edges; an example is the evergreen. Follow these steps to draw this kind of tree:

1. **Draw a slightly elongated triangle at the center of your paper (as shown in Figure 18-8a).**

2. **Draw a short triangle for the tree trunk (as shown in Figure 18-8b).**

   You want to keep this triangle shorter so that the tree is closer to the ground.

3. **Starting from the top to bottom, draw individual segments of the tree sections (as shown in Figure 18-8c).**

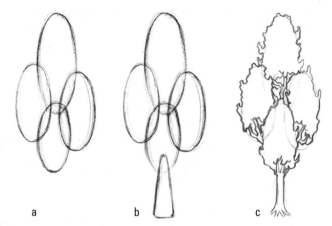

Figure 18-7:
Switching
over to
using ovals.

a   b   c

The key to getting the branches to look dimensional is leaving a gap
between the branches coming down from both sides (as shown in
Figure 18-8c). Another trick to making the tree look dimensional is
making the sharp zigzag shapes larger as segments get closer to the
ground (as objects go higher, they get smaller and vice versa).

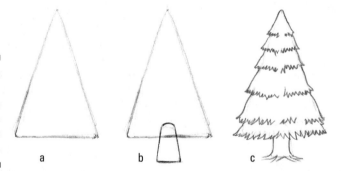

Figure 18-8:
Using a
triangle to
draw an
evergreen
tree.

a   b   c

Leaves and branches

In this section, I demonstrate ways of creating leaves and branches that you
can use in the foreground (as I mention earlier, you can get more specific with
objects that are close in the frame). I encourage you to look around and
select interesting leaf shapes that are simple enough to draw. For example,
follow along with the tear-shaped leaf:

1. **Lightly draw a circle guide at the center of your paper (see
   Figure 18-9a).**

   Don't draw the circle too large; keep it around 1 inch in diameter.

2. **Using the circle as the base, draw the leaf shape and stem (as shown in Figure 18-9b).**

   I suggest first drawing the leaf shape that resembles a tear drawn sideways. If it helps, draw the tear shape vertically and then rotate the paper so that it's resting on its side. Next, draw the stem on the left side of the circle leaf base. Draw the midsection of the stem slightly narrower than both ends to give it a natural organic look. If you look at a leaf in real life, you notice that the end of the stem has curves in a "C" shape where it connects to the branch.

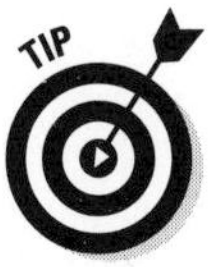
TIP

   Draw one side of the leaf different than the other; one side may have a simple curve, and the other may have an inverse curve shape. The tip of the leaf should lean toward one direction (up) over the other (down). This asymmetry helps give the leaf a more natural appearance.

3. **Add the details, starting with the center vein of the leaf, which travels from the base stem on the left to the tip of the leaf on the right, and then draw the smaller vein shapes that extend from it (see Figure 18-9c).**

   The center vein (called the *mid rib*) should curve and thin out gradually as it runs from the base stem to the end tip of the leaf. I make sure the veins that branch out from the mid rib to the edges of the leaf also curve from thick to thin to give it that organic look.

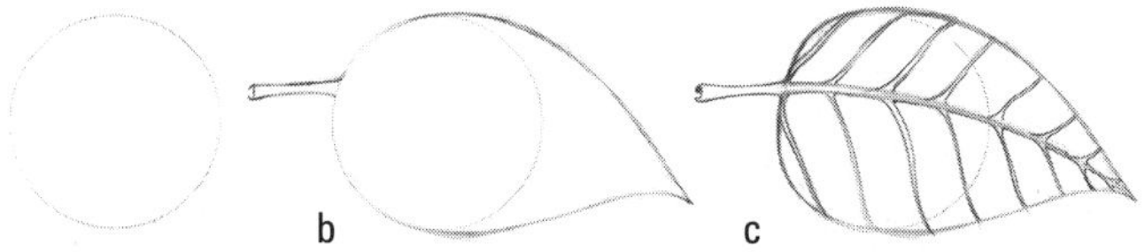
a b c

Figure 18-9: Starting off with a basic circle to draw a tear-shaped leaf.

Circle guides come in especially handy when you're determining the overall composition and structure in a frame where you have a branch with multiple leaves in the foreground. Follow along to see what I mean:

1. **Draw several bare branch shapes (as shown in Figure 18-10).**

   I show you just a few of the many types of branches that are common. Generally, straighter and angled branches (see Figure 18-10a and Figure 18-10b) are more brittle as opposed to branches that have longer curves (see Figure 18-10c).

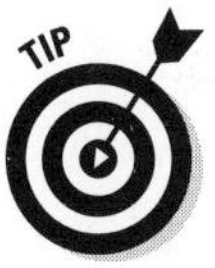
TIP

   When drawing branches, think of them as hands and fingers extending out from an arm. I find it gives more personality and feeling (plus it adds to the fun of drawing them).

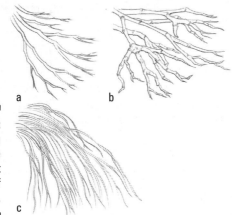

Figure 18-10:
Exploring
some
different
types of
branches.

2. **Draw a series of circles for the leaves, working from the tip of the branch and going up (as shown in Figure 18-11).**

   Don't use a template when drawing these circles — it slows you down, and imperfect circles (which are uneven and slightly different sizes) make more natural looking leaves.

   I make a point of placing the leaves opposite of each other. In addition, I don't hesitate to overlap the circles (especially if they're from different neighboring branches).

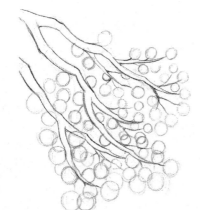

Figure 18-11:
Deciding
on the
placement
of my leaves
by drawing
the circle
guides.

3. **Finish off the leaves on the branches (as shown in Figure 18-12).**

   You don't have to draw all the detail onto the leaves if they're farther away. I like to overlap the leaves to give the branches more dimension and naturalism.

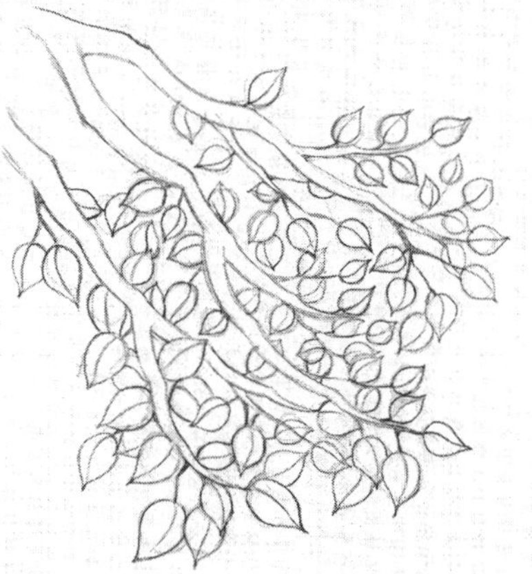

Figure 18-12: Finishing off the leaves on my branches.

Grass and bushes

Grass and bushes work well together and are fun to draw because they're quite simple and have interesting shapes. Just for giggles, look at how different manga-ka draw these items. Although they're simple in form, they play a big role in telling readers where the ground is in relation to where the characters stand and the rest of the natural environment. In this section, I start off by demonstrating how I draw grass and shrubbery that are closer as opposed to some that are farther away.

Follow these steps on how to draw an open grass field with some simple bushes off to the side:

1. **Draw two horizontal squiggle lines (one long and the other short).**

   In Figure 18-13a, I leave parts of the longer line thinner without much detail to show that the horizon is out in the distance. In Figure 18-13b, I draw the second shorter line below and slightly off to the right of the longer line. Make this line thicker with more details of the grass to show that this patch of grass is closer to the readers.

   TIP: When drawing objects in landscapes, a good rule of thumb is that objects in the distance are less detailed, and have thinner line weight and lighter value. Objects that come closer have more detail, thicker line weight, and darker value.

2. **Draw small batches of grass, which I like to call "hedgehogs," randomly on the empty area (as shown in Figure 18-13c).**

   The purpose of drawing these "hedgehogs" is to give readers something more to look at instead of staring at a blank empty space beneath the horizon line. In my drawing, it also helps to balance the weight of the overall composition so that readers aren't too distracted by the darker patch of grass off to the right from Step 1.

> **TIP**
>
> To get that random feel of placement, slightly alter the shapes and sizes of the hedgehogs. Avoid simply reproducing the same ones — if you do, the overall image appears flat.

Figure 18-13: Drawing horizon grass lines and little hedgehog grass patches.

3. **Add the bushes right above the shorter, darker grass line (as shown in Figure 18-14).**

   Lightly draw a series of overlapping, bubble-shaped guidelines right above the shorter darker grass line off to the right (as shown in Figure 18-14a).

> **TIP**
>
> The key to getting the bushes to look dimensional is to always draw the next bubble shape either slightly higher, or above and behind the last bubble. The more similar objects you draw on the same level, the more the overall image becomes flat and unconvincing.

   In Figure 18-14b, I lightly (but not completely) erase the bubble guidelines just enough that I can still see them to draw the outer edges of the bushes.

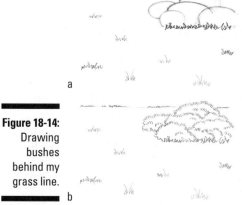

Figure 18-14: Drawing bushes behind my grass line.

When you know how to create the individual elements, combine them together to establish a clear foreground, middle ground, and background, like I do in Figure 18-15. Everything looks dimensional and shows enough information to make the readers believe the story that you're about to tell.

Rocks and bodies of water

Picture a nightmare where you're standing in front of a lake surrounded by jagged mountains and rocks. In this section, I show tips on how to draw a convincing water surface as well as various rock surfaces. So, get ready to rock on!

Water

Everybody knows that water is transparent, but you need to account for the blue color reflected from the sky, add all the detailed shadow shapes, and highlight the reflections you see at the beach or while sailing. In this section, I show you a trick to drawing water to look convincing enough for your manga audience.

I show you how to draw three types of water surfaces under different weather conditions. Keep in mind that the calmer bodies of water have less detail, thinner lines, and smoother shadows. Rougher waters have more detail, thicker lines, and jagged/harsher shadow shapes.

Figure 18-15:
Pulling everything together to create a foreground, middle ground, and background.

Follow these steps to draw a calm, quiet body of water:

1. **Draw a thin horizon line without using your ruler (as shown in Figure 18-16a).**

   This horizon line represent my viewpoint or eye level of the water. To make the water look as if it expands forever, make the horizon line as thin as possible.

2. **Starting from the top of the horizon line to the bottom of the frame, draw a series of light, sporadic, short lines (as shown in Figure 18-16b).**
3. **As the lines get closer to the bottom of the frame, switch to using very thin shapes to represent the shadows cast by the water movement (as shown in Figure 18-16c).**

   Don't make the shadow shapes wide unless you want to indicate actual objects floating on the surface area. Keep them very narrow.

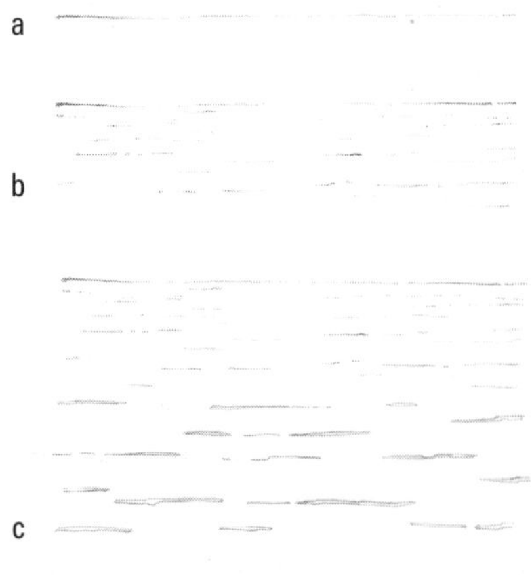
a
b
c

Figure 18-16: Drawing a calm water surface.

Next, I step it up a bit by demonstrating how to draw the same ocean, yet under windier weather. In this case, you need to draw larger water movements caused by the rising wind.

1. **Draw the horizon line with some pointed edges protruding up (as shown in Figure 18-17a).**
2. **Starting from the top of the horizon line to the bottom of the frame, draw a series of small, lightly shaded "blotch" mark shadows cast by the rising water movement (as shown in Figure 18-17b).**

   Avoid making the shadow shapes too tall, angular, or big — you're still looking on from a distance.

Although drawing this surface takes practice, the surface looks more believable the more you vary the shapes (especially the width).

3. **As the shadow shapes come closer to your readers (or your character on the boat) as you work your way down the bottom of the frame, gradually increase their size and darkness (as shown in Figure 18-17c).**

Add a variety of smaller shadow shapes to fill in the gaps between the larger shapes. Adding more detail to the shadow shapes makes the water look more dimensional. The shapes of the shadows should also become more complex. As objects approach the readers, be sure to draw more detail.

a

b

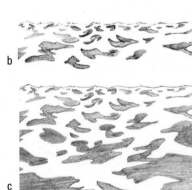

Figure 18-17:
Adding
some action
to the water
surface.

c

Now, the weather gets rough! Say you're drawing your character's viewpoint of the same ocean except she's about to experience a serious weather storm. You need to draw the waves higher and more angular.

1. **Draw the horizon line broken with bumps and small waves to show action that can be seen from a distance (as shown in Figure 18-18a).**

2. **From the top, draw a series of thin, jagged shadow shapes that get longer as you work your way down and away from the horizon line (as shown in Figure 18-18b).**

3. **As you get closer to the bottom of the frame, the shapes should have a loose resemblance to brittle tree branches (as shown in Figure 18-18c).**

Note how some shadow shapes lead and connect with other shapes. Include small shapes among the longer and larger shapes as your view gets closer to the foreground.

a
b
c

Figure 18-18: Adding even more chaos to the water surface.

Rocks

In this section, I show you how to draw the basic smooth and rough surfaces found in common rocky terrain. If you aren't familiar with cross-hatching, please turn to Chapter 3, where I demonstrate how to warm up with a series of cross-hatching exercises.

I begin with a mountain of smooth rocks (known as boulders):

1. **Start from any random point and draw a large bubble shape for your boulder guide along with other various sizes randomly placed (as shown in Figure 18-19a).**

   TIP

   The key to getting the rocks to look dimensional is letting shapes overlap one another. Also, the overall size of the shapes should get bigger as they come closer to you.

2. **Refine the rocks and draw the shadows (as shown in Figure 18-19b).**

   You want to give the rocks shadows to give them dimension. Although the rocks aren't completely round, see how similar the shadow shapes are with that of a sphere. As I shade them, I use the *hito-keta* half-tone shading technique (refer to Chapter 3). If this is your first time applying this technique, don't be frustrated if its application doesn't come naturally at first. Keep practicing in your sketchpad, and you'll develop the knack for getting it down.

   TIP

   A trick to getting the boulder to look like it's closer to you is to add more detailed and darker shadows. In contrast, by adding little or no shadow detail, you make even the larger boulders look distant.

3. **Add the finishing touches, such as the nicks and cracks, to show the age and surface texture (as shown in Figure 18-19c).**

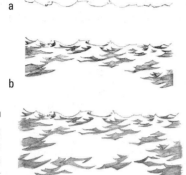

I draw some grass strands sticking out from between the boulder cracks. Straight, angular lines for cracks mixed with rounder stain marks give more realism and character to the rock.

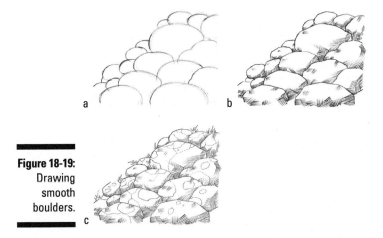

Figure 18-19:
Drawing
smooth
boulders.

Now I present to you the jagged, rough rock pillar:

1. **Starting from the top of your paper, draw the outline of the whole pillar shape measuring 6 to 7 inches tall (as shown in Figure 18-20a).**

   Keep your pillar shape centered. By nature, the smaller rocks tend to be on top while the heavier ones remain at the bottom. But just for kicks and giggles, I draw a large jagged boulder stuck at the top. Observe that unlike the smoother lines of the boulders, the outline here is angular and chiseled without any curves.

2. **Taking it from the top, draw small, abstract, trapezoidal shapes that get larger as you work your way down to the base of the pillar (as shown in Figure 18-20b).**

3. **Chisel in the shadow shapes, which are straight, without any soft edges (see Figure 18-20c).**

   I use the same *hito-keta* half-tone pattern I use in the previous smooth boulders to fill in the shadow shapes. Compare these shadow shapes to the softer, rounder shadow edges of the boulders earlier in this chapter.

4. **Give the final image more contrast (as shown in Figure 18-20d).**

   I apply the *futa-keta* half-tone pattern based on the hito-keta pattern (refer to Chapter 3).

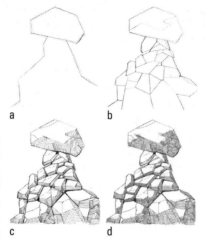

a b c d

Figure 18-20:
Drawing
the pillar of
jagged slabs
of rock.

Now that you know how to create rocks and water individually, you can
combine them to establish a clear foreground, middle ground, and background, as I do in Figure 18-21. Observe how the water surrounding the
jagged pillars has rings wrapping around the base. Also note how the
jagged objects tend to come forward while the softer boulders tend to
fade back.

Figure 18-21:
Pulling
rocks and
water
together to
create a
foreground,
middle
ground, and
background.

Chapter 19

Writing a Good Story

● ●

In This Chapter

▶ Keeping your readers on their toes

▶ Developing a strong plot with likeable characters

▶ Finding inspiration for fresh ideas

● ●

Coming up with solid stories that feature characters your readers care about is important to every *manga-ka* (manga artist). Brilliant artwork and cool special effects are initially eye-catching, but today's readers are sophisticated in taste and demands. As is the case with some mainstream movies being released today, huge special effects in manga need to be partnered with strong casting and an enticing plot. Despite an increasing amount of manga titles written and illustrated by more than one individual, a manga-ka is ultimately expected to be proficient in both drawing and storytelling. In this chapter, I ask you to determine your target audience, give you pointers on developing a plot, and encourage you to look for inspiration.

Deciding Who Your Audience Is

First thing's first: Ask yourself who your manga audience is going to be. Read through the list of different genres of manga in Chapter 1 to see which ones you find interesting. No matter how proficiently you crank out wonderful pages with stellar story concepts, your audience won't respond if your material is geared toward the wrong crowd.

To avoid writing for the wrong audience, find out what kind of manga genre best fits your story style and drawing tastes. I recommend getting several manga magazines and flipping through a number of titles. Chatting with friends and participating in online manga groups are both great ways to find out what popular titles people are raving about today. If you don't find a niche immediately, don't worry. It can take time.

The story line isn't always what triggers your interest in a specific niche — sometimes the artwork or character design draws you in. I recommend scouting out local animé or manga conventions to see what type of character art is out there. Talk to the exhibiting guest artists who have their artwork on display. If a style interests you, ask which audience the manga-ka is marketing toward.

Establishing a Synopsis and Plot

Simply put, a *plot* is what makes your manga story juicy enough to get your readers to read until the end. An effective plot begins by building up a series of sequential obstacles and events that keep the audience wondering what's going to happen to the characters. These obstacles and events build toward the very height of the story's *climax,* which is the decisive turning point in the action. From the climax, the characters resolve the obstacles and ultimately restore order.

In the following sections, I explain the purpose behind creating your own synopsis, and I break down the structural essence of an effective plot in the four storytelling narrative stages that most manga-ka professionals and amateurs observe.

Creating a synopsis

A *synopsis* is several short paragraphs in which you present your characters, the setting, and the main obstacle that your character must overcome. If you're interested in submitting work to a publisher, most editors request a synopsis along with copies of the first five pages of your original artwork. In length, a synopsis shouldn't exceed a full page. Although you don't state exactly how the main characters conquer their problems, you should include enough information to catch the publisher's or reader's attention. Your ultimate goal is to whet the appetite of the publishers by giving them something to nibble on when they look at your submission. Although readers rarely get to see the synopsis in their favorite comic book, most manga publishers in the Japan typically place a brief synopsis of the story at the beginning of the book so that new readers tuning in for the first time know what's going on before they jump in.

Look at the synopsis as a brainstorming opportunity, where you can flesh out a general proposal of what you have in mind without actually committing to a resolution.

Constructing your plot

In this section, I explain the basic stages that a manga-ka uses to create his or her original plot. The basic stages are widely embraced by the manga-ka community today, and they originate from classical Chinese poetry. After I explain the concept behind each stage, I show how to apply it by referring to page excerpts from the first issue of my original series, *JAVA!*

Stage 1: Ki — Introduction of an idea

Stage 1 basically sets up the context and scene so that the story can begin and the characters can begin to interact. To start this *Ki* (introduction) stage, a manga-ka draws the opening frame, called an *establishing shot,* to give the readers a sense of the location where the story takes place. These shots are usually larger than the average-sized frame the manga-ka draws, because he wants to include more detail in the setting. By the time this stage is complete, readers should have a good sense of who the important characters are as well as the time and location of the story.

In my *Ki* stage in Figure 19-1, readers meet my main and side characters for the very first time. I show the opening page of issue 1 of *JAVA!* where the readers see the main heroine, Java, with her sidekick, La-Té. The dialogue going on in the background leads the way into the introduction of the characters. Java (the rookie team member) is the reckless caffeine-powered girl who fights crime. La-Té is her big sister veteran figure who cautiously looks after the safety of the team (see Chapter 8 for more about this kind of sidekick). I make it clear that the story takes place in a desert (shortly to be revealed as Neo-Seattle in the year 2073). Because Java is peering through hi-tech binoculars, you know the story takes place during a technologically advanced era.

Stage 2: Sho — Developing the idea

In the second stage, you focus on building up the suspense of the story based upon the characters and concepts you introduced in the *Ki* stage (see the previous section). You introduced your readers to your characters and briefed them on the context of your story, and now you build up their curiosity. In the *Sho* (development) stage, the tempo of the story's flow should steadily increase. What kind of conflicts are your characters taking on to achieve their goal? Do you leave clues to the readers about possible danger that the main characters themselves don't know about? What are the perils or challenges ahead? In most manga, this section is crucial, because if the readers don't care about your characters, they don't care about what happens to them.

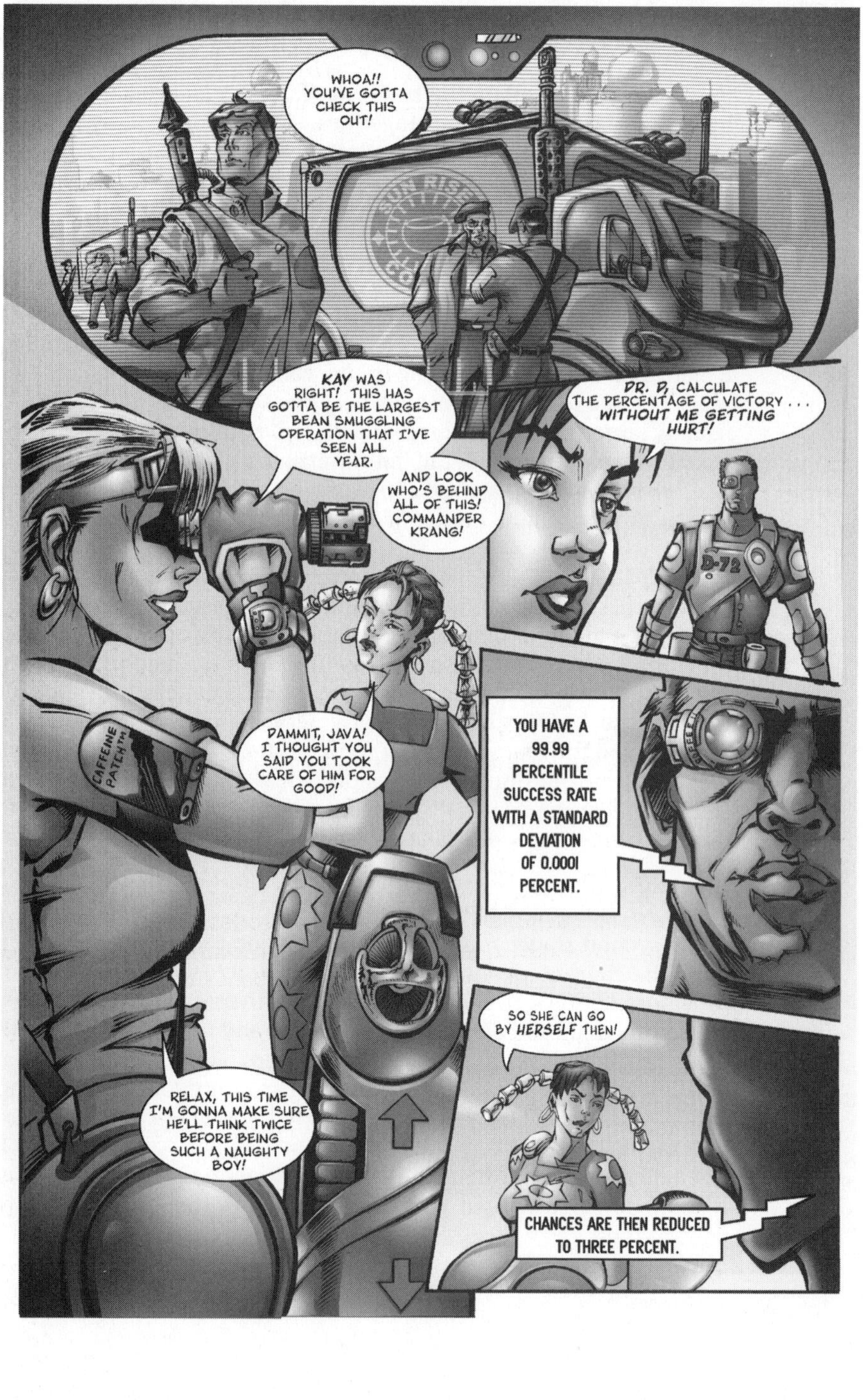
WHOA!! YOU'VE GOTTA CHECK THIS OUT!
KAY WAS RIGHT! THIS HAS GOTTA BE THE LARGEST BEAN SMUGGLING OPERATION THAT I'VE SEEN ALL YEAR.
AND LOOK WHO'S BEHIND ALL OF THIS! COMMANDER KRANG!
CAFFEINE PATCH™
DAMMIT, JAVA! I THOUGHT YOU SAID YOU TOOK CARE OF HIM FOR GOOD!
RELAX, THIS TIME I'M GONNA MAKE SURE HE'LL THINK TWICE BEFORE BEING SUCH A NAUGHTY BOY!
DR. D, CALCULATE THE PERCENTAGE OF VICTORY . . . WITHOUT ME GETTING HURT!
D-72
YOU HAVE A 99.99 PERCENTILE SUCCESS RATE WITH A STANDARD DEVIATION OF 0.0001 PERCENT.
SO SHE CAN GO BY HERSELF THEN!
CHANCES ARE THEN REDUCED TO THREE PERCENT.

Figure 19-1: The opening introduction section taken from a prelude in *JAVA!* #1.

As an example, check out Figure 19-2 to see the *Sho* stage of the first issue of *JAVA!* You see that the characters are gearing up on their hi-tech surfboards and going off to break up the illegal trafficking operations. They hope to take a sample of the tainted beans as evidence for the team's mentor figure, Dr. D. He mentions that Java's chances of survival are reduced to nil without La-Té by her side, and that builds up the readers' curiosity about the nature of these two characters' working chemistry. What makes it so special? Can the enemy exploit a certain weakness to defeat Java? From what I let the readers know up to this point, she seems confident enough to handle things by herself.

Stage 3: Ten — The dramatic, unexpected turn of events

In the third stage, you want a surprise development where your characters face a situation that throws the *readers* off guard. Note that I say "readers" and not necessarily characters. In the *Ten* (turn) stage, the result of all the building up since Stage 2 leads to the ultimate climax where readers are sitting at the edge of their seats holding their breaths. If you're looking to reveal to the readers the largest showdown of your story sequence, this is the right time and place to do so!

If you're following the events from *JAVA!* #1 that I include in this chapter, check out Figure 19-3 to see what happens next. Java's sidekick, La-Té, gets caught — an event that happens unexpectedly. Java's arch nemesis, Commander Krang, suddenly grabs La-Té and holds her hostage. The scene reaches its climax when Krang orders Java to either drop the *Decaffeinating Grenade* that she plans to use to destroy the illegal tainted coffee beans or lose her sidekick. You can tell by the way she hesitates grinningly that she's reckless; she's so confident that her friend can handle things on her own that she doesn't take Krang's threat seriously.

Stage 4: Ketsu — Conclusion

Stage 4 finishes the story. While some episodes may end by fully resolving an issue, others end by opening another can of worms, leaving the readers hanging from a cliff, wanting to know what happens in the next issue.

To find out how the action in issue 1 of *JAVA!* ends, take a look at Figure 19-4. In my *Ketsu* (conclusion) stage, everything is resolved, but not the way La-Té would have hoped for. Commander Krang yanks on the espresso shot-glass grenades she wears in her hair and accidentally triggers their detonation. La-Té's hair and makeup are ruined and Dr. D has no sample of evidence to use or analyze in his lab. Java grins guiltily, but she knows it's just another day at the office.

If the examples in this chapter leave you jonesing for another shot of *JAVA!*, go to www.javacomics.com and www.piggybackstudios.com.

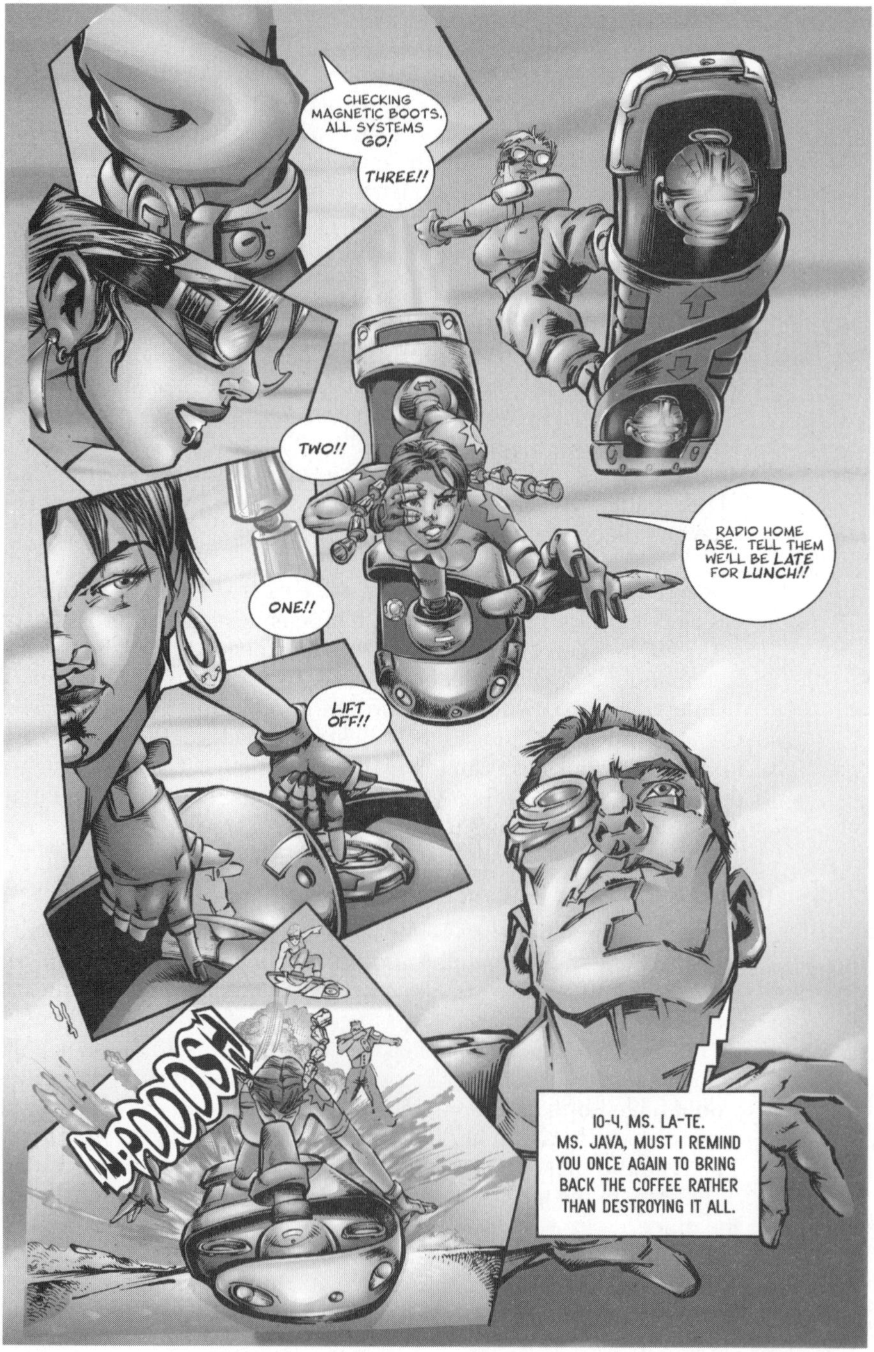
CHECKING MAGNETIC BOOTS. ALL SYSTEMS GO!
THREE!!
TWO!!
ONE!!
LIFT OFF!!
RADIO HOME BASE. TELL THEM WE'LL BE LATE FOR LUNCH!!
10-4, MS. LA-TE.
MS. JAVA, MUST I REMIND YOU ONCE AGAIN TO BRING BACK THE COFFEE RATHER THAN DESTROYING IT ALL.

Figure 19-2: The development section taken from a short prelude in *JAVA!* #1.

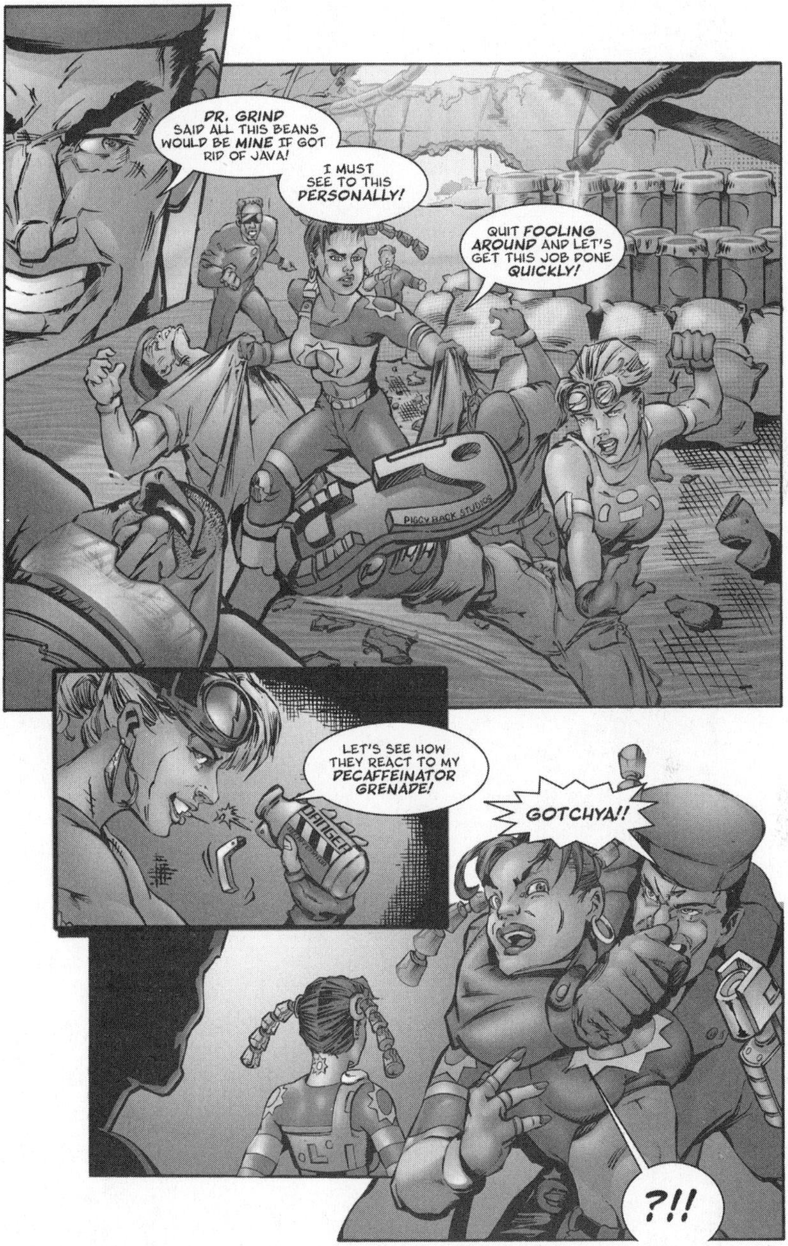
DR. GRIND SAID ALL THIS BEANS WOULD BE MINE IF GOT RID OF JAVA!
I MUST SEE TO THIS PERSONALLY!
QUIT FOOLING AROUND AND LET'S GET THIS JOB DONE QUICKLY!
LET'S SEE HOW THEY REACT TO MY DECAFFEINATOR GRENADE!
DANGER
GOTCHYA!!
?!!

Figure 19-3: The climax of a short prelude in *JAVA!* #1.

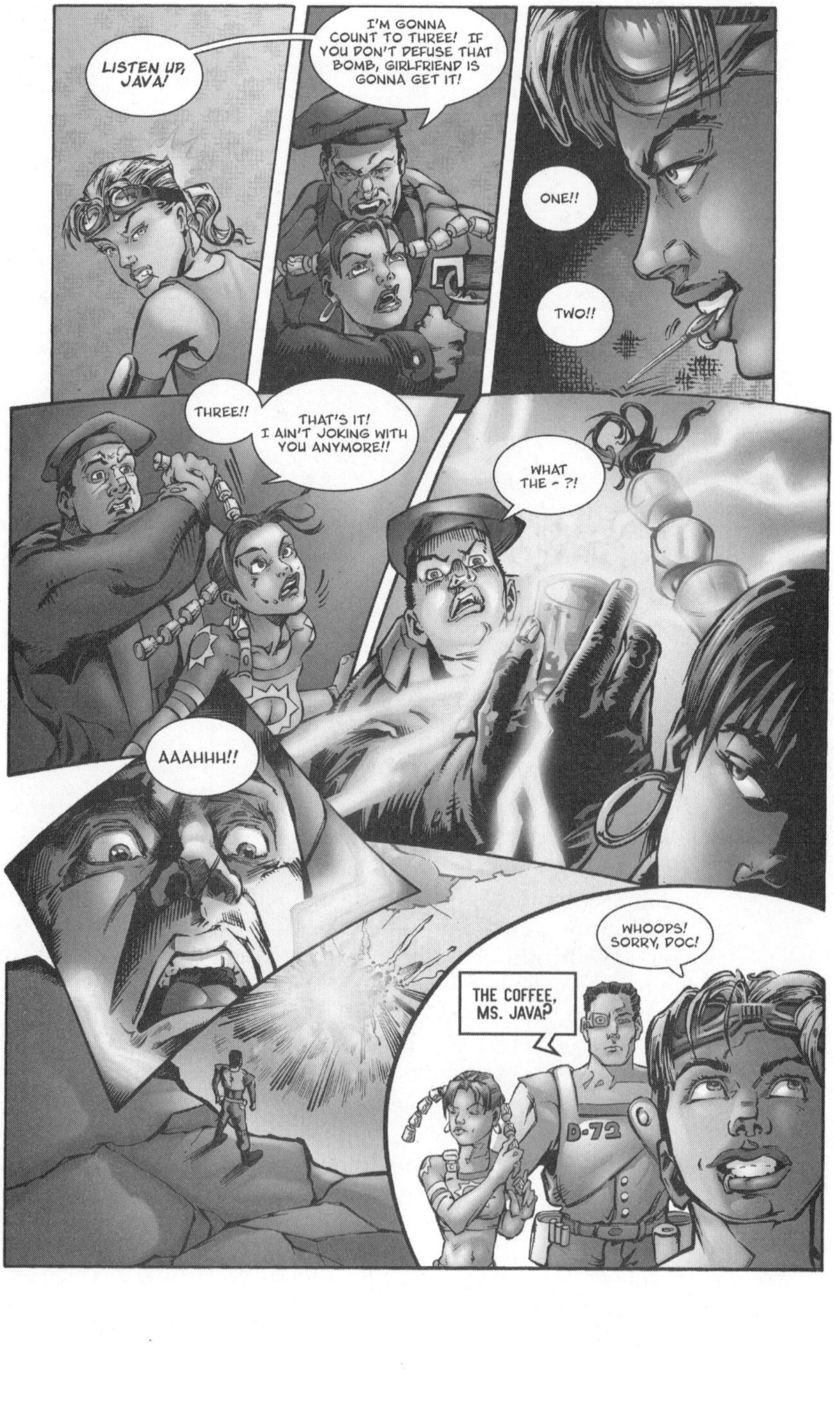
LISTEN UP, JAVA!
I'M GONNA COUNT TO THREE! IF YOU DON'T DEFUSE THAT BOMB, GIRLFRIEND IS GONNA GET IT!
ONE!!
TWO!!
THREE!!
THAT'S IT! I AIN'T JOKING WITH YOU ANYMORE!!
WHAT THE - ?!
AAAHHH!!
WHOOPS! SORRY, DOC!
THE COFFEE, MS. JAVA?
D-72

Figure 19-4: The resolution section taken from a short prelude in *JAVA!* #1.

TIP

For a helpful way of understanding this concept, look at the four steps in a graph format (as shown in Figure 19-5). As you plan the stages for your script, I recommend limiting your first story to six to eight pages.

Ten
Sho
Ki
Ketsu
1
2
3
4
5
6
Page Progression

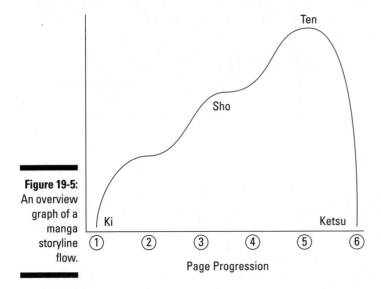

Figure 19-5: An overview graph of a manga storyline flow.

Seeking Inspiration

When you know the basic concept and structure of a story line, you're ready to explore ways of generating material to fill in that story line. Part of the challenge of writing is developing fresh ideas you care about enough to share and talk about. A popular writer's myth is that all ideas come out of the writer's head without her having to step outside her studio. In order to cook fresh food, you need fresh ingredients from outside farms. Likewise, your experiences shape your personality and strong opinions, and you can incorporate them into your story lines. You have those invaluable resources, but you need outside stimulation. Following are some tips and ways of finding various sources of inspiration:

- **Keep a diary.** One thing that helps create an interesting plot is depicting the way characters respond to their environment. The best way of personalizing any of your characters' responses is by recording and becoming aware of the way you respond to your own environment. A general rule of thumb: As long as people are nosy, they will always want to know what's going on with other people's lives. Use the interesting events that happen in your life to draw people's curiosity to your story.

✔ **Gain inspiration by sketching.** You may not read much about this fact, but whenever possible, a manga-ka leaves her studio to travel around, seeking inspiring ideas for her next manga episodes. Sometimes, the manga-ka even travels abroad! Just as a movie team scouts out locations for the right spot to start shooting, a manga-ka records her findings in her sketchbook for new visual ideas. Not all fresh story ideas can be generated from the comforts of your home or studio.

✔ **Remember that sketching isn't limited to traveling.** When you need some fresh faces for your characters to match your story, try using your friends, classmates, or family. What are friends and family for? Well, besides being great pals and lifelong friends, they can also inspire great character ideas. Just make sure you get their written permission to use their likeness in your manga.

✔ **Watch movies.** Am I actually suggesting that you can go watch your favorite movies and call it work? Yes and no. Watching *some* movies that interest you is important, but seeing movies that people are talking about and raving about is also important. Some of these movies may even include black-and-white silent movies from the past. Others may require you to make a trip to an independent film theater. After viewing a show, document your reactions.

✔ **Visit art museums and galleries.** For centuries, artists have learned from one another as apprentices, friends, and rivals. Without feeding off another's resources, coming up with a fresh approach to any story line or character is difficult. Whenever you get the opportunity, visit art shows at museums or galleries. If you have time, some museums let artists sketch or even paint a reproduction right in front of the hanging original!

✔ **Watch people.** Venture into your community to observe how people interact with one another. Spend a day at a mall or café. Take a small sketchbook with you so that you can scribble down ideas or observations based on people's clothes, gestures, or expressions. You may see someone who triggers an idea for a new character for your manga story!

✔ **Build your library.** Finally, but far from last, you should keep a diverse manga and American comic book library. When you visit your next manga or comic book convention, look around to see what's hot. Plenty of retailers are selling books that may serve as an inspiration for another creative story.

Part VI
The Part of Tens

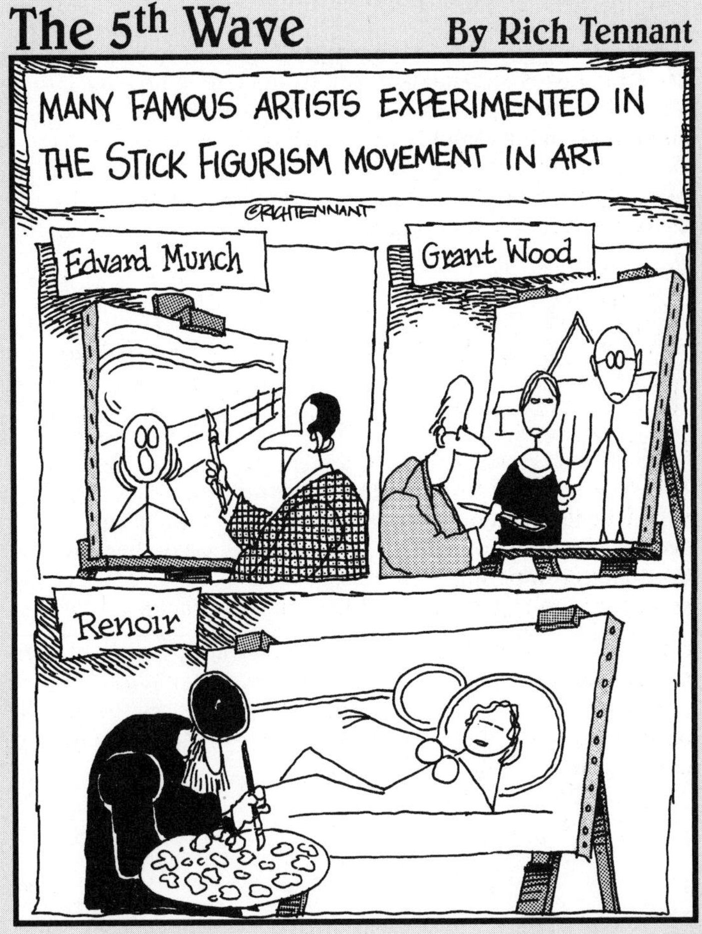
The 5th Wave
By Rich Tennant
MANY FAMOUS ARTISTS EXPERIMENTED IN THE STICK FIGURISM MOVEMENT IN ART
©RICHTENNANT
Edvard Munch
Grant Wood
Renoir

In this part . . .

As a way of wrapping things up, I present to you the famous *For Dummies* Part of Tens. The following chapters give me the chance to share additional useful information and resources.

Here, I list ten manga artists who I think reflect the highlights of the current and past classic manga hits. I encourage you to go through each name and see for yourself whether his or her work jibes with your interests in style and genre. My hope is for you to take and modify the list as you see fit, building a mini-library of manga artists and titles and updating them with new ones.

I also provide the top ten tips on getting your work out to the public. Exposure is key to generating hype among your surrounding community. No matter how small or large you start, when people begin talking about your work, word spreads quickly and increases your chances of recognition.

Chapter 20

Ten (or so) Manga Artists

In This Chapter

- Discovering a century of great manga-ka
- Viewing the life works of great manga artists

Osamu Tezuka (1928–1989)

Considered the "Father of Manga," Osamu Tezuka was born in Osaka, Japan, in 1928. He's most remembered as the prolific *manga-ka* (manga artist) who inspired artists of all genres to follow in his footsteps. Inspired by Walt Disney, Tezuka is credited with applying those large Bambi eyes to the manga characters.

His life works are simply astounding. No other manga-ka has come close to creating as many successful classics. Among them are *Tetsuwan Atom (Astro Boy), Black Jack, Tell Adolf, Hi no Tori, Jungle Emperor,* and *Buddha.*

Astro Boy, which became a hit animated series from 1963 to 1966, is about a robot, Atom, invented by Dr. Tenma as a substitute for his son who died in a car accident. However, Atom is disowned when Dr. Tenma realizes he's a robot who will never grow or become a complete replacement for flesh and blood. Holding a pure heart and knowledge of good from bad, Atom finds a new home with another genius inventor, Dr. Ochyanomizu, who builds a younger sister, mother, and father for him. Atom is equipped with super strength and machine guns on his posterior, and he can fly. Throughout the series, he fights crime and injustice.

In addition to creating shōnen manga series, Tezuka pioneered the shōjo manga genre with the hit classic, *Ribbon no Kishi.*

Fujiko Fujio: Hiroshi Fujimoto (1933–1996) and Motoo Abiko (1934–1988)

A true manga-ka dream team, the dynamic duo of Hiroshi Fujimoto and Motoo Abiko formed to work under the pen name Fujiko Fujio for more than 40 years before going on their separate creative paths.

Buddies since fifth grade, these two lit up the manga world with titles such as *Doraemon, Kaibutsu-kun, Pa-man, 21 Emon,* and *Obake Q-no Taro.* In 1956, they formed a manga alliance group with other well-noted manga-ka, Fujio Akazuka and Ishinomori Shotaro. In a megahit project titled *Manga Michi (Manga Road),* Fujiko Fujio recorded their events and experiences growing up to become professional manga-ka.

Perhaps their best claim to fame is *Doraemon,* which first appeared in 1970 and lasted for a phenomenal 40 volumes. It's about a robot cat, Doraemon, from the future, who pops out of elementary school student Nobita's desk at home. Doraemon is here to take care of Nobita because he's quite lazy as well as a social outcast. One of the many appealing factors is that Doraemon has a mysterious pocket where he stores a lot of cool gadgets, which he uses to bail Nobita out of trouble. The series continues to live on and maintains merchandise success even after the deaths of both artists.

Rumiko Takahashi (1957–)

One of the most successful female shōnen manga-ka, Rumiko Takahashi was born in 1957 in Niigata, Japan. Her claim to superstar fame came when she wrote and illustrated the satire/comedy series *Urusei Yatsura,* which was published by *Shōnen Sunday,* spanning a decade from 1978 to 1987. It's about a high school playboy, Moroboshi Ataru, who saves the world by beating the daughter, Lum, of the head of a group of alien invaders in a game of "catch me if you can." In the process, Ataru inadvertently proposes to Lum while thinking of his current girlfriend, Shinobu. Although Lum is very pretty, for some reason, Ataru refuses to tie the knot with her and thus triggers the series of this wacky romantic comedy that spans 34 volumes and animated movies.

Rumiko Takahashi's other titles include *Firetripper, Mermaid's Flesh, One or W, Laughing Target, Dust in the Wind, Bye-bye Road, Surimu Kannon, Dutiful Vacation, Maris the Chojo,* and many more.

Leiji Matsumoto (1938–)

A legend in the science-fiction manga genre, Matsumoto Leiji was born in 1938 in Fukuoka, Japan. Ironically, he began his career drawing shōjo manga series (much to his dislike). It wasn't until he met his wife, Miyako Maki, also a shōjo manga-ka, that he got his chance at drawing shōnen manga magazines.

His claim to fame came with his classic space opera series in 1974, *Space Cruiser Yamato* (later translated as *Star Blazers* when the series came to the U.S.). The saga went on to become a successful animated movie series. The opening premise is about Earth on the brink of death as invading aliens in search of a new living planet pummel it with radiation meteorites. Facing death, scientists engineer the ultimate fighting battleship using the remains of the battleship Yamato, which sank during World War II. Armed with a powerful Wave Motion Gun and warships, the crew must travel light-years away to acquire machinery that will restore Earth to its normal state. They're ultimately successful despite the fierce and devastating battles and death tolls that occur during the mission.

His fame is also manifested in the space opera work he created in 1977, titled *Galaxy Express 999.* His other titles include *The Cockpit, Queen Millenia, Queen Emeraldas, Gun Frontier, Sexaroid,* and *Otoko Oidon.*

Takehiko Inoue (1967–)

One of the most popular young superstar manga-ka in Japan, Takehiko Inoue was born in Kyushu, Japan, in 1967. His exceptional storytelling skills, popular subject matters, and incredible artwork have made his works top sellers worldwide.

As a huge fan of basketball, he debuted with the hit shōnen sports series *Slam Dunk* (1993–1996). The story focuses on a new high school transfer, Sakuragi Hanamichi, who joins his basketball team with little or no experience. However, what he lacks in experience, he makes up for with reckless and daring courage and attitude. Sakuragi's extreme athletic ability helps propel him and his team to the national championship. Although sports manga isn't a new concept, the dynamic chemistry between the characters makes this series incredibly fun to read.

Upon completing the series, Inoue re-created the adventures (fictionalized) of the legendary samurai, Miyamoto Musashi, in his action manga *Vagabond.* Inoue's other titles include *Kaede Purple* and *Real.*

Suzue Miuchi (1951–)

One of the most prominent class shōjo manga artists, Suzue Miuchi was born in Osaka, Japan, in 1951. Although some view her style as a bit conservative, her works continue to retain their popularity in the shōjo manga industry.

Miuchi is most noted for her megahit shōjo classic series *The Glass Mask* (also known as *Garasu no Kamen*) in 1976, published by Hakusenshya. The series is currently running at 42 volumes (and still running!). She won the Kodansha Manga Award in 1982 and the Japan Cartoonists Association Award in 1995.

In addition to *The Glass Mask,* Miuchi's other shōjo manga titles include *Akai Megami (The Red Goddess)* and *Moeru Niji (The Burning Rainbow).*

Katsuhiro Otomo (1954–)

One of the most controversial and innovative creators of his time, Katsuhiro Otomo was born in Miyagi, Japan, in 1954.

Both a manga-ka and animé director, he is most known for his work *Akira,* which opened in 1988. Based upon his manga series that was being published simultaneously, the animated movie focuses on social unrest surrounding a group of teenage delinquents in Neo-Tokyo, 31 years after a mysterious explosion demolishes the Tokyo Bay. Readers discover that the explosion is caused by Akira, who is a boy possessing powerful psychokinetic abilities. The climax peaks when one of the delinquent teens, Kaneda, confronts his friend, Tetsuo, after finding out that he too possesses a similar psychokinetic ability that is just as destructive as Akira's.

Otomo is also noted for his works, such as *Memories* (1996), where the same themes of social unrest, religion, and political corruption are apparent. His most recent mega-feature, *Steamboy* (which hit theaters in 2004), is the most expensive and costly animated film to have been made. Other well-known animated titles include *Robot Carnival* (1987) and *Metropolis* (2001).

Yoshiyuki Okamura (1947–) and Tetsuo Hara (1961–)

Yoshiyuki Okamura (known as Buronson) and Tetsuo Hara are credited for their work as a writer and illustrator team. A former manga assistant, writer Okamura was born in Nagano, Japan, in 1947. Illustrator Hara was born in Tokyo, Japan, in 1961.

As a writer, Okamura has written stories geared toward adults. Many of his stories deal with the Japanese *yakuza* (mafia), politics, and sex. His popular works include *Sanctuary* (which ran from 1990 to 1995) and *Strain* (which ran from 1997 to 1998).

However, his biggest claim to fame is the apocalyptic, violent manga series that Hara illustrated, *Hokuto no Ken* (better known in the United States as *The Fist of the North Star*). The premise focuses on lead character Kenshiro, who's a master of one of many clans of deadly martial artists that uses human pressure points to kill. During its release from 1983 to 1988, it caused a controversial stir as body parts were graphically illustrated exploding or splitting in half. It was so violent that many parts had to be censored during overseas translation. Despite this, it ran as a successful television animated series and was embraced by many youngsters in Japan.

Hara joined forces with Okamura to illustrate the prequel *Fist of the Blue Sky* in 2001.

Akira Toriyama (1955–)

Akira Toriyama was born in Aichi, Japan, in 1955 and combined master storytelling with meticulous line work.

Starting his career in his early 20s, Toriyama rocked the manga world with *Dr. Slump.* The comedic anthology (which is full of funny bathroom humor and silly puns, openly pokes fun at sexuality, and mocks Hollywood celebrities) ran from 1980 to 1984. Personally, this is one of my favorite manga series. The story takes place in Penguin Village, where a genius inventor (and pervert), Dr. Sembei, builds a female robot whom he names Arare-chan. Although powerfully strong, she's also silly, witty, and clueless.

After completing *Dr. Slump,* Toriyama created the series *Dragon Ball,* which propelled his name to worldwide fame. The series ran from 1984 to 1995 with a whopping 42 volumes. The adventure series begins with the funny bathroom humor surrounding a little boy named Goku. However, as the story progresses, Toriyama shifts the overall tone of the manga to a more serious action-oriented theme as Goku becomes an adult and faces one powerful enemy after another.

Riyoko Ikeda (1947–)

A prolific shōjo manga artist, Riyoko Ikeda was born in Osaka, Japan, in 1947.

Her fame struck the nation when her manga *The Rose of Versailles* was published in 1973. It's based on the historical French Revolution and the accounts of Marie Antoinette. The main character, Oscar, is a woman who was raised as a man by her father, who wanted a son. The tale blossoms into a love story between Oscar and the servant Andre. Both die on the day of the Taking of the Bastille.

The series was adapted into an animated series as well as a live drama presentation.

Riuoko's other works include *Claudine, Ohiisame e, Jotei Ecatherina,* and *Eiko no Napoleon.*

Chapter 21

(Nearly) Ten Places to Strut your Stuff

In This Chapter

▶ Attending comicons

▶ Looking into schools, competitions, and publishers

▶ Checking out online resources

So where do you go from the end of this book? In this chapter, I give you some tips and advice on places and ways of getting your work out to the public. You really need only a handful of people to ignite the buzz surrounding your work. Word of mouth travels more ground and distance than the fastest car or plane.

Don't become discouraged if you aren't published or established immediately. Success rarely happens overnight. Although your first manga project may need to be refined, be open to the possibility that sometimes publishers aren't ready to see the marketing potential in your ideas or artwork. Like all artistic careers, a satisfying manga career takes time to nurture and mature. Aspiring to become successful is okay, but be careful for what you wish for. Many of my students expect overnight fame — after all, we live in a society of instant gratification. But if you rush through your studies impatiently, chances are good that you'll have problems. My advice is always to take advantage of the times when your primary focus is education instead of rushing off to try to become the youngest, most successful manga phenomenon ever.

For even more great information and advice on showing off your work, head to www.dummies.com and search for the title of this book. There, you'll find some great bonus content.

Animé/Manga Conventions

Going to conventions is one of the best ways to get your work noticed. Following is a list of several conventions that are currently receiving a lot of buzz.

International San Diego Comicon

Probably one of the world's largest comic book shows takes place on the West Coast in California every July. Over the years, the International San Diego Comicon has grown larger and more popular than ever. Plenty of animé and manga publishers and artists attend, and panel series focus on the especially famous. In addition, you can meet editors and directors of some of the most prestigious companies at portfolio review booths.

It's the only convention that currently runs for five days in a row. If you register in advance as a professional, you can get in for free. If you can afford to make the trip, I highly recommend doing so! On a side note, seeing downtown San Diego transformed into a thriving comic book community is fascinating.

For details about this convention, call (619) 491-2475 or check out `www.comic-con.org`.

Wizard Comicon

Wizard Entertainment, which publishes popular comic book news magazines, organizes a series of conventions in major cities across the United States. Depending upon the location, bigger cities provide better space locations for exhibitors and artists. Wizard Comicon conventions are a great place to meet other professionals and amateurs who are currently making it or trying to make it into the industry. These shows run for three days. You can check to see whether a Wizard Comicon is happening in a city near you and download an application for it from the Web site at `www.wizarduniverse.com`. Check the dates for each event (time and locations vary depending on each city). Currently, Wizard Entertainment holds events in Los Angeles, California; Philadelphia, Pennsylvania; Chicago, Illinois; and Arlington, Texas. Call (845) 268-1377 for details.

Pittsburgh Comicon

Although Pittsburgh Comicon is geared toward a smaller crowd, this convention is a great place to show your work to other artists because it's not as crowded as other conventions and you still see seasoned professionals exhibiting their work. If you're traveling with another person who can watch your table, walk around the convention hall to meet and greet them during the slow days (typically Fridays). In addition to a friendly environment, artist tables are very affordable compared to other conventions. If all goes well, you should be able to recoup the cost of the table with little difficulty. Held in April in Pittsburgh, the show runs for three days.

If you're interested in Pittsburgh Comicon, call (814) 467-4116 or go online to www.pittsburghcomicon.com.

New York Comicon (Jacob Javits Convention Center)

Although new, New York Comicon is potentially the next big East Coast convention. During its opening year, the floor became so crowded that fans waited in line for five hours just to get in! Organizers are currently expanding the floor space to accommodate an even larger attendance. Even if you can't get a table, it's a show worth attending. Held in February in New York City, the show runs for three days. For additional details, call (203) 840-5321 or go to the Web site at www.nycomiccon.com.

Katsukon and Otakon

Katsukon and Otakon are great places to meet and greet other animé fans. Take a camera with you to record all the cosplay that takes place at these animé conventions. Although both are geared toward animé fans, you won't find an artists' alley registration for Katsukon. If you're looking to just soak up the animé and manga mania, Katsukon (held in February in Washington, D.C.) is the place to go. Otakon (held in August in Baltimore, Maryland) has been around longer and is larger. If you're thinking of selling your first manga project, Otakon has an artists' alley (just like the other shows I mention in this section). It's a great place to begin if you're just starting out because the environment is laid back and friendly. Although you're not going to find top-notch professional artists exhibiting next to you, it's a great place to get to know other artists while selling your artwork. Grab the opportunity to compare and research what your fellow artists are using as their influences, materials, and current aspirations. Don't forget to bring your business cards! The shows run for three days.

To download the registration form for Katsukon, check out www.katsukon.com. If you're interested in the artists' alley registration information for Otakon, head to the artists' alley section at www.otakon.com.

Art Schools

Although you can select from many art schools, make a point to visit them and see what the facilities and faculty are like by calling to schedule a campus tour. You also need to find out what their admissions requirements are; most, if not all, schools require a portfolio in addition to the standard SAT scores and letters of recommendation. Most schools have an application form that you can download from their Web site. I list some of the current top-contending schools in the United States along with their admissions phone numbers and school Web sites:

- **School of Visual Arts, NY:** (888) 220-5782; www.schoolofvisual arts.edu
- **Parsons School of Design, NY:** (212) 229-7001; www.parsons.edu
- **Pratt Institute, NY:** (800) 331-0834; www.pratt.edu
- **Rhode Island School of Design, RI:** (800) 364-7472; www.risd.edu
- **Art Center of Design, CA:** (626) 396-2373; www.artcenter.edu
- **University of the Arts, PA:** (800) 616-ARTS or (800) 616-2787; www.uarts.edu

Before committing to any school, ask your peers or current students who study in the major of your interest for their feedback.

Manga Competitions

Get online to see what manga competitions are taking place. Major publishers sponsor events where you can win cash or an opportunity for your works to be published. The common myth is that smaller competitions aren't worth the time to apply. When starting off for the first time, you need to go for every possible chance at public exposure and recognition.

Manga Publishers

During your visit to animé/manga conventions, find out which publishers are taking submissions. Pick up your favorite manga and any similar styles that you like. Use the manga you pick up as your "hit list" to see what kinds of manga the various companies are publishing. Most manga books list an address or Web site where you can visit to gather more information about submitting work to those publishers. As of the release of this book, the top manga publisher in the United States is Tokyo Pop — check out their Web site at www.tokyopop.com to obtain information about submitting your work.

Small Galleries and Art Shows

Most galleries have competitions or submission guidelines that you can easily obtain. Although fine-arts galleries are unlikely to be interested in looking at manga work, illustration galleries may be interested if the style is unique. If you're a student, galleries (such as The Society of Illustrators) have student competitions where the school may sponsor your entries.

Also keep in mind that art shows don't necessarily take place in fancy galleries. Many cafés, coffee shops, and eateries exhibit artwork to promote the ambience for the customers. Walk downtown to visit these places and ask whether they're interested in letting you exhibit your work for several weeks. Remember to bring your contact business card or a postcard that has a sample of your artwork attached.

Friends

Show your artwork to your friends. Let them spread the word around about your artwork. The more people talk about your work, the more curious others are going to be about what your artwork looks like.

Online Portfolio

With the Internet becoming ever more popular and integral in society, look into having your own Web site with your portfolio images. A lot of programs are being developed that allow artists to pop in their work and post it with little difficulty. Seeing how rapidly Web technology has advanced over the past ten years, I'm sure that shopping your portfolio via the Internet is going to get even easier and more efficient.

For a freelance artist (either an illustrator or a manga-ka), not having a Web site is a major *faux pas*. Rather than sorting through a pile of submission materials, many art directors and editors prefer to access your work with the click of the mouse from their cozy offices.

If you're just starting off, attempting to set up your own simple Web site is completely okay. Software such as Microsoft FrontPage, Apple Transmit, Adobe GoLive, and Dreamweaver (formerly owned by Macromedia) are just a few of many ways to create and broadcast your personal Web page. However, if you're turning professional, you should get a professional Web designer to create and maintain your online portfolio for you. Unless you're already well versed in designing Web sites, you don't want to go through the additional stress of constantly adjusting and re-creating yours. If you're on a budget, post the job at an art school bulletin board.

Before you set up a Web site, you need to create and register your own unique domain name. Many artists use their own full name, while others use their studio name. It's crucial that the domain name be unique and easy to remember. Avoid using obscure abbreviations or long numerical sequences.

Small Press

Don't discount the status of small press publishers who don't have the same elite status as the top large publishers enjoy. If a small press offers to publish your work, make sure you retain as many rights over your creation as possible. Avoid publishers who require you to sign away your rights as a "work for hire" artist. Also make sure you get a valid contract with them — don't settle for "verbal agreements."

Most small presses start off when an artist self-publishes her own works. Depending upon the success of their sales, many artists who initially self-publish go on to publish other artists' works and eventually become a small publisher.

Although starting off by self-publishing your works under a tight budget is completely acceptable, it can be rather financially risky and time consuming to take on other artists' works. Make sure you have your own personal project completed before joining forces with another artist. If you really want to start your own small press, I suggest grouping with your close friends or peers who are on the same level and with whom you can get along.

Index

• C •

• F •

• G •

• H •

• I •

• J •

• K •

• L •

• M •

• N •

• O •

• P •

• T •

• U •

• V •

• W •

• X •

• Y •

• Z •

BUSINESS, CAREERS & PERSONAL FINANCE

Fundraising
FOR
DUMMIES
John Mutz
Katherine Murray
A Reference for the Rest of Us!

0-7645-9847-3

Investing
FOR
DUMMIES
A Reference for the Rest of Us!
Eric Tyson, MBA

0-7645-2431-3

Also available:

- Business Plans Kit For Dummies 0-7645-9794-9
- Economics For Dummies 0-7645-5726-2
- Grant Writing For Dummies 0-7645-8416-2
- Home Buying For Dummies 0-7645-5331-3
- Managing For Dummies 0-7645-1771-6
- Marketing For Dummies 0-7645-5600-2
- Personal Finance For Dummies 0-7645-2590-5*
- Resumes For Dummies 0-7645-5471-9
- Selling For Dummies 0-7645-5363-1
- Six Sigma For Dummies 0-7645-6798-5
- Small Business Kit For Dummies 0-7645-5984-2
- Starting an eBay Business For Dummies 0-7645-6924-4
- Your Dream Career For Dummies 0-7645-9795-7

HOME & BUSINESS COMPUTER BASICS

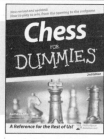

Laptops
FOR
DUMMIES
A Reference for the Rest of Us!
Dan Gookin

0-470-05432-8

Windows Vista
FOR
DUMMIES
A Reference for the Rest of Us!
Andy Rathbone

0-471-75421-8

Also available:

- Cleaning Windows Vista For Dummies 0-471-78293-9
- Excel 2007 For Dummies 0-470-03737-7
- Mac OS X Tiger For Dummies 0-7645-7675-5
- MacBook For Dummies 0-470-04859-X
- Macs For Dummies 0-470-04849-2
- Office 2007 For Dummies 0-470-00923-3
- Outlook 2007 For Dummies 0-470-03830-6
- PCs For Dummies 0-7645-8958-X
- Salesforce.com For Dummies 0-470-04893-X
- Upgrading & Fixing Laptops For Dummies 0-7645-8959-8
- Word 2007 For Dummies 0-470-03658-3
- Quicken 2007 For Dummies 0-470-04600-7

FOOD, HOME, GARDEN, HOBBIES, MUSIC & PETS

Chess
FOR
DUMMIES
A Reference for the Rest of Us!

0-7645-8404-9

Guitar
FOR
DUMMIES
A Reference for the Rest of Us!

0-7645-9904-6

Also available:

- Candy Making For Dummies 0-7645-9734-5
- Card Games For Dummies 0-7645-9910-0
- Crocheting For Dummies 0-7645-4151-X
- Dog Training For Dummies 0-7645-8418-9
- Healthy Carb Cookbook For Dummies 0-7645-8476-6
- Home Maintenance For Dummies 0-7645-5215-5
- Horses For Dummies 0-7645-9797-3
- Jewelry Making & Beading For Dummies 0-7645-2571-9
- Orchids For Dummies 0-7645-6759-4
- Puppies For Dummies 0-7645-5255-4
- Rock Guitar For Dummies 0-7645-5356-9
- Sewing For Dummies 0-7645-6847-7
- Singing For Dummies 0-7645-2475-5

INTERNET & DIGITAL MEDIA

eBay
FOR
DUMMIES
A Reference for the Rest of Us!
Marsha Collier

0-470-04529-9

iPod & iTunes
FOR
DUMMIES
A Reference for the Rest of Us!

0-470-04894-8

Also available:

- Blogging For Dummies 0-471-77084-1
- Digital Photography For Dummies 0-7645-9802-3
- Digital Photography All-in-One Desk Reference For Dummies 0-470-03743-1
- Digital SLR Cameras and Photography For Dummies 0-7645-9803-1
- eBay Business All-in-One Desk Reference For Dummies 0-7645-8438-3
- HDTV For Dummies 0-470-09673-X
- Home Entertainment PCs For Dummies 0-470-05523-5
- MySpace For Dummies 0-470-09529-6
- Search Engine Optimization For Dummies 0-471-97998-8
- Skype For Dummies 0-470-04891-3
- The Internet For Dummies 0-7645-8996-2
- Wiring Your Digital Home For Dummies 0-471-91830-X

*** Separate Canadian edition also available**
† Separate U.K. edition also available

Available wherever books are sold. For more information or to order direct: U.S. customers visit www.dummies.com or call 1-877-762-2974. U.K. customers visit www.wileyeurope.com or call 0800 243407. Canadian customers visit www.wiley.ca or call 1-800-567-4797.

WILEY

SPORTS, FITNESS, PARENTING, RELIGION & SPIRITUALITY

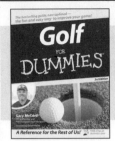

0-471-76871-5

0-7645-7841-3

Also available:

- Catholicism For Dummies
  0-7645-5391-7
- Exercise Balls For Dummies
  0-7645-5623-1
- Fitness For Dummies
  0-7645-7851-0
- Football For Dummies
  0-7645-3936-1
- Judaism For Dummies
  0-7645-5299-6
- Potty Training For Dummies
  0-7645-5417-4
- Buddhism For Dummies
  0-7645-5359-3

- Pregnancy For Dummies
  0-7645-4483-7 †
- Ten Minute Tone-Ups For Dummies
  0-7645-7207-5
- NASCAR For Dummies
  0-7645-7681-X
- Religion For Dummies
  0-7645-5264-3
- Soccer For Dummies
  0-7645-5229-5
- Women in the Bible For Dummies
  0-7645-8475-8

TRAVEL

0-7645-7749-2

0-7645-6945-7

Also available:

- Alaska For Dummies
  0-7645-7746-8
- Cruise Vacations For Dummies
  0-7645-6941-4
- England For Dummies
  0-7645-4276-1
- Europe For Dummies
  0-7645-7529-5
- Germany For Dummies
  0-7645-7823-5
- Hawaii For Dummies
  0-7645-7402-7

- Italy For Dummies
  0-7645-7386-1
- Las Vegas For Dummies
  0-7645-7382-9
- London For Dummies
  0-7645-4277-X
- Paris For Dummies
  0-7645-7630-5
- RV Vacations For Dummies
  0-7645-4442-X
- Walt Disney World & Orlando
  For Dummies
  0-7645-9660-8

GRAPHICS, DESIGN & WEB DEVELOPMENT

0-7645-8815-X

0-7645-9571-7

Also available:

- 3D Game Animation For Dummies
  0-7645-8789-7
- AutoCAD 2006 For Dummies
  0-7645-8925-3
- Building a Web Site For Dummies
  0-7645-7144-3
- Creating Web Pages For Dummies
  0-470-08030-2
- Creating Web Pages All-in-One Desk
  Reference For Dummies
  0-7645-4345-8
- Dreamweaver 8 For Dummies
  0-7645-9649-7

- InDesign CS2 For Dummies
  0-7645-9572-5
- Macromedia Flash 8 For Dummies
  0-7645-9691-8
- Photoshop CS2 and Digital
  Photography For Dummies
  0-7645-9580-6
- Photoshop Elements 4 For Dummies
  0-471-77483-9
- Syndicating Web Sites with RSS Feeds
  For Dummies
  0-7645-8848-6
- Yahoo! SiteBuilder For Dummies
  0-7645-9800-7

NETWORKING, SECURITY, PROGRAMMING & DATABASES

0-7645-7728-X

0-471-74940-0

Also available:

- Access 2007 For Dummies
  0-470-04612-0
- ASP.NET 2 For Dummies
  0-7645-7907-X
- C# 2005 For Dummies
  0-7645-9704-3
- Hacking For Dummies
  0-470-05235-X
- Hacking Wireless Networks
  For Dummies
  0-7645-9730-2
- Java For Dummies
  0-470-08716-1

- Microsoft SQL Server 2005 For Dummies
  0-7645-7755-7
- Networking All-in-One Desk Reference
  For Dummies
  0-7645-9939-9
- Preventing Identity Theft For Dummies
  0-7645-7336-5
- Telecom For Dummies
  0-471-77085-X
- Visual Studio 2005 All-in-One Desk
  Reference For Dummies
  0-7645-9775-2
- XML For Dummies
  0-7645-8845-1